Your
Psychic
Soul

Your
Psychic
Soul

Embracing Your Sixth Sense

Judith Pennington

4th Dimension Press ■ Virginia Beach ■ Virginia

4th Dimension Press
215 67th Street
Virginia Beach, VA 23451-2061

ISBN 13: 978-0-87604-700-2

Cover design by Christine Fulcher

To Edgar Cayce, with love and gratitude for your many gifts to the world.

CONTENTS

Preface

*All of us have wonderful and amazing stories about our life jour-*neys. I want to tell you a little about mine and what prompts me to use the word "soul," which so many people equate with religion. "Soul" is really a much more ancient idea, dating back to the earliest people who simply felt its presence.

Perhaps you, too, could sense the presence of your soul as a young and innocent child. I was aware of *being* a shimmering, light–filled soul in communion with a sacred presence in nature. While fishing the lazy bayous and rivers of South Louisiana with my loving parents, I felt quiet and happy inside, as if I were one with the land, water, sky, and all living things. I found the same sense of mystical oneness in the colorful, stained glass windows, fragrant incense, flickering candles, and soaring harmonies sung in my neighborhood Catholic church. But due to heart–breaking events within my family, at age fifteen, I drew away from my spirit's inner peace. After that, I felt lost.

As I grew older, I knew that something was missing but did not know what it was. Perhaps it was my unconscious longing for mystical union that drew me back one sunny day as I drove to a follow-up appointment with my gynecologist. The doctor had found a large ovarian growth and was concerned enough about it to ask me to return on Monday for a special, more thorough examination. By then twenty-five years old, I left work that day in my red Karmann Ghia and sped up a downtown ramp onto the busy interstate that runs through Baton Rouge, Louisiana. Over the weekend, I had forgotten about the appointment. By now, though, I had grown fearful. I sent up a silent, heartfelt little prayer: "I don't know if there is a God or not, but if there is, please don't let anything happen to me. There's no one else to take care of my little girl."

Before the end of that sentence, a cold chill swept over my body and changed into a sensation of warm, radiant bliss. Waves of light poured into me and intensified until my heart overflowed with awe and gratitude. I gazed into my rearview mirror and saw tears of joy and wonder streaming down my face. I was who I was, but I was more than just myself. Somehow I was inside and outside of my body at the same time. Everything was radiant with light—the car, the highway, the sky, and my entire being. The pouring light intensified, and I expanded into an infinite sea of joy. It came to me, suddenly, that being filled with light is what it feels like to die, and the body is a prison that separates us from this sweet bliss.

I was not aware of driving the car—*who was driving?*—but as the interstate exit approached, the warm light slowly ebbed away. Sensation came back into my hands, and I carefully steered the car down the ramp in what seemed like slow motion. At home, I prepared for the doctor's appointment and telephoned my charismatic Christian mother-in-law to tell her what had happened to me. She was the only person who, at that time in my life, understood.

In the gynecologist's office, I was still exhilarated and overflowing with joy when he examined me and announced that the large tumor on my left ovary had disappeared. "It must have been the prescription I gave you to take over the weekend," he said. I knew better. I had been healed by radiant light and the blissful love inside of the light. Some mysterious force had touched me, and I would never be the same.

Over the next twelve years, I could neither doubt nor deny this healing. Was the light inside or outside of me? How could I get back to it again? Not knowing where or how to get logical answers to my questions, I stayed busy working as a freelance writer, directing a peace and justice group, and managing two headstrong daughters as a single mother.

It was years before I recognized it, but an invisible current was directing me to the answers to my questions via story assignments on psychic phenomena, altered states of consciousness, and creativity and the brain. Everything converged in late 1987, at about two o'clock in the morning. I had just finished writing an eye-opening article about a social justice advocate that was powerful enough to make a difference in people's lives. So I was happy and unusually quiet as I closed down my computer and roamed around in my bedroom—a little sleepy yet exhilarated—when an indefinable urge came over me to sit down with pen and paper, listen inwardly, and write down what I heard.

Thus began my relationship with my soul, whose kind, gentle wisdom in hundreds of meditative writings led me out of a dark pit of self-hatred and worthlessness and into the clarity, peace, and light of my spirit. Twelve years later while in Virginia Beach, VA writing a book about this transformation, I asked inwardly for a scientific explanation of my journey in consciousness—without which I would not have published the book. The next day, I was intuitively urged to visit the A.R.E. Bookstore to find an issue of *Common Boundary* magazine, a national publication for which I'd written in previous years but had not seen since.

Emblazoned on the magazine cover was a headline, "Evolving Consciousness," which struck an instant chord of recognition. This interview about Electroencephalography (EEG) with the awakened-mind pioneer, Anna Wise, scientifically explained the brainwave development that opened up my psychic abilities. The information was the first of three logical proofs that I'd sought for my first book on inspired writing and the science of spirituality, titled *The Voice of the Soul: A Journey into Wisdom and the Physics of God*.

Little did I know, as I reluctantly followed my writings' guidance to study with Anna Wise seven years later, that I would assist her at the

Esalen Institute and succeed her as a world authority on EEG and the development of consciousness. Teaching this work across the United States and writing about it in international publications turned out to be my soul's destiny, a fascinating and deeply fulfilling lifework that is more than I ever hoped for or could have imagined.

Soul guidance in dreams led me to record meditation CDs and to write this book, a scientific and mystical explanation and experience of intuition that comes out of some thirty years of investigation—all of it incredibly synchronistic—of the brain, meditation, consciousness, and how the psychic soul manifests in our daily lives.

You will find in these pages the compelling stories of meditation masters, professional psychics, angel communicators, hands-on healers, neuroscientists, physicists, and many other credible people engaged in the experience and study of consciousness and intuition. Foremost among them is Edgar Cayce, whose psychic readings helped bring about the spiritual awakening that is now taking place all over the world.

Writing this book has been a joy and a privilege. It motivated me to delve more deeply into the Cayce readings on psychic material, where I was delighted to find the language and concepts used by quantum physicists to describe the intuitive process and the nonlocal mind of God. The brainwave research and two new superconscious patterns I present here for the first time validate the Cayce readings about the psychic soul as well as the scientific findings of quantum physicists.

On a personal level, the revelations in this book have inspired me to open up to new psi experiences that have expanded me into deeper and higher states of awareness. For this personal growth, I am inexpressibly grateful.

I hope and trust that this book's journey into the superconscious will be equally as exciting and rewarding for you.

Introduction

This is an extraordinary time in the history of humankind. Just below the surface of every city and nation is a powerful current of change that is churning up the promise of a new reality on Earth. In America, the current runs through television shows hosted by psychic mediums, yoga studios and meditation centers popping up on every Main Street, new scientific disciplines like bioenergetics and neurotheology, and spiritual themes in art, music, literature, theater, and film that were once considered "New Age" but are now mainstream.

One of my favorite signs of this spiritual awakening is the number of movies in which the protagonist dies in what might have been a trag-edy, except that he or she rises up out of the body into eternal life!

Worldwide, we are seeing a paradigm shift in consciousness. There's a new kid in town, and it's the psychic soul, the subconscious source of our natural intuitive abilities, and here is its message: everyone has psychic abilities, and there's nothing strange about it.

Listening to the voice of the soul in dreams, meditation, inspired writing, and everyday life expands the mind into heightened sensory perception and higher levels of awareness that transform and evolve consciousness in amazing ways. Not only great psychics like Edgar Cayce say so. Science now shows how meditation and intuition evolve the brain and body, how we telepathically communicate with each other on an unconscious level, and how the nature of God as a quantum sea of light connects each and every soul to a superconscious intelligence made of pure, perfect love.

The purpose of this book is to show you, the reader, how to tap into the knowledge and wisdom of your soul and its higher self in order to reach your highest potential and perhaps teach others how to do so. In this book you will find fascinating stories, exercises, and meditations meant to give you direct experience of your soul's inner wisdom and peace. Also available is an EEG-tested, guided meditation CD titled, *The Meditation Experience: Listening to Your Psychic Soul.*

Anyone can do this intuitive work. Everyone is built for it.

While reading this book, I hope you will keep in mind that the intuitive life is a journey of the heart. Edgar Cayce believed that true knowledge is the understanding of only one law: the law of love. It is to love that the psychic soul always guides us.

The Chandogya Upanishad of the Hindu religion, in 3:13.7, expressed this idea with great eloquence:

> There is a light that shines beyond all things on earth,
> Beyond us all,
> Beyond the heavens,
> Beyond the highest, the very highest heavens.
> This is the Light that shines in our heart.

Let us be lamps to one another, even as the psychic soul is to each and every one of us.

1

Awakening to the Psychic Soul

"Each person enfolds something of the spirit of the other in his consciousness."—David Bohm, PhD, physicist

Even as we struggle to stay balanced amidst the hustle and bustle or worries and concerns of daily life, the psychic soul finds ways to guide us; and indeed, when we are at our worst, the soul does its very best work. It speaks to us in the "languages" we speak best and in a "voice" that is crystal-clear. Here are some examples:

Perhaps you thought about a long lost relative or friend and, completely out of the blue, that person telephoned or knocked at your door. Or perhaps, when you phoned someone you hadn't talked to in a while, the person exclaimed: "I was *just* thinking about you!"

You might have been driving a car when suddenly you had an overwhelming impulse to turn left. The impulse turned out to be the correct choice, although you had no logical way of knowing it. Or you may be one of the many people who, while driving along on a highway, instinctively obeyed an inner voice that shouted an unmistakable warning like, "Switch lanes now!" By doing so, you narrowly avoided a tragic accident.

Perhaps your soul awakened you in this way: needing help, you asked for it inwardly. Shortly thereafter, the name of a bookstore repeated itself in your mind until you went there, whereupon a book or magazine containing exactly what you needed to know jumped into your visual field and leapt off a shelf into your hands or fell at your feet. (This phenomenon is so common that it has a name: bibliomancy, meaning divination by books.)

Or perhaps you have had a spiritual experience like that of my very logical and pragmatic chiropractor, Terry Hafer. While practicing stop-and-go landings in her airplane, she heard through her headphones a strangely metallic male voice that knew her call numbers, telling her that she had a visitor waiting for her in the tower. Terry landed her plane, and moments later the engine catastrophically (meaning irreversibly) failed. Shaken but safe, she climbed the steps of the tower to greet her visitor. The two air traffic controllers on duty, both women, knew nothing of a visitor and had not contacted her in the air.

Dr. Hafer told me that story after hearing from me about an angel communicator featured in this book. She confided a startling angel story of her own, which she has shared with very few people until now. One day, she accompanied her husband on a visit to his eye doctor. A typically courageous man, her husband admitted to being afraid: for the second time, a long needle would be inserted in his eye to relieve glaucoma, and the pain would be unbearable. Terry reassured him and prayed with all her might. The room grew very quiet, and when she looked up, to her utter astonishment she saw three tall angels with their wings folded around her husband and the ophthalmologist. She had not previously believed in angels, nor had her husband. But during the treatment, he had felt no pain at all. They changed their minds about believing in angels.

Sometimes when we ask for help, it shows up in an outer experience, such as an unlikely coincidence or a snatch of conversation heard from a passerby. At other times, helpful insights arise out of the quiet inner depths of the subconscious mind.

Perhaps you are a soul writer and listen intently to lyrical words of wisdom that spill into your fingers with guiding insights that you use in every aspect of your life. Or perhaps you are so intuitive that people look to you for wisdom that wells up on its own.

Dreams awaken many people to the genius of the psychic soul. Have you ever awakened with a dream fragment that flickered across your mind until you sat down, closed your eyes, and received its symbolic message, which brilliantly spelled out your next, most favorable steps in life? Perhaps you have awakened with crystal-clear insights into a work project or relationship.

There is nothing magical or mysterious about psychic abilities. In everyday life we "pick up" the thoughts and feelings of other people. Business people act on hunches all the time, and police officers live by them. So do most parents, who are in telepathic touch with their children's unspoken wants and needs. Everyone has psychic abilities, although their power and accuracy depend on how often and how consciously they are used.

Intuition is the ability to sense or know information that is not available to the logical mind. Where does it come from? Brainwave mapping shows that our intuitive abilities reside below ordinary awareness in the subconscious mind—the boundless realm of the psychic soul.

Edgar Cayce placed the soul in the subconscious, too, but pointed out that we do not *possess* a soul; rather, we *are* a soul with a sixth sense that is constantly in touch with a higher self, or oversoul, an immortal spiritual essence and ideal being residing in a superconscious dimension next to the throne of God. (5754-2 and 900-31)

You may not feel like an immortal soul. Yet on the level of your godlike or angelic nature, which has lived " . . . throughout the *eons* of time . . . " said Cayce, you are. (5754-2) The prescient and mystical experiences featured in this book are proof of your soul's ability to penetrate time and space with its sixth sense to draw higher wisdom and knowledge from your superconscious spirit.

Awakening to the power and presence of the soul changes us in every way, since once we know our true potential, we can't "not-now" it again. And who would want to? Getting in touch with the psychic soul is like falling in love. "I knew there was something else," we breathe. "This is it." We rejoin the lost piece that was missing, empty places inside us disappear, life takes on new meaning, and the world grows brighter and more beautiful.

The beauty of attunement with the psychic soul is its instant access to what cannot be known or understood by any other means.

Which job serves my soul growth? Deepen into your soul's awareness to feel the answer. Why are my relationships so painful? Close your eyes and listen for the truth. Shall I move to Boise, Idaho? Quiet your thoughts and mind-travel to Boise!

Our psychic intuition—psychic referring to the "psyche," or soul—easily and quite naturally reaches into an infinite sea of light flowing within and all around us to obtain ideas, insights, and information that answer any need. Our entire cosmos, radiantly alive with every thought, feeling, intention, word, and deed that has occurred and ever will occur, opens with perfect ease to the psychic mind that seeks to know.

Psychic intuition is the birthright and common language of every living thing. Whether our questions concern our destiny, animals, other people, spirits, or even other worlds, there is no limit to what we can learn and experience through the soul.

Just imagine what it would be like to close your eyes, rest in the loving embrace of your psychic soul, and see, hear, sense, and know how to create and enjoy a happy, productive life that serves you and everyone else. What would it be like to go through each and every day so attuned to your psychic senses that you know what to do in every moment and the best way to do it?

Life can be just this smooth, easy, and free of distraction. While there will still be bumps on the road (unless you are perfect), you will psychically sense how to go over or around them. As a master and servant of the inner light of intuition, you hold a lantern that illuminates inner and outer worlds for the good of all.

Opening the Doors of Perception

The purpose of this book is to teach you to receive not just occasional intuitive insights but instead a steady stream of psychic information that enlightens you and lights up the world. In truth, you are already enlightened—on the level of your pure spirit—and it has already awakened you to the beauty of spiritual and psychic realities beyond the physical world.

. . . Or you wouldn't be reading this book.

Can you recall one or more intuitive events that may have led to your interest in intuition? If so, you may wish to jot these examples down in a journal that you reserve for this specific use. The writing hand links to the unconscious mind, so you may receive information as you write. Be sure to note what type of intuition you experienced. Was it a dream, a waking vision, a voice, an inner sense of knowing, or a synchronicity involving people or events?

Replaying intuitive memories in your mind—if they are pleasant, of course—reconstructs *the feeling of the state* of consciousness and reawakens it. If you do not remember an intuitive event in your past, then simply draw your attention to your heart and state clearly and firmly that you are open to soul guidance. Clarifying such an intention, without reservation, attunes the levels of your mind to each other for intuitive success.

Hopeful expectation opens the doors of psychic perception and the infinite dimensions lying beyond them. Soon you will see just how psychic you are!

2

The Soul's Psychic Senses and Infinite Source

"I do not ask to see. I do not ask to know. I only ask to be used."—Sufi prayer

Everyone—and everything—is a soul. Sometimes we humans are aware of our soul. Most of the time, absorbed as we are in the life of the mind, we forget that we have an essential being. Consequently, the soul must guide us back to the higher awareness in ourselves and in all else. The soul speaks to us in the languages of waking life, nature, psychic inquiry, meditation, dreams, inspired writing, and life's synchronicities.

Soul messages travel through every channel in the sensory system, lifting the physical senses into a high-sense perception that enables us to intuitively hear an inner voice, have a vision, feel a gut instinct, or know things in a flash.

Just imagine that you are a soul—which you are!—with a message to send your conscious mind. Which channels would you use? Obviously, the ones that best fit the need. If the conscious mind needs a picture, the soul sends a vision; if it needs to taste, smell, and feel something, the soul sends a multisensory message through those several psychic channels.

The soul can use every sensory channel, or just one, to shout out a warning that keeps us safe; and when it does this, the message is always loud and clear. Otherwise, the subconscious soul whispers its messages through the one or two organs of perception that we use most in waking life and thus are wide open.

For example, writers and musicians attuned to words and sounds are well-developed aurally—their psychic sense is *clairaudience,* meaning clear hearing. People with a great deal of empathy who relate to others through emotional feelings receive intuitive messages via *clairsentience,* meaning clear feeling. Artists, architects, and airplane pilots with keen vision are usually *clairvoyant,* while high-powered intellectuals who think and move rapidly, receive lightning-quick flashes of *prophetic knowing.*

When the conscious mind's ego is attuned to inner awareness, the voice and languages of the multisensory soul are much more easily heard. Soul attunement evolves the mind's consciousness faster than anything else, since impressions streaming into the psychic senses unite the conscious and subconscious and thus awaken the mind to its spirit and source. This self-integration is the sole purpose of our slow voyage through the psychic waters of this fantastic planet.

Since we value the conscious mind's intellect and want it to cooperate with the soul, this chapter features a wealth of scientific research on four psychic reception areas and the personality traits associated with each, courtesy of Pete A. Sanders, Jr., author of the intuitive person's bible, *You Are Psychic!* Sanders, who learned to see auras as a child, used an MIT laboratory and scientific methods to conduct intuitive experiments on himself, other students, and professional psychics in the Boston area. His research proved so valid that he passed up a scholarship to Harvard Medical School in order to open a psychic training school, Free Soul, write his *You Are Psychic!* book and train thousands of people to develop their intuitive abilities.

If you are an amateur or a professional intuitive, you know it's not necessary to understand how high–sense perception works. It just does! We were made for this awareness. Still, most readers will find the information very useful. Identifying our natural psychic senses gives us the confidence to open up all the way to the voice and languages of the soul.

The Inner Vision of Clairvoyance

Clairvoyance is likely your primary psychic sense if you think in pictures and experience life visually. The psychic reception area for clairvoyants is in the "third eye" of the forehead, in front of the frontal cortex of the brain, which also processes ordinary vision, sleeping dreams, and daydreams.

Identified by Eastern mystics as the fifth chakra, a spinning wheel of light in the body's subtle energy system, the psychic third eye turns inward to look into itself and turns outward to see into other people. To tap into this psychic center, close your physical eyes and relax them; otherwise, you will stimulate busy thoughts that will distract you or block your psychic vision.

Once your eyes are completely relaxed, lift them slightly to the third eye area of your forehead just between your eyebrows. Then, mentally walk through a room in your house. Notice each item of furniture, the quality of light, the colors, textures, shapes, forms, and patterns in the room. Are the images sharp and clear, or vague and indistinct? If they are sharp and clear, then you are probably a psychic visionary with the gift of clairvoyance.

Sanders found that the visual clairvoyant who needs to see the "whole picture" seeks out open horizons and scenic views, enjoys reading maps, and may enjoy photography or art. In restaurants, offices, and living spaces, this person probably grabs the seat with the best view and the most light.

What If I Can't See?

Even if you are not primarily clairvoyant, you may see meaningful visual imagery when you ask yourself a question or give a psychic reading to someone else. Students in my intuition development classes worry that they might not see imagery, but most people do—if not right away, then with a little practice. There are good reasons for this.

Statistics report that one-half to two-thirds of any population is primarily visual because, in sighted persons, this physical sense is active throughout the day. Vision is processed in the visual cortex, which resembles a "projection screen" in the back of the head. Images travel from the visual cortex to the frontal cortex for processing in the front of the brain behind the forehead, the location of the psychic third eye.

When the eyes of a sighted person are open, this brain circuitry is always at work. When the eyes are closed, the frontal cortex processes daydreams, sleeping dreams, and psychic visions.

To sharpen your psychic vision, notice colors, textures, shapes, forms, shadows, and light. Looking deeply into the natural world will sharpen your outer vision so that your inner imagery is vivid and clear. Ask your soul to help with your clairvoyance. It will show you ways to strengthen this psychic sense, as its deepest desire is to open every possible line of communication with your conscious mind.

The Eyes of the Soul

The eyes of the soul are able to see into the past, present, and future. Perhaps you have had this experience: while shopping for groceries, a book, or hardware item, your eyes unexpectedly dart, seemingly of their own accord, to a particular item. If you buy it, later that day or the next you discover that it's exactly what you need to have on hand for an unexpected guest, free time, or a house repair.

Once, during meditation, I asked for an inspiring idea to use as the basis of a Sunday talk to be given in a church. Nothing arose, but when I opened my eyes, they darted to a book I didn't remember buying or placing on the shelf. I *felt* that it was the answer to my need. Sure enough, it fell open to a scholarly study on the stages of enlightenment, which I have since taught in dozens of classes and publications.

Your soul eyes will also guide you to safety. Some years ago, I flew with my young grandson from the East Coast to Los Angeles, California, rented a car, and started out on a long drive to Arizona. Exhausted and dazed from the long flight, I drove into rush–hour traffic in L.A. with no map, no GPS, and only a list of the *names* of highways leading to my destination. Seeing an interminable line of cars ahead of me, I pulled over, closed my eyes, and asked for help. In lightning–quick time, a simple line drawing of a map flashed into my mind's eye: I saw a road running from the freeway to a right–hand exit in the shape of a fish hook.

"But how far ahead is the road?" I asked, knowing that I was tired and could easily miss the turn. I heard and saw the number "40," but could not get any elaboration. Edging into the bumper–to–bumper traffic, I found myself driving at close to 40 miles per hour. Some 40 miles and 40 minutes later I reached the fish–hook exit leading to Arizona! I arrived at my destination with the understanding that there's more than one kind of map.

Clairvoyance is usually associated with precognition, or future seeing. It is actually much more than that. You can use your psychic vision to see distant people and places in real time, as in remote viewing, and in dreams wherein the soul is free to soar. Robert Monroe, the 1950s consciousness explorer who projected his spirit out of his body while asleep, visited many other dimensions around and beyond the earth during astral travel.

Edgar Cayce was a prolific dreamer in the sleep state and a powerful clairvoyant during unconscious trance. The most compelling stories of clairvoyance that I've ever heard are recorded in the transcribed readings given by Mr. Cayce, America's best known psychic and the father of holistic healing.

In giving a physical reading, Cayce suggested that the sick person use a certain medicine, but the person's family was unable to find it in drug stores. In a follow–up reading, Cayce's psychic eyes spotted a dusty bottle of this out–of–production medicine on the back shelf of a pharmacy in another state. He gave the client the address of the drug store, but the pharmacists employed there could not find it. In the third reading, Cayce, by then losing patience, told the family to tell the pharmacists to look on the back of that dusty shelf, and sure enough, that's exactly where they found it. (294-1, Report #4)

Of course, Cayce's clairvoyance is unparalleled. Lying down, loosening his tie, relaxing, and then tuning in to the client's name and address, the "sleeping prophet" could describe in fine detail what the client was wearing and the contents of the room. On several occasions, he even commented on the progress of the bus transporting the tardy client to his residence.

A classic remote viewer, Cayce was best known for his psychic ability to look into people's bodies, describe the status of internal organs, see the cause of illness, and suggest explicit remedies for people who were often beyond medical help. Physicians marveled at his knowledge, which could not have come from medical books, as Cayce attended school through only the eighth grade in rural Kentucky.

While you may not yet be as psychic as Edgar Cayce, whose clairvoyance was so finely tuned that he could see the body's energy field, the aura, as well as nature spirits and the spirits of the departed, you can certainly develop the natural clairvoyance of your soul. Today, many medical intuitives are able to look at the body's subtle energy system and diagnose illnesses and cures, even before diseases manifest.

Seeing is believing, and believing is seeing. Belief in the existence of this psychic channel is what allows it to open.

Clairaudience: The Still, Small Voice

In 800 BCE, Jezebel's Baal priests chased the Hebrew prophet Elijah across ancient Palestine until he took refuge in a cave where he prayed for an end to his life, as he felt that he had failed his God. In the Judeo-Christian Bible, 1 Kings 19:11–13 states that the wind rent the mountains and then came an earthquake and fire. But the voice of God was not found in these forces of nature, as Elijah realized for the first time in Jewish history: God speaks in a "voice of gentle stillness" heard from within, in the silence of loving contemplation.

Elijah's epiphany marked a radical shift in human consciousness, yet nearly three thousand years later, people are still struggling to believe in the psychic soul that so readily speaks when we slow our thoughts and listen. Believers know that this deeper voice often helps us make positive choices in our lives or protects us from harm.

If you listen to and heed the voice of your soul, its guidance will never fail you or falter. You will find this still, small voice to be your wisest teacher, most loving parent, and dearest friend.

Gifts of Clairaudience

You are primarily clairaudient, or clear hearing, if you process conversations in your head and admire the intricacies of language and music. Preoccupied with language, clairaudients practice conversations that they expect or hope to have with other people; edit their internal dialogue to crystallize what they mean to say; and, due to their love affair with words, gravitate to careers as writers, journalists, and musicians. Their psychic reception center is just above the ears in the temporal lobes that process sound, speech, and various aspects of memory.

When musically inclined, and that is almost always, audients are greatly entertained by an "inner jukebox" which cues up the appropriate song for the moment. From listening to my inner jukebox day and night, I know that it is incredibly original and at times comedic.

For example, I awakened one morning in a bad mood about having been too cold throughout the night. Before I could open my eyes, I heard the sixties' folk musician Donovan singing, "I'm so mad about Saffron/She's so mad about me." I wondered why this song was coming up, when I heard the refrain: "They call her Mellow Yellow." I got the message. Everything made me laugh that day, which no doubt was my soul's purpose in selecting that song.

The inner jukebox cues clairaudients to self-reflect. One day, while standing in my clothes closet looking for something to wear, I caught myself humming the beautiful theme from the movie "Titanic." Wondering why, I remembered that I'd just been balancing my checkbook! While I wasn't sinking financially, I realized that I must need to address childhood-related issues about money. (Otherwise I might get stuck in that old rhythm and blues song, "You Really Got a Hold on Me.")

The clairaudient involved in a tempestuous love affair might hear "Stormy Weather," or, if the relationship has run its course, "Stop Dragging My Heart Around" or "The Thrill is Gone."

The still, small jukebox of the unconscious mind, while amusing at times, is plugged in to the higher self. Its music calls the clairaudient to listen deeply in order to search the soul for truth and guidance.

Best of all, clairaudients need not insert quarters to hear the inner jukebox. It's free and it's always turned on.

Simply close your eyes and play a song in your mind to determine whether you are primarily clairaudient. If this channel is wide open, the music will sing out and you will hear it.

Separating the Signal from the Noise

Clairaudients face unique challenges. Sanders points out that because clairaudients are logical, systematic, and skeptical by nature, they tend to doubt the existence of a psychic inner voice since the only voice they hear is their own. The clairaudient's verbal brain constantly names, discusses, and edits, so psychic information can easily slip into this stream of dialogue without making much of a splash. (Did you hear that image or see it, or both?)

Even more challenging is the clairaudient's self-doubt. Here are two ways to distinguish inner dialogue from a psychic insight. If your conscious mind is inactive, as in daydreaming or meditating, the words flowing into your mind may be clairaudient insights. You can also tell the difference by reviewing the quality of the message. Is it random mind chatter or more information than you knew before?

Psychic information is super-ordinary and more than we knew before. The audient can best hear it with a quiet, clear mind that is able to listen deeply.

The Clairaudient Cat

Easily the strangest story of clairaudience that I've ever heard involves telepathic communication with an elderly tabby cat, Richie, who was dying from a large, malignant tumor that had formed between his eyes. Richie's owner took him to a holistic veterinarian who performed acupuncture on him, but the treatments did nothing until they were used to attune the cat to the higher consciousness of the cosmos. Intrigued by this concept, Richie's owner called in an animal communicator who psychically taught the cat to visualize that his tumor was shrinking. One week later the tumor began to shrink, and the next week, it disappeared.

I might have doubted this story—a clairaudient cat that heals himself?—except that it was too bizarre to have been fabricated. Several years later I traveled across the state to present an all-day seminar. That evening I wired my EEG biofeedback device (called the Mind Mirror) to a woman who said she wanted to communicate with her recently deceased cat. She did talk with her departed cat during the session, and afterward she told me the cat's story, which sounded eerily familiar. I knew that cat! It was Richie, who had eventually died of old age. What were the chances? I'd written about him in my online newsletter. Richie's clairaudient owner confirmed every detail of the story I'd heard and reported. (Now, that's synchronicity!)

True synchronicity, defined as a meaningful coincidence of inner and outer events, provides meaningful lessons. I was recently plagued by three unsightly moles (not the animal) that took up residence on the sides of my knee and face. I must have unconsciously remembered Richie's story. Not wanting to cut off the moles, I asked them to go away. Believe it or not, they disappeared within days and in one case, sloughed off within hours! I was astonished and from this experience learned that everything has ears to hear.

If a part of your body needs attention, sit quietly in a meditative state and dialogue with it. Listen to what comes into your mind, and if the insights make any sense at all, honor them.

Deer That Hear

You will see in upcoming chapters how everything on earth is connected on an unconscious level. I experienced direct proof of this idea late one afternoon while racing a truck for lead position just before a slow crawl up a long, steep, two-lane road. Just as I won the sprint, I heard an inner voice say, "Oh great, now *I'm* going to be the one to hit the deer." I was startled by these words, which rippled into my mind out of the blue so that when I approached a deer crossing, I slowed down and extended my peripheral vision. When the huge, antlered buck leapt out of the field onto the road in front of me, I was able to stop the car a few feet short of him. We stared at each other for about fifteen seconds until he jumped back into the field. I drove away feeling like we'd had a friendly conversation.

Clairaudience increases quickly when we listen all the time. I developed my inner hearing through inspired writing, the subject of a later chapter. Perhaps you will try this way of listening, too. It is very freeing to know that you can connect at any time with an inner voice that *exists* to offer guiding insights, solutions, comfort, and assurance.

The "Gut Instinct" of Clairsentience

Clairsentience is a holdover from prehistoric times, when "gut instinct" taught people to dodge dinosaurs and forage for edible food in a world without grocery stores.

Then and now, the psychic reception area for clairsentience is the solar plexus, extending from the base of the ribcage to just below the navel. This area, densely packed with nerves, is the perfect location for psychic feeling, which you may have experienced as the "butterflies" of excitement or stage fright. When endangered, cave people felt the unconscious mind's powerful warning signals: the gut spasms, a gasp of fear, or the surge of adrenaline that speeds up the heartbeat to rapidly push more blood and oxygen to the extremities. Clairsentience was and still is the perfect evolutionary mechanism, as proved by the fact that we are not extinct.

Who is clairsentient? Everyone is. Clairsentience is the only psychic sense shared by humans and animals—and the plant kingdom as well, according to *The Secret Life of Plants*, a remarkable book by Peter Tompkins and Christopher Bird that chronicles the clairsentient ESP of the plant kingdom. I always talk to my plants, and they love it.

The Sentient's Psychic Field

You may be clairsentient if you walk into a busy department store during the holidays and suddenly feel dazed and confused. Psychic feelers "pick up" the energies of people around them and very often cannot tell the difference between other people's thoughts and feelings and their own. This ability is especially true of people who have been traumatized in childhood and consequently develop a clairsentient radar for hypervigilance that guards and protects them. The "psychic empath," whose radar is extended out too far, feels the thoughts and emotions of other people, which can be chaotic, upsetting, and even painful.

Clairsentients live by their feelings about people, places, and things. Cluttered places and chaotic people and locales make them feel very uncomfortable, Sanders points out. You are not likely to find a chaotic mess on the clairsentient's desk. Confusion of any kind feels too painful.

Clairsentience enables us to "feel out" the past, present, and future of people, places, and the environment. Because retrocognition and precognition (psychically reading the past and future) often occur in our feeling centers, we don't easily forget these experiences.

Several years ago I was in a copy shop, happily duplicating a sheaf of papers to be delivered to government offices down the street. Suddenly, out of nowhere, powerful stirrings of fear and foreboding gripped my abdomen and took my breath away. The clench of fear was too strong to ignore, so I did an inner check to see if the source were physical, mental, or emotional; and to my surprise, it was none of these.

When a car rear-ended my Toyota Camry at a stoplight a few minutes later, the shallow breathing caused by the tightness in my solar plexus instantly released and my usual equanimity returned. The other driver was visibly surprised by my lack of concern over the accident. In fact, the perplexed expression on his face made me laugh out loud. I had already experienced the shock wave of the collision in the copy shop, and now the foreboding was over and done with!

The driver and his wife questioned me about what looked to them like surreal calmness. I let them believe it was simply because I am a meditator—and that was true enough. It is the quiet, self-aware mind that is best able to pick up psychic signals and "feel" ahead, which is what I had unconsciously done.

Why did my clairsentience bother to forewarn me about a minor accident? No doubt it was on-the-job training meant to convey a reassuring message: everyone possesses gut instincts that will warn him or her of danger. Only the psychic soul is with us all of the time to perform such a protective function. Our responsibility is to attend to our feelings and ask where they are coming from. If we listen deeply, the soul will tell us.

Dealing with Doubt and Ambiguity

It can be difficult to distinguish a clairsentient alarm bell from an unfounded fear rooted in the memory of an unresolved experience. In other words, is the woman sharpening a knife at the kitchen counter a real threat, or does she resemble someone who once was?

Negative emotional experiences are stored in the subconscious mind in long-term memory alongside the soul's sixth sense. Both control the involuntary nervous system. Once an instinctive warning sets off the fight, flight, or freeze stress response, adrenaline surges through the body, and the rational mind is overtaken by the primitive reptilian brain, which strikes first and asks questions later.

The best way to resolve ambiguity is to clean up the subconscious. How do we stop people from pushing our "hot buttons"? We get rid of them (the hot-buttons) through personal transformation. Until then, we can mitigate the potential damage done by the reptilian brain. When we catch ourselves flaring up in anger or defensiveness, we can quickly relax, grow quiet inside, and psychically look at the buried memories that created those buttons. Mastering the inner reptile increases the power of the intellect, and tossing out the garbage leaves the subconscious calm and clear. Once we have clarity, we can trust our psychic feelings.

By far the best way to transmute emotions is to meditate. Happily, meditation is the natural way to increase psychic sensitivity, as it puts us in direct touch with the psychic soul.

Powering Up Clairsentience

Besides emotional transmutation, what powers up clairsentience the most is the loving intention to heal or to help, as I discovered in an EEG-monitored study on healers and healing carried out in early 2011. Six healers were transmitting spiritual energy to a single recipient lying on a massage table, and toward the end of the session, I followed a hunch and asked them to send distance Reiki (a type of energy healing) to their loved ones. Later, they reported that compared to the stranger lying on the table, the distance healing felt much more effective because they were emotionally connected to their loved ones.

While they were sending distance Reiki, their brainwave patterns showed a clear rise in consciousness, due entirely to the transformative power of love. Clairsentience similarly amplifies when two people have an affinity for each other. People who live together often know what the other person is thinking or feeling, and this connectedness is the reason why.

The principle in physics that governs the transmission of healing energy is sympathetic resonance, wherein similar frequencies connect and communicate with each other as in cell phones and radio telescopes. Musically, the sympathetic resonance of a fundamental frequency with multiple harmonics, as in thirds, fifths, and octaves, is called harmonic resonance. Everything in life—especially psychic perception—is governed by sympathetic and harmonic resonance.

This law of nature gives the psychic empath a means of self-protection. Since we are always in resonance with environmental energy fields, we can choose to resist them. Resistance only creates pain. Or we can surrender to the energy while producing positive emotions that shift surrounding fields, as shown in the story below.

In laboratory studies, neuroscientists working with the Mind and Life Institute studied the interaction between a placid Tibetan Buddhist monk—a longtime meditator—and an infuriated history professor who was ranting about the stupidity of the rising belief in reincarnation. The orange-robed monk continued to nod his head benevolently and smile in understanding. Soon the history professor, who had become increasingly aware of his inappropriate behavior, sat down and calmly asked the monk what he thought about reincarnation.

Serenity in the midst of a raging storm usually causes overexcited people and events to calm down, too. Sympathetic resonance works! It's a law of physics, playing the music of the universe.

Naturally enough, psychic feelers are exceptional at psychometry, the psychic technique of attuning to objects to read their history. Vibrations travel from the hands to the energy field and then into the solar plexus and brain for perceptual processing by any or all of the psychic senses. Since everyone is a psychic feeler, anyone can succeed at psychometry.

Clairsentience is a wonderful gift that draws us to like-spirited people, places, and things. Similar, like-spirited people are drawn to us by our good vibrations. Continually monitoring our feelings keeps us moving in the safest and best directions.

The Prophetic: Psychic Knowing

The psychic sense of intuitive knowing is found in high-powered, quick-thinking people who simply know what they know. Prophetics, as Sanders terms them, don't know *how* they know what they know or *where* the knowledge came from, but they are certain of it and will go the distance to uphold or defend their intuitive knowing. Religious prophets have had precisely this strong sense of knowing for thousands of years.

Naturally enough, prophetic insights stream into the crown of the head, according to Sanders. I haven't seen anyone else correlate the crown chakra, a spinning wheel of physical and subtle energies, with the brain's two parietal lobes, which are located at the crown of the head. Nevertheless, the correlation is real.

The parietal lobes govern our sense of personal separation in time and space. Researchers have found that in people meditating on compassion, the cessation of the neural stream into the parietal lobes gives rise to divine union, spiritual ecstasy, and super-ordinary psychic insights. By their consistent use of the crown chakra, prophetics might get a jump on enlightenment.

Do You Know a Prophet?

Prophetics proliferate in our busy modern society. Sanders cites a few examples. The stock broker gets a sudden intuitive "hit" on a commodity; the real estate salesman spots the serious buyer in a crowd of strangers; the business traveler knows, despite misleading timetables, which train to catch to a critical meeting. Prophetics are smart, super-charged people who operate on the "high octane" of the crown chakra.

Steve, a theoretical mathematician, university professor, and author of eleven books, is a classic prophetic, and I mildly envy him. While I, as a clairaudient, tend to question my psychic insights, Steve just *knows* the truth of his. Prophetics have the wonderful ability to trust and act on their knowing without the slightest doubt. And they are usually right.

Sanders notes that the life of the prophetic is not always rosy. Prophetics can be impatient with people who talk or walk slowly, because, after all, they have things to do and places to go. They tend to interrupt other people's conversations with a "Yes, I know," because they do know what the person is going to say. Prophetics think and talk so quickly that their words jumble together. Because they are moving so fast, certain details may be ignored or pushed aside in favor of more important projects.

Prophetics may be overwhelmed by the sheer number of thoughts in their minds and the unlimited number of things that are possible for them to do; consequently, some prophetics do not accomplish much of anything. The saving grace for the "ideaphoric" prophetic is a creative project or a contemplative activity that quiets the mind. These calming activities allow this kind of person to sort things out and make a sensible plan to follow from beginning to end.

One of my favorite modern-day prophets is spiritual leader, James Twyman, who acts without hesitation on his psychic knowing. In 1995, Twyman, a former Catholic monk, dreamed about the biblical story of Joseph and his coat of many colors. He awakened with a clear vision of a project that he knew would make a difference in the world.

Being a meditator and contemplative by nature, Twyman was able to follow through with his vision. Using email blasts and the broadcast media, he asked individuals and spiritual communities throughout the world to donate swatches of material that contained vibrations of love and the intention of world peace. He received tens of thousands of colorful patches of material which, when sewn together, extended for more than a mile. He and a group of volunteers wrapped this "multi-colored dream coat"—the Cloth of Many Colors—around United Nations buildings and the base of the US Capitol and Pentagon, and then transported it to countries in conflict or at war to seed peace in the world. Today, the Cloth of Many Colors project has involved hundreds of thousands of people and more than fifty countries.

Twyman prophetically knew that this project would touch the minds and hearts of peace-seekers everywhere. Because he followed through on his dream inspiration and his waking sense of prophetic knowing, individuals, churches, and government officials in the United Nations and their many countries opened to the prospect of world peace through prayer.

How can you tell if you are a psychic "knower"? You already know it.

Multisensory Remote Viewing

Although remote viewing, the art of mind travel, is typically associated with clairvoyance, it is actually a multisensory experience that relies on all of the psychic senses. The most convincing demonstration of remote viewing that I have ever seen—or even thought possible—took place in November 2003 during an historic conference, Remote Viewing: Beyond Time and Space, hosted by Edgar Cayce's A.R.E. in Virginia Beach, VA. Stephan A. Schwartz, anthropologist, author, and remote-viewing pioneer, convened the scientific and military founders of remote viewing and opened the event with an experiment for the three hundred scientists and healers in attendance. (*See* Resources at the end of this chapter.)

Schwartz introduced two people who would serve as monitors and asked them to draw a number from the basket of a random number generator. The number drawn by the monitors directed them to one of four locations within a twenty-minute drive of the A.R.E. Schwartz led a discussion on remote viewing until the monitors phoned to let him know of their arrival at the target location. At that point he asked us to close our eyes, relax, and draw our attention to the target. "Sketch what immediately comes to mind," he instructed.

I drew a tall, narrow, vertical object rising out of a round base and to the right of it, little peaks of water. Next, Schwartz asked us to imagine ourselves as being "life-size" at the site. Standing there, what were our sensory impressions?

I wrote the words: blue skies, surf, asphalt, grass, birds, and the sounds of people on a boardwalk. This gave way to clear visions of two places in Virginia Beach that I had visited: a museum related to boats and the sea, and the city's contemporary arts center and museum.

When the two monitors returned with digital photos of a historic lighthouse on Cape Henry Beach, a collective gasp of surprise rolled like a wave through the auditorium. I wasn't the only one who had tuned in to the target: ninety percent of the people in the audience—some 270 people—had drawn and verbally described the tall lighthouse in striking detail.

The compelling story of remote viewing held the audience spellbound for four days. During a follow-up intensive workshop, Schwartz asked the hundred or so people attending to remote-view the location of Saddam Hussein. Several months later, Schwartz reported that the vast majority of trainees, with me included, had closely described the underground hiding place, nearby structures, and bedraggled condition of the newly captured Iraqi dictator.

The Inner Certainty of Higher Awareness

Practice develops the psychic senses more than anything else, as remote-viewing studies have shown and Edgar Cayce discovered over the forty-three years he gave readings. What also helps is the inner certainty of higher awareness that comes from deep within and feels "realer than real." This sentience is what propelled Jesus, Buddha, Mohammed, Krishna, and many other great seers to stand by their prophetic knowing, sometimes at the risk of death.

The prophetic person's quick and sure sense of conviction comes naturally, while the rest of us must listen, see, and feel the information until the sensed knowledge of higher awareness builds to inner certainty.

When soul messages are vitally important, they flash through any and every available channel. If you want to open up channels that you seldom use, the meditation and psychic inquiry techniques provided in upcoming chapters will show you how to do that. Simply quieting thoughts to access the deeper awareness of the psychic soul stimulates inner imagery that will give you the answers to everything you want and need to know.

The Soul's Essence and Source

Although we use terms like "higher consciousness" to describe levels of awareness that exist beyond ordinary states of mind, in actuality we *are* this eternal higher consciousness living in a temporary physical body, as described so beautifully by the Cayce readings on page 9 of the Meditation chapter that opens the first book of *A Search for God*:

> It is through meditation that we may become aware of the existence of the spiritual forces within, that we unlock the door between our physical and spiritual bodies. Through this door come impulses from the soul, seeking expression in the physical.
>
> Our souls are endowed with many faculties that are limited and bound by our impressions in the physical. The soul is always present, always willing to express its true purpose, its true relationship with the Creator. Through meditation we make this possible; we open the way.
>
> Some say that we are not conscious of possessing a soul. We should know that each of us is a soul. This body in which we live is only our house for the moment, and then out of it we go on to other states of consciousness and other experiences.

Understanding the nature of the soul is central to intuitive development. Your psychic senses are not "out there" or "in another realm"; they exist in your spirit, which interpenetrates your physical body and is in and with you always.

We can say something more: your spirit, simultaneously existing in non-physical and physical realms, has immediate access to any and all information and energy. When you turn your attention to your solar plexus to feel, to the temporal lobes above your ears to hear, to your third eye to see, and to the crown of your head to know, you are tuning in to the spiritual matrix of your brain and body.

The ability to concentrate the mind is essential to the psychic, due to the fact that intuitive impressions usually stream into the senses very fast. Blink and you miss them. The remedy is to keep your mind as calm as a glassy lake—a lesson taught by nature.

Everything on earth contains the potential to lift the ordinary senses into the psychic awareness of the higher mind—from nature, animals, and people to inspiring art, music, and literature. Nature, creativity, and anything else that stirs the senses and opens the heart lifts the mind into the soul's sixth sense: " . . . a faculty of the soul–body itself . . . ," said Cayce. (5754–2)

Inner Paths to the Sixth Sense

While earthly pleasure is the outer path to the sixth sense, according to Edgar Cayce, the inner path consists of meditation, dream study, and inspired writing. These practices create a sensory bridge to the subconscious mind, where the soul's higher awareness resides.

Extraordinary results occur during meditation, dream study, and inspired writing. When we focus our attention and awareness on a spiritual ideal, the kundalini life force coiled in the lower body rises up through seven major chakra centers and concentrates its high-frequency energies in the crown of the head and third eye.

This shift in consciousness from lower to higher vibrations enables the soul to calibrate the body–mind to the superconscious realm in which its sixth sense communes with its godlike, angelic nature (the higher self, or oversoul) that is " . . . built by the entity through its experiences as a whole in the material and cosmic world . . . ," according to the Cayce readings. (5754–2) The godlike, angelic self is " . . . ever on guard before the throne of the Creator itself . . . " (5754–1)

Contact with these superconscious energies "spiritualizes" the body–mind and rewires it to a higher vibration that can sustain high–sense perception in ordinary life.

Superconscious Awareness

The Cayce readings traced the effect of the rising kundalini and its activation of high–sense perception for a group of people who met with him in 1931 to ask how they might become more spiritual and psychic. To answer this request, Cayce gave 130 psychic readings that became the basis of the two volumes titled *A Search for God*, which were compiled and used as texts by this original study group of thirteen people. Today, more than five hundred active study groups in the United States and thirty-three other countries meet weekly to discuss the readings in the text, meditate, and practice lessons that invariably amplify the members' spiritual attunement and psychic powers.

The Meditation chapter, which opens the first book, states on page 11 that people "who by constant introspection are able to bring to the surface their experiences as a whole are called 'sages' or 'lamas.'" When this spiritual ability is made practical, the person becomes a master.

The chapter also traces the upward movement and effects of the kundalini force, a powerful reservoir of physical and spiritual energy, as it rises up through the spinning wheels of light known as the chakras.

A sensation experienced in the eyes indicates a healing vibration, according to the Cayce readings on page 13 in that Meditation chapter. If energy runs up through the body and ends in sensations of fullness in the head, pulling these vibrations down to the "disseminating center"—the spiritual third eye in the forehead—enables the meditator to heal others magnetically through the laying-on of hands.

Hearing an inner voice signifies an awakening to God. This awakening stimulates other faculties until we pass "into the presence of that which may materialize in voice, feeling, sight, and a consciousness of oneness with the Whole," said Cayce's Source. (p. 13)

Meditation consistently and reliably develops psychic abilities over time. When we purify with water, sanctify with incense and candles, relax the body, and quiet the mind, we find in the stillness of meditation a sense of inner unity and a thirst for the presence of the infinite. Meditation, dreaming, and inspired writing deepen the mind into the light-filled awareness of the multisensory soul which lifts us into the superconscious realm of the divine.

(*See* the chapter entitled "The Light of Consciousness" to learn more about the chakras and kundalini life force.)

The Sources of Psychic Information

With a spiritual intention, a subject treated in the next chapter, those who believe in their intuition can read someone else's mind—called telepathy—or preferably, their own soul and the souls of others. Everything has a soul—an energetic template that gives rise to physical forms—from people and animals, to plants, minerals, and stars, as well as "light beings" in dimensions beyond the earth.

Setting a spiritual intention establishes this higher connection and provides access to the Akashic Library, a record "written on the skein of time and space," (1574-1, et al.) as Cayce described it. The Akashic Record is a symbolic representation of the superconscious, a quantum sea of light that contains every intention, thought, feeling, word, and deed that has ever occurred or ever will.

Kevin J. Todeschi, author of *Edgar Cayce on the Akashic Records: The Book of Life*, describes the Akashic Library as a storehouse of information —an infinite, interactive "database"—that contains the history of every soul and connects us to one another.

Connecting with the soul and the Akasha—meaning "boundless space"—enables us to be guided by the possibilities and potentialities in the Divine Mind to the future that is our highest destiny.

The highest destiny of the soul, as mystics have known since the beginning of time, is to grow in spiritual awareness and serve others. Motivated accordingly, psychic abilities naturally awaken.

The Thousand Names of God

When I joined an Edgar Cayce study group in 1993, I was relieved and encouraged to find in the *Search for God* texts an energetic concept of God that transcends religious distinctions. Cayce was deeply religious and devoted to the God of the Judeo–Christian Bible and the Christ pattern attained and lived by the man, Jesus. Yet in psychic trance, below everyday awareness, he perceived God as the love and light vibrating in waves of energy through all of reality. His psychic information came out of those waves of light in Universal Consciousness.

Scientists working with the Institute of HeartMath and the Institute of Noetic Sciences, two leading organizations in research on intuition, have unwittingly confirmed Cayce's view of God in new theories that the source of psychic information is a quantum sea of light in which waves of energy encode and carry information. This quantum energy field is the chi (or qi), pranic life force, and biblical light out of which everything emanates.

Many people have been hurt by their experiences with narrow-minded religions and consequently want nothing to do with spirituality. If these are your feelings, then you may wish to think of your soul's source as your Higher Power, Peace, Love, Essence, Pure Spirit, or one of Edgar Cayce's names for God: Universal Consciousness, Universal Mind, and the Creative Forces, to name a few.

Whatever you call it, the "Field" out of which everything arises intuitively informs and evolves human consciousness. There is nothing more freeing than the realization that some benevolent force, in the most intimate sense of a companion or friend, informs us from moment to moment so that we are never alone. Feeling connected to something greater inspires us to take an evolutionary step in consciousness toward this Greater Whole.

The word "evolutionary" describes the person who is consciously evolving the mind, body, and spirit for the greater good. Psychics are evolutionaries first, because their rise into universal light assists and evolves others, and second, because this spiritual light transforms them, as well. In a very real way, the energies carried by the psychic back into the physical world lift our dimension and others in service to the divine.

Mental Imagery Scale	Rating
Perfectly clear and as vivid as the actual experience	1
Very clear and comparable in vividness to the actual experience	2
Moderately clear and vivid	3
Not clear or vivid but recognizable	4
Vague and dim	5
So vague and dim as to be hardly recognizable	6
No image present at all, only know that you're thinking of the object	7

This scale has to be matched to: 1) visual imagery; 2) touch, pain, heat, and cold (skin senses); 3) taste and smell; 4) sound; and 5) kinesthesia (sensation of bodily movement). The score can vary, therefore, from $5 \times 1 = 5$ to $5 \times 7 = 35$, where the higher the score, the poorer the mental imagery. The ability to think in sensory imagery instead of in words is an absolutely essential first step toward the mastery of higher states of consciousness, self-control of pain, and so forth. –Comments by C. Maxwell Cade

Note: The above Mental Imagery Scale is excerpted from: Cade, C. Maxwell. *The Awakened Mind.* Element Books, 1989, p.48, with permission from Isabel Cade.

Resources:

"Orange Trees by the Ocean," *a meditation, will help you identify your strongest psychic senses and which ones need development. This series of sensory images ends with a guided meditation.*

"Autumn Woods," *a guided reverie into the sensory beauty of nature, relaxes the body, opens the mind, and uplifts the spirit.*

(For the above meditations, *see* Selected Bibliography for track information regarding: Pennington, Judith. *The Meditation Experience: Listening to Your Psychic Soul.* A.R.E. Press, 2011, CDs.)

Visit *StephanASchwartz.com* for links to books on remote viewing and remote-viewing CDs. His daily newsletter, "The SchwartzReport," tracks trends in consciousness that affect our future.

3

Psychic Explorations:
How to Read for Yourself and Others

"I hear and I forget. I see and I remember. I do and I understand."—Confucius

Linda Schiller-Hanna settled into a comfortable chair in her hotel room, closed her eyes, took a few deep breaths, and went inside herself, as if between two doors. When her awareness of the outside world slipped away, she prayed silently, "Tell me what to say and how to say it," and then imagined a violin string connecting our two hearts.

All four of her psychic channels instantly opened. She heard, saw, knew, and felt my life story as it flowed into her mind; she even felt my feelings, and in a rush of words told me what came to her. The story tumbled out, as she expressively nodded, laughed, waved her hands, and shifted in her chair in response to the energetic impressions streaming into her mind.

Linda was joyful during this thirty-minute reading, and I watched her connection with her Source intensify moment by moment. She was wired up to my unique electroencephalograph, the Mind Mirror, and it showed that she was channeling pure energy. Within four minutes, her brainwave pattern shifted from the awakened mind of psychic mastery to the superconscious mind of the higher self. When she asked me to close my eyes and feel the love of my divine teachers and guides, her brainwaves suddenly shifted into the highest-known brainwave pattern of the angelic, godlike nature. Today we know this as the higher self, or the oversoul.

To make sure that Linda's movements had not influenced her extraordinary brainwave patterns, at the end of the reading I asked her to close her eyes and connect with her Source. The evolved-mind pattern of illumination, a circle of blissful oneness with the divine, appeared on the EEG and then returned to the superconscious mind, in which very high frequencies of light evolve the brain and consciousness. (See the next three chapters for the significance of these brainwave patterns and how to develop them.)

It was a magnificent display of the psychic's rise in consciousness, made possible by Linda's meditation mastery and nine months of psychic training at a California school, Heartsong, in 1980. She has been a professional intuitive ever since. (See Resources at the end of this chapter.)

"Psychic readings are meditations for someone else," Linda told an audience of ninety people at a psychic training intensive seminar hosted by Edgar Cayce's A.R.E. on that February weekend in 2012. The next day she stated, "A psychic reading is a healing." She would know. She offers free intuitive counseling to HIV and AIDS patients through her Angel Love Healing Center and, as a Reiki master, gives hands-on healing to people in need. In two cases, she prayed deeply, applied Reiki, and was "coincidentally present," she said, when Spirit awakened the recipients from comas. One woman had been in a coma for several years and awakened on the spot. The other person, a young man who had been shot in the head, awakened the next day.

People with a high spiritual intention to help and heal others can do "all of these things and more," as Jesus promised. It's a simple matter of deepening into the quiet awareness of your soul and allowing it to resonate with the energy and information you seek. Your soul will draw intuitive imagery and healing energy from the superconscious realm of Universal Consciousness, where Edgar Cayce believed the most accurate readings were produced.

Psychic perception and transmission are the natural abilities of the soul. Every soul can do these things, as you will see for yourself in trying out the powerful intuitive techniques presented in this chapter.

Seven Steps to Psychic Awareness

Linda Schiller-Hanna's seven steps to psychic awareness quiet and center the mind while raising sensory awareness into the high-sense perception of the soul. After years of practice, Linda needs only a few moments to deepen into her alpha brainwaves, the doorway to intuitive awareness. Practice will teach you to shift your brainwaves and consciousness into this higher state of awareness very quickly, and eventually you, too, will consciously live the intuitive life of your soul.

If you are new to psychic inquiry, you will find these seven steps immensely helpful. I learned them in one of Linda's Lightworker Intensive trainings and have taught them to hundreds of people in community college classes, with terrific results.

Whether you use the seven steps for self-guidance or to intuitively "read" someone else—an animal, object, or place—this preparation will enable you to access information about the past, present, or future. You may wish to read others in person to begin with, but with practice you will be able to "tune in" to the vibrations of the person, place, or thing without regard to distance.

When two people pair up to read for each other, the sensory-rich seven steps guide the speaker (reader) and listener (recipient) into a shared intention, subconscious awareness, and an intuitive heart connection. Experience these steps and their shifts in consciousness alone, as you begin. Then, after reading the guidelines in the rest of this chapter, get together with a friend or friends to practice paired readings with the help of these seven steps.

1. Breathe. First, breathe in through the nose and out through the mouth seven times. Immerse your mind in your deep, slow, and steady breathing.

2.   Affirm protection. Say out loud or inwardly: "I set my intention that this reading is for the highest good of all concerned. This reading will be truthful, non-judgmental, non-manipulative, caring, and in divine order."

3.   Ground yourself. Imagine your body as a tree with roots extending from your tailbone and your feet all the way into the center of the earth.

4.   Center yourself. Successively move your attention to the center of your forehead, the center of your heart, and your center of gravity (just below your navel).

5.   Cleanse. Imagine a white shaft of light flowing from above you (and from God, if you wish) down into your heart and through your spine, carrying all negativity, fear, prejudice, and anything that is not perfectly *you* into the center of the earth.

6.   Make a heart connection with your partner. Imagine a violin string of energy extending from heart to heart. You may feel a little tug indicating that this connection has been made. (Be sure to disconnect this heart string at the end of the reading.)

7.   Open "banana" fingers. The speaker widens the fingers of both hands and extends both palms toward the listener to sense his or her energy field. At this point, the listener clearly states his or her name three times to attune the speaker to the vibration. The speaker's eyes close, and the listener's eyes remain open. The speaker says whatever comes to mind without any editing at all. The listener listens without comment and gives feedback afterward.

Schiller-Hanna advises the reader to "blurt out" whatever he or she receives, which is great advice. Sometimes people working in groups hesitate, as if looking to each other for permission to begin. But once the first person begins to read, so does everyone else.

Some people receive information more slowly than others, and that's fine, too. Just take your time and allow the words, images, feelings, and inner knowing to surface in their own way.

Setting an Intention or Ideal

Psychic inquiry must always begin with a spiritual intention, as you have seen in the seven steps. Intention is everything in psychic readings, as it unites the body, mind, heart, and spirit into a single-pointed awareness that frees the soul to journey through the superconscious to the sought-after information.

The recipient's intention is equally important; if it is only one of idle curiosity, there will not be enough resonance to make the connection, according to a Cayce reading (294-131) and the science of intuition presented in later chapters of this book. Resonance is the law in physics and metaphysics by which two vibrations attune to one another.

If you don't already have a clear intention for your life, which Edgar Cayce termed an ideal or guiding aspiration, you may wish to set one now. Simply close your eyes, relax, and get in touch with what you need most in life. If that is peace and joy, create an affirmative "I am" statement along the lines of "I am peaceful and joyful."

A good addition to your ideal would be something like this: "I am peaceful, joyful, and in touch with my psychic soul." Use whatever words feel right to you, but be clear that you wish to open up to your soul's intuitive awareness. Think, feel, and experience your ideal, and repeat it in meditation and waking life as a kind of mantra.

Cayce maintained that repeating an ideal builds it into every atom and cell of the body. Your ideal will radiate into your subtle energy field (the aura) and attract people and situations that serve your goals. If your ideal includes soul attunement, it will help your conscious mind's ego to get on board with your practice.

Guidelines for Psychic Readings

Listening to inner guidance is a simple matter when only you are involved: you tune in and perhaps record on paper what arises. Readings for others bring ethical matters into play, as well as considerations about how to open up, receive, interpret, and report the information to the listener. Be sure to read all of these guidelines before you get started.

It's always best, at first, to do intuitive readings for people you don't know. This way, the thinking mind is not as likely to intrude with its memories and what it thinks it knows.

For the Intuitive Speaker/Reader:
How to Receive and Report Information

Don't try to force it. Wait patiently for a vision, inner voice, feeling and/ or sense of knowing to surface in your awareness. On the other hand, recognize that psychic information can and often does flow very fast, streaming into the mind within seconds like water through an open dam. If it flows this fast for you, blurt it out without any censoring. If there is a lull, allow the imagery some time to form in the depths of your subconscious mind.

Keep the channel open. Do not judge or analyze the information, as scrutiny will block the flow. Your attitude should be that of hopeful expectation. Build this expectancy, and all will come. Even if what you receive is puzzling or seems unlikely, go ahead and say it aloud. If you are working alone, jot down your impressions on a piece of paper.

Report the information exactly as it comes to you and leave nothing out. For example, "I see a white picket fence in the front yard of an attractive white cottage, with a child riding a bicycle on the street in front of the house. I get the feeling that the child is very happy and that you are that child. But now I see another image of the child, who is a little older. She falls off the bicycle, hurts her arm, and lies in the street crying. I get the feeling that this is not an actual event, but is symbolic: that in childhood you were hurt and felt lost because of painful events in your family life. Now I see your stepfather appearing in the doorway and yelling at you for falling down; you are very frightened. I'm not sure of this, but I get the sense that you haven't been able to trust being happy since then."

In this example, all of the reader's psychic senses were active. Still, the reader was unsure in places and had the wisdom to say, "I get the feeling" and "I get the sense that . . . " The listener will interpret the images. Don't guess about anything; give only what you receive.

Do not frighten the listener. If what you perceive could worry or harm the listener, convey your impressions carefully or not at all. If you decide to share the information, do not say that such–and–such (a heart attack, a car wreck, a death in the family) will happen; you could be wrong and cause unnecessary worry. Instead, tell the listener what you picked up, and then ask if someone has a fear or concern about such-and-such.

Schiller-Hanna added a comment about this practice in an interview with me, saying: "Sometimes I'll be guided to talk in more general terms. Instead of telling an elderly woman that I see her husband passing in the next year, I may be guided to say, 'I feel you will be having a change before too long. It will be helpful to learn to be more independent.' This gives her tools but doesn't burden her with anxiety and fear about the loss of her partner, if Spirit has not told me to reveal this loss directly."

Be sure to point out to the listener that the future depends on the choices and decisions we make. Changing the present changes the future. Simply alerting the listener (or, if you are reading for yourself, your own conscious mind) of the possibility of a problem is the extent of your responsibility. After the reading, the listener must use his or her instincts, intellect, and intuition to determine if some kind of action needs to be taken.

Stop when the flow ends. The reading continues until nothing more surfaces for you. If the listener has questions, you may wish to return to your intuitive state to ask for more information.

For the Listener/Recipient: How to Listen and Give Feedback

If you are the listener, listen quietly without distracting or interrupting the speaker. Volunteering information could derail the stream of information or change its direction entirely. It's better for the information to come from the intuitive reader, unless he or she seems stuck or unsure, in which case it may be helpful for the listener to supply a missing piece of information.

Despite this instruction, some listeners can't help but respond to the speaker with a supportive "Mm-hmm." This kind of agreement is human nature, but it is better for the listener not to comment. Besides breaking the speaker's flow, the speaker may begin to listen for confirmation, and this delay could take the reading down a psychic alleyway that might be a detour from the soul's original path.

When the reading is over, the listener is invited to give feedback to the speaker. The listener should report what resonated and what means nothing at present. Later on, the information may become meaningful.

I experienced this delayed understanding in my first psychic reading of someone else. A city magazine had assigned me to write a cover story on a well-known local psychic, so I attended her intuitive training class. Some thirty people sat in a circle in a large room, and during a psychometry exercise, each of us picked a name out of a basket. I unfolded the piece of paper and was astonished to get a clear, distinct impression of green leaves on a curving stem placed against a purple background.

The person who owned up to the name I drew said that image meant nothing to her. But later on, she took off her jacket and, lo and behold, her purple sweat shirt was decorated with a winding stem of green ivy leaves. This design was exactly what I had seen, but if she hadn't removed her jacket, I would have assumed that I'd been completely wrong.

What does not make sense to the listener at the moment might become clear minutes, days, or even weeks later. So don't worry about what seem like intuitive "misses." They may turn out to be "hits."

Extending the reading. During the feedback session, the listener may ask for details on certain aspects of the reading. Whether to go back for more information or not is the speaker's choice. If the speaker is willing to give more, he or she may be able to do so immediately. There's a simple explanation for this ready availability: the speaker and listener are still in the channel, much as the dreamer, immediately upon waking, is still in the dream.

The speaker may be able to answer questions by looking inward with the eyes open or may need to retreat inward by repeating the seven steps to get back into the channel.

Interpreting Imagery

Your subconscious soul is a brilliant playwright, director, and producer who uses the symbols stored in your mind, and some physicists theorize, in universal awareness, to communicate complex ideas quickly and succinctly. These images spring to life in multisensory plays with plots, settings, and characters that speak to you on many levels and in ways you can understand.

No one can interpret your inner imagery better than you can, as it comes from your life experiences and their associations with specific symbols. Your psyche uses these symbols as a kind of shorthand to telegraph richly meaningful messages to you.

For example, if you are reading for someone else and see an image of a house surrounded by a picket fence, your interpretation will depend on what this image means to you. You may have lived in such a house and had an idyllic childhood—or a miserable one. What you are seeing, then, may indicate the same situation for the client as what you experienced, or it may simply mean that the next few intuitive impulses will relate to the person's childhood.

Could it also indicate that the person is living in such a house right now? Of course it could! Such is the ambiguity of psychic symbolism. Because of this ambiguity, it's best for the new psychic reader to merely report what arises, unless the imagery is accompanied by a distinct sense of inner certainty (and even then, the wise speaker says tentatively, "I feel" or "I get a sense").

It's also possible that the symbols you see and sense are not part of your inventory at all and instead mean something to the listener, since it's his or her reading. In both cases, it's best to allow the story to emerge, image by image, until the meaning is clear.

If the listener has no idea of the meaning and you suspect that you do, share what you know. Couch it as, "This is what I feel/suspect/guess is the meaning." Perhaps your insights are correct or will stir comprehension in the listener.

Paying attention to your dreams will better acquaint you with your symbol system. When a minister friend of mine shows up in a dream, I know the dream refers to my spiritual life. Similarly, the appearance of the color green, coupled with pictures of outdoor scenes and a tingling feeling in my palms, tells me that the recipient of the reading is a healer (the tingling in my hands indicates that idea) or a gardener, farmer, or landscaper who works outdoors in some way.

How you give a psychic reading is entirely your own choice. As in everything else, you will learn from your mistakes. I prefer to report—at least early in the reading—only what I see, hear, feel, and even taste, touch, and smell *without* giving any interpretation until other images tell the full story. I might say to the listener: "I see the color green and my hands are tingling, so I sense that you either work outdoors or are a healer. Let me see what else I can get about this . . . ." Then I will be quiet again while receiving the next few clarifying images, which will explain what the reading is about and what it means. (But that's my way!) Follow your own path, which you will discover with every step forward.

Distinguishing Ego from Soul

Psychic information typically comes with some degree of inner certainty: the vision, voice, feeling, or inner knowing wells up on its own, and we feel the truth of it. Even with this validation, the new psychic may doubt the source of his or her guidance and wonder if it's coming from the voice of the ego or the voice of the soul.

To discern the difference, simply go back into your psychic state to evaluate the message. Use your clairsentience to check the validity of the information. It's always wise to do this same reality-check on intuitive guidance received from others as well.

If the guidance you receive tells you what to think or what actions to take, the ego is definitely involved, as the soul never impinges on our free will. The transcendent soul is unemotional (it never worries), and it never dictates a course of action. The soul leaves choices to the heart, mind, and body, since it is only through our choices—and the wisdom of experience—that we grow.

The intuitive soul evokes feelings of peace, comfort, and spaciousness while presenting information that provides context for decisions. It encourages us by pointing out our goodness and potential. It never sets us apart or makes us feel superior to others. Only the ego plays that role.

To distinguish the two voices, ask this simple question: "Does this psychic voice, vision, feeling, or inner knowing stir sensations of panic and uncertainty or spaciousness and promise?"

The ego's monkey-mind feeds on worry, dread, and fear. The Spirit comforts, loves, and encourages us. These are two very different movements: one urges us to spiral downward, and the other urges us to spiral upward. Each indicates the fundamental nature of its consciousness.

The Role of Resonance in Readings

Because I love the question "why," my readings tend to paint an over-all picture that reveals the person's life story, purpose, destiny, and how to attain soul growth. Psychics who are hypervigilant might pick up threats to the recipient of the reading. It's all about resonance: what's in *you* determines the type of information you tune in to as well as the content of your readings.

Here's a good example of resonance. Professional intuitive, Mary Roach, guided the audience at a psychic training conference through a psychometry exercise directed to a past life that would relate in some meaningful way to the person's present life. I was paired up with a woman named Gail. She held my Southwestern-style necklace and saw a past life in which I was a nurse or doctor in the Old West and was surrounded by people who wanted and needed healing. She intuited that my stress relief in that life was to ride off into the sunset on a horse with a dog at our heels.

While holding Gail's necklace, I saw a quick image of a small gold cross that gave way to a cinematic vision of her wearing a saloon-gal's outfit of bright red satin and black lace and singing and dancing with considerable talent. Singing and dancing were her diversion from the family she loved, as shown in a quick image of a filigreed piece of jew-elry kept in a round jewelry box.

Both of our readings proved accurate. I am indeed surrounded in this life by people who need healing, and I was grateful for Gail's clos-ing comment that I no longer need to spend most of my time healing other people. I have always felt drawn to horses, although horses don't seem to like me at all. Gail's connection with a Christian group (the small gold cross) led her to singing and dancing, at which she is very talented. She owns a piece of jewelry and a jewelry box similar to what I described, which she received from her loving family.

The point of this example is resonance. Gail and I could easily get on each other's "wavelength" for the readings because we shared similar interests. I saw her singing and dancing because I love to sing and dance. She saw me as a healer because she is a healer.

Did we actually have past lives in the Old West? Who knows? Something much more important came out of the psychometry exercise. In talking with Gail over the lunch break, I learned that she lives on the northeast coast of Scotland at the Findhorn Foundation, a spiritual intentional community that is one of my favorite places on earth. This discovery led us to still another resonance. I wanted a personal story of a kundalini awakening for this book, and Gail has had a kundalini awakening of major proportions. You will find her story in the chapter titled "The Light of Consciousness."

The imagery you obtain in a reading will usually emanate from your resonance with the listener. Resonance explains why you will pick up, out of the entire content of the listener's soul, a particular piece of information. It happens because it means something to both of you!

Resonance also provides an inner certainty of higher awareness by "striking a chord" of truth in the reader and/or listener. If the reading or guidance in meditation, dream interpretation, and inspired writing does not feel true to you, accept what did make sense, and leave the rest behind.

Here's an example of how resonance works—and does not. A professional and highly reputable psychic once gave me a lengthy reading about my upcoming move to Tacoma, Washington, and how I, with my companion (a beautiful red setter), would explore wooded mountains near the sea in what would prove to be the pinnacle of my life. I loved the idea, as this terrain is similar to that of Scotland, and living in that kind of landscape has always been my dream.

What she predicted just did not ring true, and several months later, I learned that *she* had moved to Tacoma, Washington! She displaced, as it's called in remote-viewing research, to a probability that did not manifest, because what resonated the most was in her future rather than in mine.

This curious situation is worth a closer look, as it involves two of the five known reasons why intuitive predictions fail: she missed the mark, and my direction changed.

Potential Futures, Displacement, and the Power of Coherence

When intuitives scan for outcomes, they pick up the probability that is the most highly charged, or numinous. Numinosity, as remote–viewing expert Stephan A. Schwartz explains, is created and influenced by "acts of intentioned, focused awareness," meaning that the more often and the more intensely an idea or place is visited by the fired–up mind and emotions, the higher its psychic "charge," and therefore the easier it is to see, hear, sense, and feel. The reason that remote viewers succeed so well at locating historical artifacts and places is that people have repeatedly invested mental and emotional energies in them over the course of time.

I had certainly revisited my dream of living in the Pacific Northwest, and so had the clairvoyant who read for me; therefore, her psychic prediction—called a probability observation, in remote–viewing terms—described the most numinous outcome for us both at the moment the question, "What does my future look like?" was asked in space–time.

Complicating her reading was another factor that added to the numinosity. Soon after the reading, my husband considered a job possibility in Eugene, Oregon. Due to my uncertainty about various issues, he did not apply for the job. So the numinosity for the Pacific Northwest was very strong: not only was I attracted to the area, as was the psychic, but a choice point in my future also made living in that area of the country a very real possibility.

Because the electromagnetic brain, heart, and auric field imprint our thoughts, feelings, intentions, words, and deeds on the Akashic Record—which exists beyond time and space and yet is very much like a biofeedback device—potential futures coexist with ultimate outcomes. This potential coexistence makes it possible for an intuitive to displace information. An incorrect reading is inevitable when people change their life directions, and both the potential futures and ultimate outcomes will change accordingly.

The other three reasons that predictions fail relate to distortions in energy fields. Solar and/or geomagnetic disturbances in the earth, the reader's fatigue or illness, and the doubt or distrust of people involved in the reading contribute to flux and static that may cause a psychic to displace.

How, then, can any intuitive be accurate? The short answer is coherence in the mind, heart, body, and spirit. Coherence, referring to internal clarity, enables the intuitive reader to pick up the resonating signal without distortion or displacement.

Remote-viewing (RV) research has pinpointed what makes intuitive inquiry, or "anomalous perception," as RVers prefer to call it, work best. The most important factor in probability observation is the remote viewer's (that is, the psychic's) state of mind. Seasoned meditators with high levels of mental coherence make, by far, the best remote viewers. The highest accuracy occurs in people (like meditators) who are inwardly disciplined enough to control internally-created "noise" like mind chatter, analysis, and imaginings that might distort the psi signal.

Let's remote-view this critical factor by zooming into the brain for a closer look at what creates mental coherence.

In the book, *Evolve Your Brain: The Science of Changing Your Mind,* author Joe Dispenza, DC, explains that when we do not pay focused attention to what we are doing, the brain activates other synaptic networks that might distract us with electrical "noise" that confuses consciousness. Concentrated attention, by contrast, causes associated neurons to fire with greater strength and excites new teams of neurons to engage in the point of focus.

To be a better psychic, use your powers of concentration to create the mental coherence that increases attention and brainpower! The new science of neuroplasticity states that "What fires together, wires together." (Originally: "Neurons that fire together wire together," by Donald Hebb.) So it's easy, with practice, to rewire your brain cells and circuitry—which also rewires the body—to a new way of being in the world. The highly adaptable brain accommodates our intentions and desires, whatever those might be.

Schwartz agrees that clear intention, body-mind coherence, and practice all increase "nonlocal perception," or intuitive accuracy. "You have to actually work at it," he emphasizes. "It's not like a free lunch. It's not like a good fairy comes down, waves her wand, and says, 'Now you're a great remote viewer.'"

"You have the innate ability," he continues. "That's in you. That's just a part of being alive. But you've got to use it to get good at it. You've got to develop it as a discipline. It's very much equivalent to a mental martial art." (Visit my international e-newsmagazine at www.oneworldspirit.com to read a lengthy interview with Schwartz on remote viewing.)

Over the years, Edgar Cayce's ability to receive information steadily improved, and so did the scope of that information.

Climbing the Stairway to Heaven

Since intention is the energetic force that propels the soul's sixth sense through time and space, one simply decides whether to read the past, present, or future, and then the soul retrieves that information. Clear spiritual intention enables the soul to resonate with the non-local energy and information in the quantum sea of light that permeates and interpenetrates all of reality.

Schiller-Hanna's teaching partner is Mary Roach, a professional intuitive whose heart-centered work brings understanding, healing, and hope to her clients from all over the world. She presented at the A.R.E. conference a powerful and effective intuitive technique that was used with great success by the people attending. I call it a "stairway to heaven," because that's just what it is. (*See* Resources at the end of this chapter.)

To use this technique, sit comfortably, close your eyes, relax, and conduct yourself through Linda's seven steps to clarify your spiritual intention and to clear, center, and ground yourself and the other person if you're giving a reading for someone else. After you've completed your preparation, begin to imagine yourself walking up a staircase while counting the steps: one, two, three, four, five, six, and seven.

On the seventh step, you arrive at the landing and walk down a hallway. You see a door bearing your name or the listener's name. Open the door and walk into the room to find the information you seek. It will come in the form of an image, symbol, or cinematic movie that gives you a message. Understand what the message means if it's for you, or report your impressions to the recipient of the reading.

Spend as much time in this room as you want or need to. When ready, walk back down the steps one at a time and arouse yourself by wiggling your fingers and toes. Take a few deep, sharp breaths and enjoy a full-body stretch to return completely to the outside space.

This powerful intuitive technique can be used in many different ways. You might walk up the seven steps and at the landing meet an angel holding a box. Inside the box is an object or a symbol. The box may already be open; if not, open it up, and give yourself a little time to fully understand what the symbol means. If the reading is for someone else, describe the symbol. If you are reading for yourself, once you fully perceive the symbol and its meaning, walk back down the steps, open your eyes, and draw the symbol or object with colors or colored markers on a piece of paper, and then write about what you learned. Using the information will encourage your soul to give you more!

Mary Roach of Virginia Beach, VA has been a professional intuitive for more than twenty-five years. She learned how to use her natural psychic abilities in classes on psychic development and assures the reader that anyone can learn. Linda and Mary, a resonant and complementary pair of intuitives, teach together. Linda teaches how to do readings for others, while Mary focuses on accessing your own inner guidance to receive day-to-day insights and solutions.

Both of them advise people to consult a professional psychic when blocked; otherwise, depend on your psychic soul for everyday guidance. Seeking inner guidance on a daily basis is the quickest and best way to build your psychic powers and evolve your consciousness, as you will see and experience in upcoming chapters.

In readings for clients, Mary makes a heart connection with the listener and tunes in to the soul to give life-reference readings that center on past lives. She always looks for the spiritual lessons. "I find the purpose of the whole life and go from there," she said in an interview. "It's sort of like a puzzle. Once you find the purpose, you know the whole thing."

Mary has been hypersensitive to subtle energies as far back as she can remember. She emphasizes that, because the psychic is so wide-open energetically, it's important to use Linda's seven-step preparation with reverence, focus, and the protection of prayer before opening up the soul to give a reading, especially before mentally climbing the seven steps. Not only does this preparation provide coherence and protection, it also ensures that the seven steps will take you as high as you need to go to receive the desired information.

Whether you are reading the past, present, or future for yourself or someone else, you will find Mary's stairway to heaven to be a solid and uplifting structure to stand on while you tune in to psychic information.

Use your soul's creativity to come up with other pathways to higher consciousness. For example, you might imagine entering a garden and looking for the most brilliant flower, one that will contain an intuitive insight. You could walk through a forest in your mind to meet an animal with a message for you. Or you might want to simply close your eyes and remote-view a distant location. Feel how it feels to you, and then try another location. The one that makes you feel happy and spacious is better.

Hypnosis offers a good technique for reading a past or future life. In the quiet of your mind, drift up into the sky and stand on a timeline that stretches ahead of you into the future and behind you into the past. Proceed in either direction toward a bright spot. If you are interested in a past life, ask to see the one that contains the most important insights for you or perhaps the life in which you expressed gifts and talents that would be useful to you now.

Be sure to use the insights you obtain. That's how you will receive more!

Exploring Past Lives

You can use the techniques taught by Linda and Mary or the ones previously mentioned to access a past life of your own or someone else's. Past-life recall reveals patterns of consciousness that extend into our present life. We can change, or reframe, past lives so that no part of us remains "stuck" in the past. Remaining stuck causes a pattern to continually manifest in the present.

Understanding the idea of the Akashic Records as a kind of interactive database reveals the importance of reframing past lives and transforming troublesome patterns of consciousness in the present life. From the Akashic Records, we continually "download" our previous patterns of consciousness and repeat them until we change them and "rewrite" new patterns into boundless space. Looking into past lives often reveals why certain people and situations crop up again and again to teach us the same lessons. People and situations are patterns in consciousness, and all of these reappear until we address and transform them.

How can you tell if a past-life memory is true? Your clairsentience will tell you. Deep inside, you will feel whether it is true or not. But in the end, it doesn't really matter. What is real in the mind is what is real in your present life.

In the chapter on inspired writing, I sketch the stories of three past lives that surfaced in my mind during meditation. Once I recognized their commonality of stubborn willfulness, I did not know what to do next. Inner guidance directed me to transform these lives. I did so by injecting the thought of love into each life, whereupon that past life changed itself—and so did my present life.

Shakespeare wrote in his play, *As You Like It*, that, "All the world's a stage/And all the men and women merely players/They have their exits and their entrances/And one man in his time plays many parts . . . " From my experience of meditative reframing, I learned that we do indeed play many parts on the stage of the mind, and whether those stories from the past are real or imagined, rewriting them changes our character in the present and in the Akasha.

And why shouldn't you change the past if it improves the present and future? It's your mind and your life! Just be sure to realize that it is not a game. It is real. Remote viewing research has proved that anomalous perturbation—that is, influencing reality with the power of the mind—can physically change the past, as long as no one else witnesses what is being done. Rippling into the present, the change that was made in the past changes the future, too.

If an unpleasant past life comes up in a reading, and you or the listener wish to change it, simply hold that past-life story in mind during meditation (the subject of the next chapters) and bring to it the thought of love. The presence of love will unfold a new story with a happy ending. You don't have to imagine the new story; it unfolds on its own. All you need to do is watch what happens, and jot down a few notes to firmly plant the change in your consciousness.

People go to psychics to learn about their past lives, but as Mary Roach points out, you can have this experience for yourself in the privacy of your own home. If you do so, be sure to use Linda's seven steps to prepare, and if you have climbed up the stairway to heaven, close the door to the past, as Mary advises, when you are finished with it.

If someone gives you a past–life reading and it does not resonate with you, toss it out of your mind. Stake nothing on what you hear from someone else. What's important is for *you* to become more psychic. That is the soul's highest purpose. On this idea, you can depend.

Calling All Angels

Not everyone sends out a desperate cry for help, turns around in her living room the next night, and finds that an angel named John Reid has come to the rescue. But that's exactly what happened to angel-communicator Kim O'Neill, a guest speaker at the A.R.E.'s psychic development conference. Kim said that everyone's angels are helping them all of the time, and, if the desire is strong enough, these angels will materialize. (*See* Resources at the end of this chapter.)

O'Neill's story is credible and persuasive. Her guardian angel guided her every step of the way into psychic attunement. She left her advertising agency in Houston, Texas, opened a professional psychic practice, and was soon led to appear on national radio and television shows and to psychic detective work with the American FBI and Secret Service. Next came the publication of her first book, *How to Talk with Your Angels.*

Still more persuasive are stories told in her new book, *The Calling: My Journey with the Angels.* This compelling autobiography traces her angelic guidance to the clearing of a past–life memory in which she was an eight–year–old Jewish girl in a Nazi concentration camp. Facing this horrific experience invoked the courage she had in that lifetime and dissipated her present–life need to hide from people, which alleviated her paralyzing fear of public speaking.

In this life, John Reid and the spirit of actress Jean Harlow alerted her to the place and the moment she would meet her soul mate. She married the man and is the mother of two children who see, play, and talk with departed spirits and their own guardian angels. Kim was in constant psychic communication with her first child from before her conception through the moment of birth and wrote a book on this subject, too: *Bond with Your Baby before Birth.*

Skeptics may question O'Neill's story, while others will be happy to hear about a leading psychic who was nudged by angels toward a destiny that surpassed her wildest dreams. For cynics and believers alike, the only way to know the truth of O'Neill's story is to experiment with angelic guidance. When you do so, be sure to keep your mind open and receptive. Kim offers readers encouragement by quoting Martin Luther King, Jr.: "You don't need to see the whole staircase, just take the first step."

The key to angelic guidance, she said, is "just to listen all the time," even if you don't have any human support in your endeavor. The angelic communication will come in your own voice. Follow the advice, and you will receive more. Keep a record of your process and progress, and keep track of predictions that prove true. As time passes, your journals and tangible signs will reveal that your angelic guidance is real and accurate.

Kim promised the audience that as we transform our consciousness, new guardian angels will come to work with us. Your angels, matched to you by personality, will "help you work with spiritual contracts" that you have committed to with others. If you begin to channel angelic guidance for others, tell people exactly what you hear.

Psychic information flows in through all of Kim's psychic centers, as it does for Linda and Mary. "We all have psychic gifts, although they are more pronounced in some people than others," Kim said in an interview with me. "If you put in the work, you get the reward. It doesn't have to run in your family. It's not about being ordained."

"Listening to spirit makes us more mature and confident, and we move ahead faster," she added. The ultimate goal is "to help people discover who they are so all of us can accrue as much independence and empowerment as possible."

Kim, Mary, and Linda agree that seeking inner guidance for ourselves is the best approach to soul growth, but if we get stuck, then it's time to get help. There's no better help, said Kim, than help from our guardian angels.

Still, everything comes down to our willingness to become as coherent as possible in order to receive and use that guidance.

The Cayce Readings on How to Enhance Your Psychic Abilities

In his book *Understand and Develop Your ESP*, Cayce expert, Mark Thurston, synthesizes and distills the Cayce readings to provide a list of suggestions (that I have italicized) on how to become more coherent and thereby enhance your psychic abilities.

The starting point, *ideals* and *self-analysis*, puts us in touch with who we really are and what we want out of life. That idea was the welcome discovery of the first Edgar Cayce study group, formed back in 1931, as its thirteen members practiced the spiritual lessons in the 130 readings given for them. They added their own experiences of these teachings to the two small volumes which became the *A Search for God* (ASFG) texts. The books are still in use today by Cayce study groups, which are sprouting up all over the world.

Belonging to an "ASFG" study group for ten years awakened my mind and ramped up my psychic abilities more than anything else, apart from inspired writing. In 1993, one of my writings predicted that something important was just ahead, and it would teach me to meditate. A light–filled series of synchronicities guided me to a presentation on Edgar Cayce study groups in a local library, and as soon as I walked into the room, my soul–eyes lit upon six other people scattered in the crowd of forty. All six of them signed up for an alternate meeting in my home, once a week on Tuesday nights.

We were resonant, to say the least, and quickly became the best of friends and teachers for one another. In our first meeting, we took turns reading aloud the content of the Meditation chapter in the first ASFG book, and I was astonished to find in this introduction to meditation everything my inner voice had been teaching me for the previous seven years. The Cayce style of meditation carried me into the same state of consciousness as did my meditative writings. In *silent meditation* my mind grew lastingly coherent, and so did my life.

Creating an ideal by which to live, practicing meditation, and reading the text's lessons on cooperation, love, the destiny of the body, knowledge, and virtue, to name a few chapter titles, provoked lively discussions that revealed our beliefs and *attitudes* and provided ample opportunity for self-analysis. Each of us looked into the mirror of the others to see ourselves more clearly, and what we did not like, we changed.

Everyone took up *dream study*, and at one point, several people experimented with sending telepathic messages to each other at certain times of the day. Continued practice increased their accuracy. As our spiritual commitment and intuitive powers grew, each of us paid more attention to our *diet*, realizing, as Cayce believed, that we are what we eat and think.

Recognizing the body's influence on consciousness, and vice versa, we steered away from overeating, unwise food-combining, and choosing hyper-acidic foods. We found that these foods do indeed congest fluids, dull the physical senses, and hamper the intuitive senses. One small step toward health led us to others, including *physical exercise*, which sharpens the psychic senses by improving general health and balancing the endocrine glands associated with the chakras and the body's subtle energy system.

All seven study group members experimented with other Cayce suggestions for psychic attunement, such as using *castor-oil packs* applied to the lower abdomen to stimulate the lymphatic system's expulsion of toxins and wastes. Besides using castor oil packs on my lower back, which gave me immense pain relief, I also began to see a chiropractor for *spinal adjustments*. Those treatments conjoin the two nervous systems and, as Thurston points out, connect the conscious mind with the subconscious soul.

I followed Cayce's recipe for physical health with great success. Eating consciously, getting regular chiropractic adjustments, applying castor oil packs, and walking around my neighborhood caused my chronic back pain to disappear entirely within three years (I was counting). Careless overwork brings it back, but it's not nearly as painful as it was. All things considered, I am much healthier today due to Cayce's guidance.

None of the young people in my study group were overly enthusiastic about reading *The Holy Bible*, but we did dutifully explore the passages referred to in the readings, giving special attention to the fourteenth through seventeenth chapters of John and the thirtieth chapter of Deuteronomy. Cayce considered these to be wisdom teachings that would enhance one's connection with the divine.

Spending time in nature came naturally to us, as we lived in the lush, semi-tropical state of Louisiana, where the warm, sunny climate beckons everyone outside. We were already attracted to *gems and stones*, which enhance psychic ability in some people, thought Cayce, by emanating and attracting helpful vibrations. Thurston notes that Cayce often recommended various types of lapis—such as malachite, azurite, lazurite, and chrysocolla—to be worn against the throat or heart. Since some people need to encase these stones in crystal, be sure to use your intuitive awareness to choose the stones that work best for you and where to place them.

Joining "A Search for God" study group increased our psychic abilities in countless and immeasurable ways, simply by bringing us into body-mind coherence and guiding us toward more spiritual lives. I recommend joining one of these groups to you, dear reader, above everything else.

Some of my study group members, including me, have moved to other parts of the country. Despite physical separation, the lessons we learned together forged spiritual bonds that will last forever.

Psychic Circles

It is also this writer's hope that you might consider forming a Psychic Circle. Such an event, held periodically, would be a great deal of fun as each person practices giving readings. Everyone would receive valuable information, and giving readings would sharpen their psychic senses and quickly widen these channels.

The people you invite will be delighted to attend. After all, who doesn't want to obtain information about their lives, especially for free!

You may wish to invite only friends and family to begin with. Since you might already know a great deal about these people, you could direct paired readings to the past and future, remote-viewing, and psychometry exercises using a photograph, for example, or a personal item. Practice meditation together, and if available listen to my CD titled *The Meditation Experience: Listening to Your Psychic Soul.* I would love to hear about your experiences for my newsletters and possibly a future book.

As time passes, friends of friends will want to join your Psychic Circle. Not knowing the new people intimately will allow you to do present-life readings and receive immediate feedback that measures your accuracy.

If this concept were to spread from city to city and nation to nation, what a wonderful world this would be! Upcoming chapters express more about the power of soul energy to uplift consciousness and heal people. I can't think of anything more beautiful than *ASFG* study groups and Psychic Circles that evolve participants' consciousness and positively transform the world at the same time!

Bioenergetic Fields of Light

While in Virginia Beach, VA attending the psychic development conference described in this chapter, I had a vivid dream about walking along a neighborhood sidewalk until I came to a tall, wooden panel strung with wire. I had to walk into the street to detour around this obstruction and then walk back to the open sidewalk to continue my journey. I awakened from this dream with the words "bioenergetic fields of light" ringing in my ears. With this phrase came a fully developed concept of how energy moves in the body and in the earth.

See in your mind's eye how energy travels the planet in ley lines that function like the meridians in the human body. The energies of the past and present travel along these circuits and determine how energy moves in the people in that vicinity: is the energy building, diminishing, or rapidly shifting?

Neither the spiritual kundalini coiled at the base of the spine, which carries the body–mind into psychic consciousness, nor the earth's creative energies can move past blockages. Because everything in existence is a bioenergetic field of light, consciousness is confined to internal and environmental fields until it can blast through blockages.

Cayce spoke in one reading (294-131) of how the vibrations of some cities are lower than others. One will have a commercial "radiation," as he put it, and another will have a healing radiation that will be much easier to read. It's easy to see intuitively how the radiation of the people and places you read will influence the accuracy of your readings.

Clear receivers and transmitters of spiritual energy create high-energy resonance, or numinosity, for the intuitive to "lock onto." In numinous places the "veil" between the physical and spiritual dimensions—lower and higher frequencies of vibration—is very thin. These are the spiritual power points of the planet, such as Findhorn, Scotland; Big Sur, California; Sedona, Arizona; and Virginia Beach, Virginia, to name a few. The numinosity of these energy-filled places is very high.

When people move into these bioenergetic fields—created by everything from *ASFG* study groups and Psychic Circles to self-realized people and mystical places like Glastonbury, England—they are profoundly affected by these fields of light.

If you want to be revitalized—to feel more vital—visiting such places on a spiritual pilgrimage will charge you up with positive energy. Perhaps you have already noticed how powerful people and places stimulate inner transformation. Bioenergetic fields, whether in people or places, harmonically resonate with the highest frequencies in the superconscious and clear away unresolved issues.

Sometimes issues fly out of consciousness, and that's the end of them; at other times, we look at them too closely and get emotionally entangled again. In the latter case, we must deepen into the meditative brainwaves of the superconscious soul to extricate ourselves.

Whatever happens to us in any given moment is inwardly initiated by past and present thoughts and feelings and our resonance with environmental fields. If the environment is shifting and changing, the fluctuating vibrations will stir change in us. If we are stagnant, this monotony will cause stagnation in our environmental field or fields. The entire organism—composed of local and global and universal fields—is interacting at every moment in a co-creative effort that is moving us toward positive change.

If you want to be a positive influence for the world, charge yourself up by clearing out what obstructs Light so that you can radiate more light to charge up and clear others and the place you live. To have even more of a positive impact on the world, live in a light-filled place and add your light to it—inhabit a dynamic area filled with creative, spiritual people devoted to enlightening the planet and All There Is.

We fill with Light to become more as-Light, and like a lantern, we illuminate the way to God's peace, joy, fulfillment, spiritual awakening, creative flow, and psychic Soul. Intuitively plugging in to the bioenergetic fields of other spiritually-minded people lifts all of us into the frequencies of the web of light that define the next highest dimension. That dimension is a world of peace created by our own consciousness, whether in this material earth or another world that looks like it but vibrates at a higher frequency where people are more evolved.

The web is infinite and so are we.

How do we recognize these places of great spiritual and electromagnetic energy? We feel them with our clairsentience! There are fewer blockages in these locations. Vistas are wide open, and our dreams are more vivid and profound. In sunlight and fog, we look beyond the floaters in our eyes and behold the charged particles of energy—tiny white pinpoints of light—that are filled with the promise of higher consciousness inside them.

Winds, tides, and sunlight clear the energies in these places, just as we actively clear, with our rise in consciousness, the inner self and our bioenergetic fields. "Stuff" in us surfaces and clears out; we are transformed, and our psychic attunement becomes more dynamic and vibrant.

In the Meditation chapter of the *ASFG* texts, Edgar Cayce describes psychic attunement as a radio. Our clarity—a matter of soul development—is one important factor in our intuitive reception; the other is the radio's position in space. Its location amidst surrounding fields also determines the strength and accuracy of our psychic abilities.

Everything in existence is a real-time biofeedback loop operating between and among these fields of light. Every positive change we make in consciousness changes the environmental fields that surround us.

How to make changes in the brain and its frequencies of consciousness in order to better attune the "radio" is the subject of the next three chapters. How the transformation of human consciousness changes bioenergetic and superluminal fields that compose the interactive Akashic Records of the past, present, and future is the subject of following chapters.

In the rest of this book, you will learn how the conscious evolution taking place on this planet today is creating a new reality that is lifting us, through interpenetrating bioenergetic fields of light, into the divine consciousness that makes the soul and everything else blossom.

Resources:

Linda Schiller-Hanna can be reached through her Web site, www.lightworker22.com for a reading. Or email her at linda@lightworker22.com if you have HIV or AIDS or wish to refer someone to her for free intuitive counseling.

Mary Roach is available for readings in person or by telephone. She lives in Virginia Beach, VA. To schedule a reading, request her telephone number by calling the A.R.E. at 1–800–333–4499.

Kim O'Neill can be reached for a reading through her Web site at KimOneillPsychic.com.

Peter Van Daam's *Exercises: Western Yoga for All*, developed using guidelines in the psychic readings of Edgar Cayce in cooperation with the A.R.E., 2006, a DVD, explains Cayce's exercise techniques and their physiological effect on the body. The DVD demonstrates gentle movements that strengthen the body and improve overall health.

4

The Brainwaves of Consciousness

*"But strange that I was not told / That the brain can hold /
In a tiny ivory cell / God's heaven or hell."—Oscar Wilde*

What part of the mind does inner guidance come from, and how
do we tap into it at any time? Why does meditation increase intuitive
abilities, and how does it awaken and evolve our consciousness? Where
does the soul reside, and how does it manifest? Who am I, really?

Nearly forty years of fascinating research into how the mind works
and how to master it will answer all of these questions for you, except
for the last one. With this information, you will be able to answer it for
yourself, if you haven't already.

The subject of brainwaves–the electrical activities of the mind–may
initially strike you as too complicated and, possibly, as unnecessary science. It is anything but that. Understanding how your brain or mind works
will provide you with an inner map for navigating with ease into higher
states of consciousness. Mastering your brainwaves will enable you to
power-up your intuitive abilities to guide your conscious mind and life.

Questions you did not even know you had will be answered in this and the next two chapters, and you will be amazed by the "aha" insights that well up in your mind. While explaining why the two intuitive techniques—the seven preparatory steps and the stairway to heaven—work so well, these three chapters about the brainwaves of meditation and mind expansion will enable you to listen to your companion meditations with greater awareness and understanding.

With this information, you will be able to guide yourself into psychic awareness in mere moments. Soon, if you like, you will be able to live in that higher state of consciousness.

Interested? If so, let's get started.

What is Consciousness?

The human brain, composed of ninety billion brain cells and about a thousand times more connections between them, entertains some 60,000 separate thoughts each day. The brain is by far the most powerful processing unit in existence. Each thought or emotion produces the electrical activity of brainwaves. Those brainwaves travel at incredible speeds through the neural (nerve) circuitry of the brain and body to regulate the nervous system and create a state of consciousness.

Consciousness is not confined to the brain. Rather, consciousness is a composite of all our aspects: the mind, heart, body, and soul—each of which influences the others. Brainwaves cascade thoughts and emotions into the body's electromagnetic auric field, which projects out into physical space to influence the consciousness of everything it touches. Similarly, the brain and auric field are influenced by environmental energies emanating from people and places, as well as by the universal field of superconscious light that so profoundly changes brainwave patterns and rewires the mind, heart, and body to a higher vibration.

Human consciousness is essentially a high-speed communication network—a living matrix of energy—that in every moment resonates with every dimension of reality, all of which shows up in brainwave patterns and states that portray a local and universal view of consciousness.

The Frequencies of the Mind

We can see brainwave patterns in real time on a unique electroencephalograph called the Mind Mirror. Unlike any other EEG, the Mind Mirror monitors, maps, and measures the subject's frequencies of consciousness. It produces a continuous picture of brain rhythms that can be read and understood by the practitioner during an EEG session and used to guide the subject into optimal states of awareness that more fully awaken and evolve the mind.

The Mind Mirror was created to map higher states of awareness. It was invented in 1974 by the English biophysicist, Zen meditator, master hypnotist, and psychical researcher, C. Maxwell Cade, with Geoffrey Blundell, electronics engineer and mind researcher. Cade connected yogis, swamis, psychics, mediums, and healers to the Mind Mirror to see what their brainwaves looked like. He discovered the brainwave patterns of meditation and the awakened mind of meditation and psychic masters.

Maxwell Cade's ground–breaking book, *The Awakened Mind: Biofeedback and the Development of Higher States of Awareness,* promised what the title says: for the past forty years, people all over the world have used his understanding of the state and content of consciousness to guide themselves into brain rhythms that develop higher awareness.

To teach you about this awareness, this chapter explores four categories of consciousness: beta, alpha, theta, and delta. Unlike the spiky "raw trace" of brainwaves produced by medical EEGs, the Mind Mirror shows a composite picture of consciousness that includes both sides of the brain and the interrelationship of the four brainwave categories. With a little practice, anyone can read and interpret these patterns. (But you won't have to.)

Fourteen horizontal frequency bars show the speed, or rapidity, of thought. The width of the frequency bar shows its amplitude, or signal power. Both are indicated in the following diagram.

BRAINWAVE PATTERNS

1. Frequency—the rate or speed of vibration, high or low (vertical arrows)

2. Amplitude—the strength of the signal (horizontal arrows)

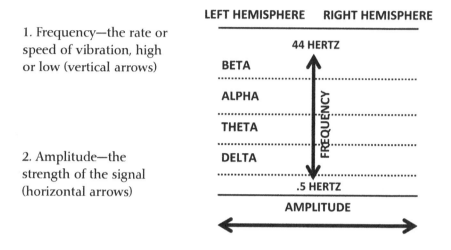

Some thirty awakened–mind practitioners in the United States, Brazil, England, Holland, and other countries use the Mind Mirror to monitor their clients' brainwaves during EEG–led meditations geared to self–discovery, healing, and transformation. Guiding people into the subconscious for personal transformation connects them with the psychic soul (my term) for creative insights and solutions used to clear repressed issues, release suppressed creativity, and awaken the mind to self–mastery, peak performance, spiritual connection, and illumination—also referred to as enlightenment or cosmic consciousness.

Acquainting people with the *feeling* of various states of consciousness—which is what we do in this chapter—enables them to access an optimal meditation state and master their brainwaves for creativity, insight, and healing. Self–mastery for intuitive awakening is the central purpose of this book, since the inner guidance of the soul awakens and evolves consciousness faster than anything else.

The Four Brainwave Categories

To begin with, here's an overview of the four primary brainwave categories and their content:

Beta (30–14 Hz)
The conscious mind of normal waking consciousness.
The intellect's verbal, linear, and logical thought
in external orientation.
High beta produces stress, anxiety, and panic.

Alpha (14–8 Hz)
Relaxed, sensory awareness produced as we shift
from the external to the internal world.
Daydreaming, visualization, light meditation, imagination.
The frequency bridge between beta and theta.

Theta (8–4 Hz)
The subconscious mind of long–term memory, dreaming, REM
sleep, emotional healing, intuition, creativity, spiritual insight.
The mind of the soul.

Delta (4–0.5 Hz)
The personal unconscious, doorway to Universal Consciousness.
Deep, restorative, dreamless sleep.
Empathy and a kind of radar that scans the environment
and psychically picks up information and energy.

You can see from these brief descriptions and their frequencies that meditation and psychic inquiry (including both inner guidance and intuitive readings for others) require a deepening of awareness from the higher frequencies of beta's external conscious mind to the lower frequencies of alpha's relaxed inner awareness, to theta's creative connection with the soul, and to delta's radar–like resonance with Universal Consciousness.

Edgar Cayce placed the psychic soul in the subconscious, and it's easy to see why. The subconscious is the repository of long–term memories accrued in this life, and according to Cayce, in past lives as well. Hypnotists conducting past–life regressions agree with this idea and so do Mind–Mirror readings. Meditation, creative work, dream study, inspired writing, and energy healing all take place in the frequencies of the subconscious mind.

It may occur to you to wonder why, if the psychic soul resides in theta, psychic awareness is associated with delta. The answer to this question is that you *are* your soul.

When your soul externalizes its awareness, it speeds up its frequencies to operate in beta's conscious mind. In alpha's sensory awareness, the soul connects with nature to look into signs and symbols for insights, or simply daydreams or meditates. Resting in subconscious theta, the soul provides creative insights and spiritual awareness for emotional healing and intuitive connection with its sixth sense. The soul deepens into the lower frequencies of delta when it does not have its own answers; then its sixth sense connects with Universal Consciousness to draw in universal insights and energies that revitalize its body, mind, heart, and spirit.

The soul, centered in the alpha–theta frequencies of meditation, intuitive inquiry, and related endeavors, attunes to a "still point" in consciousness that is much like the glassy lake mentioned in the second chapter. The same still point is reached in deep subconscious meditation, dreaming, and dreamless sleep, all of which enable the quiet, receptive mind to resonate with the high–frequency energies in the Field.

When this resonance happens, the higher vibrations of the Field rewire the brain and body to the higher consciousness of the meditation master, psychic, and healer. This higher consciousness raises the soul's vibrational level and that of every other interconnected and interdependent realm of existence.

The evolution of just one soul raises the vibration of Universal Consciousness.

Deepening into Higher States

How do we deepen into the soul's awareness? We simply go down and into our consciousness, much as you did in the last chapter with the seven–step preparation for a psychic reading. But before we explore other ways to deepen into soul awareness, let's look at a description of human and universal consciousness presented in the Meditation chapter of *A Search for God, Book I*, on page 3:

We are miniature copies of the universe, possessing physical, mental, and spiritual bodies. These bodies are so closely knit together that the impressions of one have their effects upon the other two. The physical body is a composite unit of creative force manifesting in a material world. So all-inclusive is the physical body that there is nothing in the universe that man can comprehend that does not have its miniature replica within it. It is not only our privilege but our duty to know ourselves, and to be aware of our bodies being temples of the living God.

This reading, given three-quarters of a century ago, may sound like mystical mumbo-jumbo. Instead, it is a scientific key to the conscious universe.

Today, the theory of a holographic reality is winning widespread acceptance among scientists. The theory rests on the concept of a quantum field of light that is filled with information and connects everything in existence. Physicists are now saying that the brain's sensory apparatuses, acting as converters, configure light waves into visible objects including the earth, animals, and humans, and that these physical forms are mere representations of energies that preexist in higher frequencies of the Field.

Edgar Cayce presaged this theory in his famous statement that, " . . . the spirit is life; the mind is the builder; the physical is the result . . . " (349-4)

If these physicists and Cayce are correct, then everything in the physical world—including each of us—is a hologram created by its consciousness; therefore all physical forms contain all of existence. The ultimate meaning is that the infinite knowledge of the Field resides in everything. This universal consciousness resides especially in the subconscious mind, which is the repository of the soul that is the source of the mind, heart, and physical body.

This expanded view of reality is a paradigm shifter for the busy, thinking mind engaged in the hologram of physical reality. The rational ego, always a bit hesitant about change, goes more willingly into the night with the understanding that slowing its frequencies to intuitively perceive the information in its subconscious and universal mind will dramatically increase its brainpower, thus providing an evolutionary pathway to the life of its dreams.

Quieting the Beta Brainwaves of the Conscious Mind

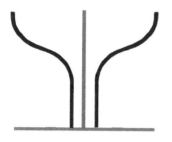

In this diagram of beta, the ego's verbal conscious mind is either thinking random thoughts or using its linear and logical intellect to analyze, evaluate, plot, and plan. Beta's normal waking awareness is externally oriented, as you can see in this upwardly spread-out, "splayed" beta pattern.

When beta speeds up to process more complex tasks like list-making and decision-making, frequencies rise and amplitudes increase. Beta's highest frequencies and amplitudes produce stress, anxiety, and panic, and what Edgar Cayce called "broken points of consciousness," wherein the mind is moving so fast that it just can't connect the dots to see the whole picture. (*A Search for God*, p. 10)

If you've ever had a restless, distracted mind (and who hasn't?), you know how stressful, fatiguing, and counter-productive high beta can be. Self-criticism, doubt, and uncertainty reside in high beta, along with the chattering "monkey mind" that swings from tree to tree in search of the next banana. Beta's chattering ego can be the biggest obstacle to meditation and psychic inquiry. Once the conscious mind taps into the inspiration flowing through the subconscious, the ego quiets down and develops the stability and continuity of consciousness that brings life into focus and gives rise to creative genius.

Beta Mastery Techniques

The companion meditation, "The Lake of Inner Peace," listed as a resource at the end of this chapter, is designed to relax beta waves. Reducing beta is easy when you remember this rule: in most people, relaxing the body relaxes the mind; and relaxing the mind relaxes the body. Beta mastery increases peace, which gives us the patience and flexibility needed to tolerate the constant changes in life.

Beta mastery also ensures that your ego will not impede, influence, or distort psychic impulses—simply because beta's ego is not present! Experiment with the following mind–calming techniques from yogic science and brainwave biofeedback to find which ones work best for you.

Diaphragmatic breathing, as seen in infants, is the healthiest and most natural way to breathe. Focusing on your lower abdomen, allow your belly to be soft. Pushing your belly out, draw air into your lower and then upper lungs. To exhale, simply let go. As your upper and lower lungs deflate, your belly will relax and contract. Expanding and contracting the lower abdomen in a bellows–like action slows respiration and relaxes the long vagus (cranial) nerve that controls the involuntary and voluntary nervous systems. The result is self–regulation: you are able to bring your whole body and mind under your conscious control.

Slow your breath. Fixing attention on the breath lessens *self*-consciousness and causes the voluntary and involuntary nervous systems and their sensory channels to overlap so that mind–body awareness merges simultaneously into a single identity, wrote Cade in his book. No wonder every good meditation begins with breath control!

In ordinary consciousness, we breathe between seven and seventeen times per minute. Body–mind arousal causes rapid and shallow breathing; conversely, slowing and deepening the breath creates body–mind relaxation. So, to relax, simply slow your breathing rate. Try this right now for one minute. Notice how you feel beforehand, and then slow down your breath as much as you comfortably can. Or breathe in for half as many counts as you breathe out: breathe in to the count of two, breathe out to the count of four, or breathe in to the count of three and breathe out to the count of six. Both of these breath–slowing techniques activate the parasympathetic (relaxation) nervous system and profoundly relax the body and mind.

Relax the back of your tongue. One of the simplest and most effective ways to quiet beta is a yogic technique involving relaxation of the tongue. Focus your awareness on the back of your tongue at its root in the back of your throat, and keep it relaxed for sixty seconds. When the tongue is relaxed, the mind can't talk to itself, and thoughts drift away. You will find your body and mind relaxing into the diffused, daydreaming alpha waves of lower frequencies.

Withdraw from the outside environment. Slowing your breath and relaxing your tongue automatically withdraws awareness into the self. However, if you find that beta's attention keeps jumping back to external awareness, you will need to exert discipline.

First, close your eyes and take a moment to notice where your consciousness is located. If your mind is very active, you may feel its electrical activity in an area that is just outside of your head. In this case, simply imagine throwing a lasso around your thoughts and drawing them into your head. Holding your thoughts inside your head, immerse them in white light flowing down from your crown chakra, located above and toward the back of your head (where a crown would sit). Next, gently draw your light–filled thoughts down into your heart and hold them there. Pour white light from your crown into the thoughts held in your heart. Soon your thoughts will slow down and drift away.

Progressively relax your body. Progressive relaxation is one of the most effective ways to reduce beta waves, possibly because it takes about five minutes to complete, and in that time, the ego gives up and goes away. Some people imagine each body part relaxing from a viewpoint outside the body. Other people relax from the inside. Both viewpoints work equally well. Start at the top of your head and work down to your toes, just relaxing and letting go of tension in each part of your body. Breathe light into especially tense areas until all you can see inside yourself is light.

With a little practice the mere thought of physical relaxation will instantly relax your body. It will remember the routine; you will sink down into deep relaxation in one fell swoop.

Expanding into Alpha's Sensory Awareness

Relaxing the body and mind into lower beta frequencies generates the diffused, detached awareness of alpha, which is most often experienced in daydreaming. Closing the eyes to relax or go to sleep generates alpha frequencies that may be present in dreams to provide clear imagery and are always present in lucid dreams when the conscious mind is awake and observing the dream.

In waking states, sensory awareness of any kind of activates alpha, which graciously lowers a frequency bridge to the subconscious for meditation and/or inner imagery. It's a two-way bridge: thoughts flow down from the conscious mind across the alpha bridge into the subconscious and unconscious; and impulses flow up from the unconscious and subconscious across the alpha bridge into the conscious mind's intellect.

The activities of gazing at flowers and landscapes, gardening, fishing, and other relaxing outdoor pursuits generate the sensory awareness and clear, vivid imagery formed in alpha, which occupies the same frequencies as the earth and its principles of healing and growth. For this reason, healing most often takes place in alpha.

The following exercises will familiarize you with how alpha feels, in case you've been too busy to live in it. Be sure to find a representative *landmark* for the feeling of this state of consciousness: a word, phrase, image, symbol, concept, or body sensation. Since the brain can't tell the difference between a real and an imagined event, reimagining a landmark recreates the original brainwaves and a return to that state of consciousness. Landmarks are shortcuts to brainwave states, and you will find them very useful.

Since not everyone sees imagery, we use the word sensualization, or sensory imagination, to describe the use of some or all of the inner and outer senses.

Alpha Sensualization: Connecting with Nature

To do the first part of this exercise, go outside in the daytime and widen your gaze to take in the whole sky. Notice how simply expanding your perspective relaxes your body and mind. Enjoy this relaxation and deepen it by noticing the colors, forms, textures, patterns, and play of light on whatever you see. Watch the wind, listen to the birds, feel sunlight on your face, and get in intuitive touch with the energy that is vibrating in everything. Imagine drawing these energies into your body, mind, and spirit. Detach from thoughts and focus only on sensory awareness.

Next, draw your attention to the space around your body. Just notice your body's position in space and extend your peripheral vision as far as is comfortable. Notice how your mind expands as your perception of space increases. Before you end this meditation, take a moment to find a representative landmark. It might be what you are experiencing. Instead, some other word, image, concept, or body sensation may come to mind.

Shifting our attention to any aspect of nature evokes positive emotions and the balanced health, harmony, and wholeness that are the governing principles of the earth. Feelings of happiness, joy, and love—more than anything else—link the soul to the divine.

Beingness Meditations

The above meditation encouraged you to generate alpha waves by attuning your physical senses to nature and the awareness of space around your body. You can also attune inwardly to generate alpha waves; simply close your eyes and experience an inner landscape with all of your senses. All good meditations begin with sensory experiences that activate the five inner senses and kinesthesia, the sense of moving around in space.

Focusing the mind's awareness on a sensory experience like the beingness meditation below engages all four lobes of the brain in alpha synchrony, which leads to deep meditation, the high-performance (or peak-performance) mind, and better health.

Beingness meditations invite the mind to project its awareness into any kind of object such as a tree, book, animal, computer, cell phone, flower, garden, or ocean. The brain plunges into enjoyable mind play to "become" that object. Sensory experience is so pleasant that the brain/mind deepens into alpha without any need for beta mastery. Beta just goes along for the ride.

You might want to have someone read this meditation to you, guide yourself through it, or record and play it back to yourself. Experience it in a quiet, comfortable place where you won't be interrupted. Jot down your insights afterward, as you will be asked to use them.

Alpha Beingness Meditation: Sensualizing a Plant

Close your eyes, withdraw into yourself, relax a little, and begin to sensualize yourself as a plant in a garden. You could be a real plant or a fantasy plant. Use all of your senses to bring this experience to life.

What kind of plant are you? How big are you and what is your shape?

What is your color? Do you have any blossoms?

Are you growing in a container, or in the ground?

What kind of roots do you have?

How deep are your roots? How far do they spread?

What kind of soil are you planted in? Is it dry . . . or moist? Fertile . . . or barren?

How are you fed? Who feeds you?

Are there any other plants growing near you? How many and what kind?

What does the rest of the garden look like, and where in it are you placed?

What makes you happy? What makes you feel sad?

What makes you feel strong? Courageous? Whole and free?

What is your role or purpose in life?

Use all of your senses to live the experience of being this plant.

* * *

Soon you are going to turn back into your human form.

But before you do, take a few moments to focus on the qualities and characteristics of your plant form that you would like to bring back with you into your human form.

What are your qualities and characteristics? Find two or three words that describe what you are like as this plant. Meditate on this idea for a few moments and crystallize these qualities into words.

When you are ready, gently come back to the outside space with the memory of your qualities and characteristics. Wiggle your fingers and toes to awaken from your meditation. Enjoy a full-body stretch.

Experiencing the inner or outer world with the senses generates a light or deep meditation state. Perhaps you felt a distinct shift in consciousness, as if, upon awakening from the meditation, you were emerging from a daydream. That's the feeling of alpha, the first stage of a silent or working meditation. If you were able to sustain your attention and awareness on being a plant, then your alpha bridge opened and your psychic soul reminded you of qualities and characteristics that you possess, deep down, and can use in your life right now.

The best way to use this information is to create an "I am" sentence out of these qualities and characteristics, and then repeat this sentence in waking life as an affirmation or during meditation as a mind-centering mantra. Consciously using the wisdom of your soul will assist you with present and future challenges that your soul perceives or foresees. This practice will attune your mind, body, and heart to the presence and high-sense perception of your soul.

For example, if the plant you became in the above meditation was a rose and your qualities and characteristics were colorful, friendly, and uplifting, your affirmation might read, "I am colorful, friendly, and uplifting." Chances are that you may not feel that way at the moment, which is why you have received this guidance. When you feel pale, unfriendly, and droopy, repeating this affirmation will shift your thoughts to these brighter and happier qualities and consequently create a positive change in consciousness that will help you through life's challenges.

(It will also rewire your brain and body to an openness that gives you greater access to soul guidance.)

That's quite a lot for one simple affirmation to accomplish, isn't it? Yet this is just the kind of practical and profound inner guidance you can expect from your omniscient soul.

Measuring Your Sensory Imagery

As mentioned in Chapter 2, most people have access to only one or two of their inner senses, and some people have very little sensory awareness: they cannot see, hear, or feel an inner experience yet may somehow sense what is taking place. In most cases, what causes sensory imagery to be hazy or sporadic is wavering attention. Random thoughts break the mind's concentration and cause imagery to fade in and out.

If you lost concentration in the plant–sensualization meditation, don't worry. It works better when we are guided through it. Try one of the companion meditations, a beingness meditation titled "What Instrument Am I," which is referenced at the end of this chapter.

Strengthening your powers of concentration will enable you to guide yourself through meditation with full access to inner imagery. The beta mastery techniques in the section above and the Sensualization Exercises in Appendix A will also help you develop a strong, stable, and multisensory alpha bridge.

If you found yourself drifting off during the plant sensualization, as if "blanking" or "trancing" out, then you were slipping down below alpha into theta. The best remedy is to sharply focus your mind on your senses. While being a plant, for example, you might listen intently to the wind as it blows through the garden and allow yourself to sway as the wind caresses your body. Zooming in on imagery as if you were a camera intensifies the quality of your attention and lifts alpha waves into higher frequencies that are closer to beta's waking awareness.

Other ways to stay awake include rubbing or pressing your fingers together and sliding your feet across the floor to arouse your nervous system. Taking a deep, sharp breath of air oxygenates the sleepy brain.

Keeping your alpha brainwaves turned on is the key to taking the brainwaves of meditation out into the world as the awakened mind of psychic mastery. Being able to maintain your alpha state enables you to have both inner and outer awareness at the same time: an important definition of the awakened mind.

Seeking inner guidance develops all of the inner senses as well as the soul's sixth sense. The more senses you develop, the more stable and continuous your alpha waves will become. And just as alpha connects beta's conscious mind with theta's subconscious, it is also the connecting link to the superconscious. In reading 5754-3, Cayce was asked how to train the sixth sense. He advised the seeker to develop the " . . . mental visioning in the imaginative forces, that which is constantly associated with the senses of the body . . . "

We know this mental visioning and sensory awareness as the activity of alpha brainwaves. With this sensory bridge wide open, you can easily slip down into your soul's subconscious to communicate directly with your superconscious higher self, gaining insights for your life along the way.

Tapping into Theta, Your Subconscious Soul

The alpha bridge opens to the calm, quiet theta waves that compose the subconscious mind, defined by Edgar Cayce as an "attribute" of the soul, or the "mind of the soul" (*see* especially reading 3744-3). Brainwave biofeedback science agrees that theta contains our essential being, as it is the storehouse of long-term memories and thus the material, or content, of the mind. We access theta's subconscious in meditation, hypnosis, and dreaming sleep to retrieve present–life and past–life memories to heal the past and create new neural pathways.

As the home of our creativity, insight, and spiritual awareness, theta is the source of the "aha" revelations that enable the deeper mind to devise creative solutions and resolve issues with little, if any, emotional discomfort. During meditation, dreaming sleep, and creative and intuitive work, the soul provides inner imagery filled with wisdom, insights, and the inner certainty of higher awareness. These ideas originate, according to Cayce, from the sixth sense—that active soul force that enables us to partake of the "other self" or "accompanying entity" (higher self) that " . . . has been built by the entity or body, or soul, through its experience as a whole in the material and cosmic world . . . ," said Cayce in reading 5754-2.

When the conscious mind is at rest, he explained in the same reading, this " . . . other self communes with the *soul* of the body . . . " to remind us of our goals and purposes. Basically, we enter the silence in theta to commune with the soul's ideal self. Infinite and immortal, the ideal self is thus completely aware of and in attunement with the divine or creative forces.

The "Magic Journey" into Theta

The best way to develop psychic ability, Cayce told one of his followers and supporters, Edwin Blumenthal, in reading 137-3, is to concentrate the body, physically and mentally, in order to enter the "magic silence" of meditation and therein contact the soul's sixth sense and higher self. Curiously, Cade used similar language on page 130 of his book, *The Awakened Mind.* He wrote that "access to the deeper layers of the mind is at first attained only during the practice of meditation itself, but as one becomes more experienced, the ability to attain the more remote depths increases, and ultimately every meditation is a *magic journey* to the storehouse of visions and ideas."

Cade points out on page 87 in a chapter titled "The Art of Meditation" that "for people generally, it is very difficult to grasp the concept that our so-called normal waking state is neither the highest nor the most effective state of which the human mind is capable, that there are other states of vastly greater awareness which one can enter briefly and then return to normal living enriched, enlivened and enhanced."

In what ways are we enriched, enlivened, and enhanced? Quite simply, the magic silence that accesses the greater awareness is what awakens consciousness to its full power and potential. The conscious mind working with the visions and ideas flowing in the subconscious gradually releases repressed issues, frees up creativity, and *becomes* its higher self. Freed of the stress created by subconscious issues, the conscious mind gains lucidity and awareness as it opens to a steady stream of ideas, insights, creative inspiration, and intuitive flashes from theta and delta. The conscious intellect unites with the subconscious mind's creativity and spiritual awareness and with the unconscious mind's psychic intuition, altogether forming the awakened mind of the meditation and spiritual master.

The early Greeks inscribed on the temple of Apollo this famous injunction: "Know thyself and thou shalt know all the mysteries of the gods and the universe." The ancients knew that the key to personal evolution lies in the subconscious, which opens the doors of perception in the unconscious to the knowledge, wisdom, and love flowing in Universal Mind.

You will find a pure and perfect aspect of yourself in theta—and the answers to all of your questions. Theta is a wonderful place to inhabit. It is a non-judgmental realm of peace, wisdom, and light where you can heal and transform any unwanted programming that obstructs your progress in life.

Theta's Role in Psychic Development

Simply put, the more time you spend seeking soul guidance in theta, the more psychic you will become. Clearing the snarled-up energies of inner conflict and confusion lifts the heart, unites the mind, heals the body, and increases the flow of light in theta. Theta amplifies its signal strength to more closely connect the sixth sense with its higher self. In the end, releasing issues in theta makes us more powerful psychics and clearer channels who are less inclined to distort information through our biases and predispositions.

Elaborating on the role of the soul, Cayce compared it to "the police" which represent the law and therefore guide and direct the enforcement of whatever serves the best interests of each individual. (900-243) Continuing with this metaphor, we can say that the soul's job is also to check in with the "police chief" (superconscious mind) and the "commissioner" (godlike, angelic nature or higher self) to ensure that their standards are being met by the mind, heart, and body.

This check-in takes place in theta during deep meditation and in dreaming sleep, when the soul is free to travel. When we descend into the light, peace, and wisdom in theta, we awaken to a finer reality that calls us to truth, beauty, and goodness. For most people, there is no turning back. Who would want to?

Transformation in the Light of the Soul

Someone wisely said that the only thing in life that does not change is the constancy of change itself. Still, change is daunting to the ego, which is most comfortable with the familiar and wants to keep things just as they are. So it was for me in my late thirties as I continued to live my life in the same old ways with the same predictable results—the definition of insanity, as some clever person pointed out. "If I change, who will I be?" I worried.

In listening to the universal guidance that flowed into my pen during inspired writings, I realized that I would be the same person, the same essential being, but without the pain and suffering. This realization proved to be the ultimate truth. Night after night, a wise, kindly voice awakened me to the wisdom in my heart and soul—in what I would learn, years later, were my theta brainwaves!

Writing down the beautiful imagery and transcendent wisdom of my soul very gently and gradually changed me, beginning with lessons on self-love—a quality that is missing in so many people. Self-love is the "carrier" of the light of the spirit, my inner teacher said, and without it we cannot grow and flourish. Hundreds of teachings made me recognize my essential worth and the worth of every soul: that none is better than another and that we are all souls on a journey of awakening. This awakening happens in theta, where change takes place easily.

Self-purification in theta enables the mind to be more present to the intuitive information that empowers and comforts us. Nothing is more empowering than the knowledge that we hold the key to our own happiness. The vast majority of people on this planet do not believe that a wise, kindhearted teacher resides within them and is their very essence. One reason for their disbelief is the lack of self-love.

Love for self, others, and one's spirit lifts us into the transcendent perspectives of the guiding soul. Setting my pen to paper and listening deeply for the past twenty-five years has taught me that my soul's primary concern is my happiness and fulfillment.

Guiding hundreds of people into brainwave meditation has further convinced me that the subconscious soul serves everyone in this very same way. The soul sees across the boundaries of time and space and knows everything: the purpose of life, the path of its destiny, why the world is the way it is, how to love and be loved, how to reconcile a relationship, and the meaning of a dream. You name it. Your soul's theta and your spirit's delta brainwaves will help you with any question or desire.

We truly awaken when the beta intellect centers itself in its subconscious soul and consciously perceives its role and purpose in life. From that point on, the protective ego does not allow negative thoughts and feelings to take root and destroy its newfound happiness. Working in harmony with its spirit, the ego systematically detects and dispels all obstacles in the way of its conscious evolution.

Working with Theta Imagery

You will be pleased and perhaps surprised by the brilliantly composed imagery conveyed in visions, voices, feelings, and inner knowing by your subconscious mind. Working with theta imagery is a skill—a mental discipline—that better acquaints us with the soul's exquisite intelligence.

Theta imagery is initially hazy and indistinct, like a watermark on a piece of high quality paper; rising into the higher frequencies of alpha, it is clothed in clear, vivid images; rising still higher into beta, it crystallizes into words. Because theta imagery is vague to begin with, some people dismiss it. I have heard people say, "Oh, I don't know if I can believe this (insight). It felt like my imagination."

Surprisingly, during a guided meditation in one of my classes in New York City, a psychic medium found an inner gift in the form of a compass and doubted the validity of her vision. I asked her what a compass meant to her. She said it meant knowing what direction you were going in and that if you had a compass you would not get lost. This symbol was an especially important theta message, as she was on the verge of moving to another state and was uncomfortable with not knowing her way around. Her theta waves were assuring her that she would easily find her way: she had an inner compass and should trust in it.

Everything in the subconscious is meaningful. Nothing irrelevant or unimportant exists within us; and within every message from the subconscious is a solution, if only we take the time to understand and use it. It's easy to interpret subconscious imagery, since it arises in symbols stored in your subconscious with feelings and/or mental associations that are unique to you.

Subconscious imagery may be quick or prolonged, and it may or may not present itself with a readily accessible meaning. If not, you will need to work with the imagery. Simply list what each image or symbol means to you and how you feel about it, and then put the images or symbols together again to understand the overall meaning, just as in dream interpretation. The questions and concerns at the top of your mind are most likely the ones being answered by the message.

If the meaning eludes you and you feel it is important, then ask for elaboration in a dream and look for outside synchronicities concerning people and events. Your soul wants you to get the message, so it will arrive in some shape, form, or fashion.

You will be amazed by the lucidity of your subconscious soul—an amazingly gifted, Oscar-winning playwright with a fascinating story to tell you—about you! The more attention you pay to your inner imagery, the more you will receive. Soon you will awaken to the brilliant flow of inner guidance from your soul. Psychic intuition will increase until your mind is alive with inner knowing.

Guiding Yourself into Theta

Deepening into subconscious memories, creativity, insight, and spiritual awareness immediately generates theta frequencies. You might want to bring to mind someone you love, and then sensualize that person with heart-centered awareness, ask a question of any kind, and then wait for insights to come. Or meditate on blues and purples to deepen into theta frequencies. Creative work such as writing, playing music, praying, or dancing in the wind also generates theta.

Feeling gratitude for your unlimited creativity and insight will strengthen your soul connection. Perhaps you could meditate on the following: what does your psychic soul look like, feel like, sound like, or even taste and smell like? What does your soul want to tell or show you? Just linger in this awareness for a while to see what surfaces.

The above suggestions access theta through its content. You can also access theta by deepening into this brainwave state. To do this exercise, let's track the descent into theta.

1) Relax your body and mind (quiet beta). 2) Sensualize an environment, preferably an outdoors setting such as a countryside, beach, forest, or park that you enjoy (generate alpha), and walk around in this environment. See, hear, taste, smell, touch, and experience this place with all of your senses. Live the experience. 3) Sit or lie down in a comfortable place that feels safe and secure. Close your eyes and drift very gently and very slowly, and then fall deeper and deeper inside yourself (from alpha to theta) until you come to a peaceful, quiet place. Settle into that place.

While you are relaxing in theta, you may wish to sit in silence. If you ask a question, wait patiently until something surfaces. If anything does, it will be of help to you in some way.

The challenge is to believe that you can do it. We are trained from an early age to ask other people for solutions. Paradoxically, we continue to ask others even after we find our answers within, despite the fact that self-inquiry, as the ancient Greeks knew, awakens and evolves the mind faster than anything else.

Studies show that theta—generated either during meditation or physical exercise that people enjoy—forms new brain cells in the frontal lobes and hippocampus with the result of powering up the mind's intellect and improving memory storage and retrieval while reducing the age-related thinning of brain cells. Perhaps neurogenesis takes place in theta because these frequencies are where the personal subconscious mind and soul come into contact with delta's universal awareness.

Only theta's psychic soul can access superconscious light. Nothing else possesses this power.

Theta Meditation: Connecting with Higher Awareness

Deepening into your theta waves will immediately connect you with your soul. You may experience a sense of vast, expansive spaciousness like a sacred presence in your subconscious, or you may feel no difference at all, since you *are* your soul. Instead, you may experience distinct sensations of light, especially in and around your head and third eye, or perhaps in your heart.

Begin by setting a clear intention to make this connection. Let your intention be a higher aspiration, or as Edgar Cayce called it, an ideal such as love, peace, joy, gratitude, or soul connection.

Now, withdraw from the outside environment and relax. Once you are deeply relaxed, allow light to enter the top of your head and forehead, your neck and the back of your head, throat, chest and upper back, stomach and mid-back, pelvis and lower back, legs, feet, and toes. Welcome this light into your entire being, so that you are filled with it.

Feel the inundation of light and become aware of a still point of light, wisdom, and peace that is deep inside of you. You may sense a loving presence that is spiritual in nature. If not, expand your awareness out into the universe and relax into the higher consciousness of your spirit. Explore your soul's spirit with your mind. Perhaps you will experience a vision, hear a voice, or sense or feel something of use to you. Or perhaps you will just rest in your soul's quiet embrace and be comforted by the knowledge that you are never alone.

Return to the outside world when you are ready, and write in your journal about this experience.

Theta Meditation: Gifts to the Altar

Someone once said that we are either the way of God or in the way of God. This theta meditation invites you to step out of your own way by forgiving and letting go of any negative feelings toward yourself or someone else.

Decide whom you would like to forgive, then sit comfortably, relax your tongue, slow your breathing, and deepen into theta by imaging yourself sinking down and in, deeper and deeper inside yourself.

Now imagine that you are standing next to the altar of God (or any healing power you can believe in for the purpose of this meditation). Place a gift box on the floor. Holding your arm above the gift box, send your hurt or anger into the box. Feel it flowing down along your arms and out through your fingertips into the box.

When you are finished, tie a ribbon around the gift box, pick it up, and put it on the altar of God. Then walk away from the altar. God will take care of the gift box. Maybe you will see what happens to it, but make sure that you walk away and leave it behind. When you are ready, find a closure for your meditation.

Healing the past makes us more loving. The heart opens like a flower. The mind is more lucid and creative. The body grows healthier, the spirit lighter.

As the Zen master said to his students: "You do not know the weight of this self you are carrying until you put it down." We feel, and we are transformed as the brain and body rewire to a higher state of consciousness.

Healing in Theta

Because destructive patterns in consciousness are frozen memories composed of atoms and molecules, you can change them. The following self–healing meditation shows how to change, heal, or transform a thought pattern or physical condition. Self–healing meditations are unlimited in scope.

The Uses of a Healing Meditation:
Healing your body.
Changing a thought pattern, emotion, attitude or behavior.
Forgiving yourself or someone else.
Soothing mental–emotional discord, pain, or sorrow.
Healing a part of you that feels abandoned or neglected.

Theta Meditation: Self-Healing

Once you have decided what you want to heal, set aside your thoughts about it and clear your mind. Relax and sensualize an environment to generate alpha waves. Walk around in this environment and use all of your senses to bring it to life. When ready, find a place to sit down, close your eyes and drift down and in, to a place of light, wisdom, insight, and peace. Settle into that place.

Now allow what needs to be healed to manifest as an image, voice, sound, or feeling, or just sense that it is present. Focus your full awareness on the image to deeply understand it. Commit to memory what you learn.

Next, allow a second image that will do the healing to manifest. Understand its meaning, and then apply the healing. Experience it with all of your senses. You will know how to do this.

When the healing is complete, create a mechanism for the healing to continue to work on its own. Find a landmark that represents the feeling of theta, complete your meditation, arouse properly, and write down what you learned.

Emerge from your self-healing meditation with the faith that you are healed. Doubt and disbelief in the conscious mind can reverse the healing. Assume the best and you will get it. Be patient and faithful. You are acquiring a powerful technique and a masterful skill that will help you give healing to yourself and others.

Of course, if you are working on a life-threatening illness, be sure to seek qualified medical help. Edgar Cayce wisely pointed out that physicians are instruments of God. So are you!

If you had any difficulty sustaining your attention during the "Gifts to the Altar" or the "Self-Healing" meditation, you may need to listen to the companion meditation, "The Healing Garden," for a little help. It will focus your mind on the task at hand. I know of one woman who listened to this meditation during radiation and chemotherapy treatments. She felt transported into the heart of healing.

Landmarking the feeling of theta will help you dive into its deep, still waters quickly and easily. With practice, you will be able to sink into the depths of your theta waves in mere moments. Each dive into theta carries the soul's spirit back to the surface until one day the soul remains conscious and becomes the conscious mind.

Joanie's Story: Coming Home

Joanie came to me for hypnosis in the hope of releasing an all-consuming rage toward her ex-husband. The breakup of their fifteen-year

marriage four years before had forced her to sell her beautifully decorated home, which she had owned before the marriage and dearly loved.
Her husband landed on his feet, but she lost the life she loved and felt
angry and sad, humiliated, rejected, and abandoned. Joanie had moved
to a small apartment with hundreds of exquisitely beautiful costumes
for theater productions that she had sewn over the years and was now
"hemmed in" by the chaos in her environment.

When she arrived for her session, she was pale, her lips were trem-
bling, and she looked twenty years older than her sixty years. She had
abandoned her meditation practice and could not seem to find a way to
let go of her past. She was stuck.

Joanie easily deepened into her theta brainwaves, as I could see on
the Mind Mirror display. When I brought up the memory of her lovely
home, she envisioned every detail in it. This time, her vision was without emotional attachment—a characteristic of soul awareness. When I
asked her what her *real* home looked like, in her mind she walked outside into nature and explored the woods and winding paths in her
garden. I asked her to sit down on a bench, go deeper inside, and ask
her soul where her real home was.

With this question, her delta waves suddenly flared out, showing
that her soul was reaching out to Universal Consciousness for guidance.
"I am floating in pure light," she said emotionally, as tears ran down her
face. "I feel so loved, and I hear a voice saying, 'Your true home is here
and only here. Forgive and let go to return to your spirit.'"

After Joanie spent some quiet time feeling her oneness with her
Source, I asked her to seek solutions, and she moved into a high-amplitude theta–delta channeling pattern. *What could she do about the costumes
that filled her apartment?* She saw a sale flyer filled with compelling text
and people arriving in her living room, where the clothing was ar-
ranged and quickly sold. (Later it was.) *What about her anger toward her ex-
husband?* "I can forgive him now," she said softly, seeing what really
mattered. "And I'm ready to get on with my life."

People who are traumatized by painful events sometimes cannot find
their way back home. Once they drift down into the light of the soul,
they realize what Joanie did: that home is where the spirit is.

She contacted me two weeks later to say that she no longer yearned for her previous home, as she was taking great pleasure in walking the wooded Appalachian Trail. She invited me to her clothing sale and said she was happy again—filled with light for the first time in years.

In this session, her soul called her back to her real home inside herself. She resides there still.

The Universal Awareness of Delta's Unconscious Mind

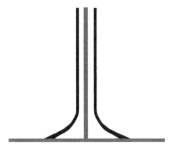 The personal unconscious rests below theta in the very slow brainwave frequencies of delta, where we connect with the universe, higher self, collective unconscious, and our spiritual source. Delta's empathy and psychic intuition access universal information that cannot be known or understood in any other way. Delta lifts information into conscious awareness during intuitive inquiry, deep unconscious meditation, healing work, empathy for others, and dreamless sleep wherein the soul communicates with its pure, perfect nature in Universal Consciousness. Becoming conscious of the unconscious awakens the mind to the soul's spirit and therefore is the key to brainwave development and mind expansion.

The mechanism for psychic attunement is a kind of radar in delta, which senses information in the physical world and extends beyond it to intuitively pick up energy and information stored in Universal Consciousness. Ever present and always on guard, delta's instinctive and intuitive radar is a powerful ally to the body–mind and the psychic soul.

When I demonstrate live brainwaves to a group of people and merely think of delta, the person connected to the EEG instantly produces it in intuitive anticipation of what I am going to say—before I say it. The audience sees what happened and is duly impressed.

So am I. I know that when people understand that delta frequencies connect us with all that is, they will open up to the soul's infinite spirit and attune to their unlimited intuitive powers. People who are already attuned will further extend this sensing device to turn up the volume.

Finding the Missing Piece

No doubt it was delta's intuition that caused me to read Cade's book repeatedly in search of what I sensed was a missing piece, an underlying structure that explains how psychic intuition works in the brain/ mind. I found this missing piece in a table that lists subjective descriptions of the descent into relaxation/meditation and correlates them to brainwave states. (See the Table of Subjective Landmarks at the end of the next chapter).

Cade notes in pages 40–41 of *The Awakened Mind* that Stage 6, the deepest level of relaxation/meditation, shows up on the Mind Mirror as very little electrical activity in the brain, except for occasional flares of delta. The subjective experience of Stage 6 is a new way of feeling intuitive insights from a higher perspective and is the synthesis of opposites into a higher union.

I was very excited by this discovery, which confirmed my long-held theory that the unconscious mind's resonance with frequencies in the Field is what stimulates the higher-state brainwave patterns discovered by Cade, as well as two still-higher brainwave patterns, the superconscious mind and the godlike, angelic nature of the higher self, both introduced in an upcoming chapter.

Essentially, the importance of this recovered information is that meditation, psychic inquiry, energy healing, and spiritual practices like inspired writing and dream study involve the steady descent of the mind into delta's formless awareness, which so easily resonates with the high-frequency, information-filled quantum Field.

When the psychic soul deepens into delta and then expands out into the Field for universal insights, any one of several possible brainwave patterns appears on the Mind Mirror. The most common is the dreamless sleep or unconscious trance pattern depicted in the diagram at the beginning of this section. Deepening further into delta stimulates yoga nidra—the super-intuitive, mind-awake, body-asleep state of awareness cultivated by yogic meditators. Still further deepening generates the very low frequencies of epsilon, where consciousness enters the suspended animation cultivated by spiritual masters and the sleeping prophet, Edgar Cayce.

The deep unconscious trance of yoga nidra and suspended animation can give rise to waking or sleeping out-of-body travel wherein there is little to no brainwave activity (because nobody's home). The disappearance of the personal self into the unconscious field of light can produce the spiritual unity and oneness of the evolved-mind pattern and its bliss and illumination. Read the next chapter for more information about the evolved mind.

Low delta and epsilon in advanced meditators, psychics, and healers can generate super-high-frequency gamma waves that produce the brainwave patterns of the higher self—the superconscious mind and godlike, angelic nature—described by Edgar Cayce and introduced in a later chapter.

Because delta's unconscious is resonating with Universal Mind, these brainwave variations yield powerful psychic insights, the nonduality of spiritual union, and spontaneous healing.

The Psychic Sleep of Yoga Nidra

There is a Hindu spiritual practice called *yoga nidra,* or psychic sleep, wherein the mind is awake and the body is asleep. Yoga nidra takes place in low delta and/or the still lower frequencies of epsilon (see below). Yogis and swamis teach the art of psychic sleep to transform consciousness. The meditator surrenders to delta's universal awareness and repeats a sankalpa—a positive affirmation or resolution of some kind, like smoking cessation or spiritual oneness—that is sent into universal awareness with the expectation of spiritual support that will reprogram the mind's awareness.

Most people lose awareness at the beginning of yoga-nidra meditation during the "rotation of consciousness" which quickly and successively focuses the mind on various body parts. The bored conscious mind, tiring of the tedium, absents itself, and as the body falls asleep, the spirit comes to consciousness, as in sleep, but is now in a superconscious waking state.

When this state is achieved, rejuvenating energies flow into consciousness and clarify the mind and body in wonderful ways. Sometimes I slip into yoga nidra during meditation, especially while relaxing in a hot bath, and awaken feeling intensely energized and lucid, with a strong inner certainty of higher awareness. The insight that I needed but did not consciously seek is always in my mind, and my work that day is crisp and creative. At other times, I receive a stream of powerful psychic insights.

The following streamlined meditation invites you to try this practice on your own.

Yoga-Nidra Meditation: Into the Infinite

Either lie down in a comfortable place or sit with your back fairly straight in a shallow tub of warm or hot water. Set a high spiritual intention that includes a heartfelt desire to enter yoga nidra. Decide on a sankalpa—a resolution related to health, happiness, or spiritual insight—and deepen into meditation by slowing your breath and relaxing your body.

Drifting deeper and deeper into yourself (in your mind and body), relax your physical eyes and focus your awareness on your third eye. Continue to relax into yourself, and find a still point in your mind. Keep your whole body deeply relaxed and your mind quiet and clear.

When you feel your body begin to fall asleep, repeat the sankalpa and then allow your body to "blank out" into a sleep or trance state. Just go with it. Surrender completely to the experience of deep relaxation.

If your head drops to your chest and you begin to snore, the sound will wake you up slightly. Notice where your mind's consciousness is located, and then continue to meditate until your meditation feels complete. Before you awaken from meditation, bring your loved ones to mind one by one and send to them your accumulated light. Close your meditation by distributing the light that has coalesced in your crown and third eye into the rest of your body. Mentally usher the energy into your arms, hands, and fingers, and then into your legs, feet, and toes.

If this meditation worked for you, you will notice the clarity in your mind and the coherent energy flowing in your body. If this advanced practice did not work for you, try again. Eventually, it will work.

Epsilon's Suspended Animation

Since no one connected Edgar Cayce to a brainwave device, we cannot know with absolute certainty whether his readings were given in low–delta's yoga nidra or epsilon's suspended animation. If I were to bet, I'd put my money on epsilon, since Cayce's Source told him in one reading that he was the perfect channel because he went into "suspended animation." He achieved such a deep, unconscious trance that the Universal Forces could use his organs to communicate. (507-1, Report #24)

Occurring below delta, epsilon frequencies range from 0.5 to 0 hertz. These are the lowest and slowest possible brainwaves. As such, they induce a state of suspended animation with little to no breath, heartbeat, or pulse.

Out–of–body experiences, also known as astral travel, take place in very low delta and epsilon. Brainwave activity all but disappears until the spirit gets back into its body and mind.

Epsilon is cultivated by Hindu yogis who can maintain this state for three to six days at a time, taking in no food or water during demonstrations for crowds of people who gather to pray and absorb the spiritual light that concentrates around the yogi. This stillness in consciousness causes super–high frequencies to "ride" above low delta and epsilon in light waves that transmit energy and information through harmonic resonance.

Sustained focus and attention enable meditators, psychics, and healers to ride these low–frequency light waves up into the high–frequency superconscious that so powerfully refreshes the body–mind. (More is written about this topic in upcoming chapters.)

Epsilon is also associated with a Tibetan spiritual practice called Tummo, meaning Inner Fire. Buddhist monks standing in the Himalayan snows descend into epsilon's super–low frequencies and raise the kundalini energy from the navel to generate an intense heat that dries their seven layers of frozen clothing. Scientific experiments completed by Dr. Herbert Benson of Harvard Medical School in 1982 confirmed that Tibetan monks are able to raise their body temperature by more than 8.3 degrees Celsius, which equals 15 degrees Fahrenheit. Since the kundalini fire is associated with high–frequency gamma brainwaves and an inward state of religious ecstasy or divine union, we can infer that the monks are entering a superconscious awareness in which the real "fire" is Universal Consciousness.

Tum–mo is cultivated by Sufi mystics in the Islamic religion, as well, and by Kundalini Yoga practitioners who breathe up the inner fire of kundalini through concentration on the navel.

Hypervigilance and Psychic Empathy

The low–frequency delta radar that picks up psychic impulses from the Field can pose challenges for people who grew up with physical or emotional abuse and as a result developed the super–sensitivity called hypervigilance. People who unconsciously "watch their backs" all the time become psychic empaths who pick up and often confuse other people's thoughts and emotions with their own, as mentioned in Chapter 2's section on clairsentience.

What hypervigilant people need is a healthy delta. Short of healing the patterns of consciousness that created the hypervigilance in the first place, the empath can turn off delta by retracting his or her energy field closer to the body. You will instinctively know how to retract your energy field—just pull your awareness in—and your clairsentience will feel that it is occurring. Suddenly you will feel like you're back inside yourself instead of everywhere else.

Some teachers suggest placing mirrors around the waist or soaping the auric field to deflect other people's energies. This deflection is not the purpose of delta, which is to open up as fully as possible to pick up universal energy and information. One of the best solutions I know was taught to me by Anna Wise, successor to Max Cade. Open your heart and auric field as widely as possible to allow other people's energies to travel through the empty spaces between your atoms. Nothing gets stuck, this way, and you can stay calm and centered no matter what is coming at you.

I have recently found another solution to psychic empathy, and that is to center in the heart and expand outward to "plug in" to the energy currents in the superconscious which naturally protect and guide us.

Practice will teach you to plug in to this protection. When another person is the source of disturbance, you can plug in to that person's higher self and hope that he or she also rises in consciousness.

If so: end of difficulty; if not, you can always head to the hills.

Delta Meditation: Activating Your Intuition

Sitting on a park bench or some other quiet public place, use your delta radar to tune in to the person closest to you. Expand your awareness into his or her energy field. Follow your radar outward and open your intuitive awareness until impressions come to your mind.

Notice what you see, hear, feel, taste, or smell, and anything else your sixth sense tells you. It's as if you are sensing the other person from deep inside yourself, possibly from the navel or heart. Perhaps you will feel your intuition arising in your gut or in the upper chakras in your head—your crown, third eye, and throat. Let the information flow, and once you have gathered several clear impressions, try this exercise with another person.

If you are courageous enough, engage these people in conversation. Just tell them the truth: that you have sensed these feelings and wonder if they are true or not. (I've admitted my sensations many times, and people don't mind at all; it's a great conversation starter.)

Try as often as you can to open your psychic channels; it will build up your confidence. Notice whether time, place, or similarities between you and the people you are reading make any difference in your accuracy. Exercising your delta radar and auric field will increase your awareness of each condition. This practice is the way to master your energy system and your mind's consciousness.

Now that we have explored the categories of consciousness and you know what they feel like, you can orchestrate them into the symphonic brainwave patterns that play the music of the psychic soul—the meditative, awakened, and evolved mind of higher consciousness.

Resources:
"The Lake of Inner Peace" *track is designed to quiet beta brainwaves. It will guide you into the still waters of your subconscious to experience the deep peace and*

tranquility of your psychic soul.

"The Healing Garden" *track is a guided journey into the heart of nature and self-healing.*

"What Instrument Am I," *a beingness meditation, invites you to sensualize yourself as a musical instrument.*

(For the above meditations, *see* Selected Bibliography for track information regarding: Pennington, Judith. *The Meditation Experience: Listening to Your Psychic Soul.* A.R.E. Press, 2011, CDs.)

The High-Performance Mind, Mastering Brainwaves for Relaxation, Insight, Healing and Creativity, is an audio CD of guided meditations by the late Anna Wise (Relaxation Co., 1998.) and includes tracks that evoke and train each of the four brainwave categories.

5

The Symphonic Brainwaves
of the Psychic Soul

"To the mind that is still, the whole universe surrenders."
                                                    —*Lao Tzu*

Now that you understand how to produce beta, alpha, theta, and delta frequencies, let's see how to orchestrate them into three higher states of awareness: meditation, the awakened mind, and the evolved mind. Experiencing and conditioning the brain to these open, flowing states of consciousness lifts the psychic soul out of the subconscious into conscious awareness so that we become the conscious spirit we were born to be.

The shapes of these three brainwave patterns show how accurately the Mind Mirror, a biofeedback device, reflects states of consciousness. Everything that happens in consciousness shows up on the Mind Mirror screen, as Cade and Wise discovered in their observations of thousands of advanced meditators, psychics, healers, swamis, and other spiritual adepts, and as I, too, have seen without exception in the hundreds of people I've worked with.

The meditation pattern, for example, is shaped like a person with the outstretched arms of the open heart and no head, as we do not think in meditation. The awakened mind is a meditation pattern with a head that is quietly processing thoughts. The evolved-mind pattern of transcendence is a circle of unity and oneness showing the merging of the self with divine consciousness.

In this holographic Field of light, the whole universe is in every atom and cell. And so it is with consciousness and brainwaves: as above, so below.

The Magic in the Silence

Edgar Cayce did not maintain a formal meditation practice; instead, he joked that his psychic journeys were his "little meditations." And indeed they were. As you will see, Cayce lived in an awakened-mind state—a waking form of meditation—due to his heartfelt connection with nature and his psychic readings, dream studies, and spiritual pursuits, all of which constantly attuned him to the dimensions out of which his incredibly accurate readings came.

Cayce urged people to meditate in order to awaken their psychic faculties. There is magic in the silence of meditation, he believed—the magic of prolonged bonding with the psychic soul, out of which derives an amazing array of benefits to the body, mind, heart, and spirit.

On the most fundamental level, the peaceful awareness that is immediately engendered by meditation soothes the emotional peaks and valleys that afflict us with stress, diffract thinking, and destroy the body's health. When we condition the brain and body to calmness, meditation, and the ensuing two brainwave patterns—the awakened-mind and the evolved-mind—we become happier, healthier, and increasingly psychic.

Meditation is the most consistent and reliable path to self-actualization, psychic mastery, and spiritual enlightenment for these reasons:

• Lowering the frequencies of consciousness relaxes the body, reduces respiration, slows the heart rate, decreases blood pressure, and brings the left and right hemispheres of the brain into balance. Bilateral symmetry in the brain reduces the "noise" that stresses the electrical nervous system and its cells, tissues, and organs.

• The reduction of stress enables the brain, a command center, to communicate better with itself and increase coordination with its central nervous system in order to repair cells, tissues, and organs, balance systems in the body, and restore physical health and well-being.

• While beta, alpha, theta, and delta (each with a "mind" of its own) operate semi-independently in most people, the open flow of consciousness in meditation unites these brainwave frequencies with each other. The result is lucid awareness flowing with the clarity, creativity, insight, intuition, and spiritual awareness in beta, alpha, theta, and delta.

• The theta waves generated in meditation form new brain cells in the intellectual, memory, and creative centers, thus increasing the meditator's capacity to think and create.

• The coherent mind looks into itself and removes mental-emotional issues to release suppressed creativity and power up the brain. Personal transformation opens the heart, calms emotions, frees the mind, refines the body's health, and increases the spirit's happiness.

• The meditator's sensitivity to subtle energies now increases so that spiritual energies are felt and recognized for what they are: pure light that is available for healing and transformation. The meditator draws these higher energies into the body-mind to heal self and others.

• The brain wires these new patterns of consciousness into its circuitry and body, and gradually externalizes the meditative mind as the awakened mind, bringing it to conscious awareness while retaining its clarity, creativity, insight, intuition, and spiritual awareness. Self-mastery develops with the ability to respond to internal and external events in appropriate and beneficial ways. The awakened mind projects this mastery into everyday life.

• The awakened mind, open to a continuous stream of intuitive insights from the subconscious soul, experiences peak moments of insight and joy that "spiritualize," illuminate, and evolve it. The enlightened soul rises into conscious awareness and projects the light of love and service out into the world.

Meditation is the fundamental way to evolve because it is the key to physical and mental-emotional health, self-mastery and inner guidance, the awakened mind of the psychic soul, and the evolved mind of cosmic consciousness. But what makes people want to meditate is that it feels extraordinarily good to be calm, united, and lucid. Life becomes so much richer and easier that the new meditator will want to return to this practice day after day.

It may take some effort to deepen into an alpha–theta meditation state to begin with, but with mental training you will be able to reach meditation in minutes and then moments. For many people, a twenty-minute meditation once or twice a day or every other day is enough.

The best psychics and healers maintain and take great pleasure in regular practice, as silent meditation gives voice to the soul as nothing else can.

The Brainwaves of Meditation

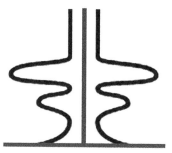

Silent meditation is a combination of alpha and theta without beta; delta is present, unless the meditator is self-absorbed. Between alpha and theta is a crossover frequency at 7.83 hertz that is a "still point" in consciousness. Finding this still point is the key to meditation and all healing.

People who access this still point in meditation resonate with universal awareness and feel the soul's connection with the spirit's infinite wisdom and knowledge. It is this feeling of expansiveness that draws most people back to meditation. Emotional healing takes place in this still point, where imagery from the unconscious and subconscious arise with insights provided during meditation and dreaming sleep, which share this pattern.

Cayce said that meditation makes us more sensitive to influences of every kind, and you will experience the truth of this idea. Meditation heightens perceptions—we see, hear, and feel the pumping of the blood in the body, the subtle rise of the kundalini, and the light–filled imagery of the psychic soul, which reveals what we need to know and helps us heal what does not serve us. The psychic soul, in touch with its higher self, feels the spiritual oneness and love in the superconscious and brings this awareness back into the earth.

Coming out of meditation, the mind remains united while the subconscious soul is still in charge of the sensory system: our "soul eyes" and other psychic senses view life through the higher perspectives of the spirit. Creativity and intuition flow freely, work is performed easily, and we are kinder, more patient, and compassionate with self and others.

No other endeavor produces the benefits that result from meditation. Even when our only immediate goal is to calm the mind, reduce stress, and improve our health and well–being, meditation also gradually awakens us to a perceived awareness of the spiritual light at the core of our being.

Heart-Brain Synchrony

The following technique, called the Heart Breath, is an excellent entry into silent or working meditation. You may also use it in daily life to create a calm, coherent state of mind that will vastly improve your physical health.

The Heart Breath was developed by the Institute of HeartMath®, a research organization whose scientists spent fifteen years mapping the psychophysiological effects of emotion. They discovered that breathing positive emotions like love, joy, and appreciation into the heart synchronizes it with the brain and body and produces a high level of coherence in each.

Heart–brain synchrony generates a coherent waveform that brings the sympathetic (arousal) and parasympathetic (relaxation) nervous systems into synchronous operation at the same frequency, tips their balance toward relaxation, increases the brain's clarity, and cascades electrochemical hormones through the body to power up the immune system.

The Heart Breath accomplishes all of this coherence in three to five minutes, which means that everyone can do it while riding a subway or recharging during the lunch hour. The Heart Breath can also be used as a quick entry into meditation, since it relaxes the body and expands the mind. Over time, the Heart Breath improves heart–rate variability, which determines the body's ability to adapt to stress and environmental demands.

Meditation: Self-Regulating with the Heart Breath

Closing your eyes, place your hands over your heart. Bring your awareness to your heart and breathe into your heart. Breathe deeply and evenly, with an equal number of inhalations and exhalations, until you feel relaxed.

Now bring a positive emotion like appreciation, care, or love into your heart, or relive a happy memory of a person, place, or event. Relax into this positive emotion. Breathe it into your heart for several minutes to create coherence in your body and deepen into an alpha–theta meditation state. Continue with your meditation for as long as you like.

Be sure to create a landmark for what it feels like to meditate with the Heart Breath. It will help you attain inner peace and the single-pointed consciousness enjoyed by spiritual masters.

Preparing for Meditation

The ritual use of candles, incense, spiritual icons, and inspirational readings trains the conscious mind to be still and at the same time uplift the spirit. It is not necessary to use any of the following rituals, except for the light of protection, which also sets a high intention. Nevertheless, rituals create a sense of the sacred and serve to focus the mind. Once you learn how to discipline your mind, nothing else will give you as much pleasure (and as many good ideas) as a deep, satisfying meditation.

No one will give you this time for your meditation practice. You must give the time to yourself.

First consider the best time and place for your practice. Find a chair or set up a meditation room that will accumulate your vibrations and carry you into relaxation. To time your practice, set a watch alarm with a gentle chime or trust your inner clock to reawaken you in twenty or thirty minutes.

Traditional wisdom and remote-viewing research agree that the best times to meditate are at dawn, noon, and dusk—or in the middle of the night when there is less geomagnetic activity since other people are asleep; the quiet in the atmosphere resonates quiet in us. I like to meditate after getting dressed in the morning as a way to sharpen my mind, strengthen my spiritual awareness, and set the tone (and my priorities) for the day.

The Cayce readings offer the new meditator many helpful suggestions. First, minimize caffeine and food intake before your practice so as to avoid disturbances in the body. Purify by washing your face and hands (or showering) and by drinking water, a conductor of electricity. Loosen any binding clothing and stretch like a cat by rising up on the balls of your feet and reaching your arms one at a time toward the ceiling, gradually moving the stretching motion down to the floor. The stretching helps energy move more easily through the body–mind. Sit in an upright chair that supports your spine, and place your feet flat against the floor.

The body is a battery, so it's useful to close the circuit by resting the tongue against the roof of the mouth or the back of the teeth. Holding the hands together in some way finishes closing the circuit. Some people gently press the thumb and forefinger of each hand together in what's called a mudra. Both methods will help you retreat from the outside world into yourself.

With your back straight, try this head–and–neck exercise to further relax your body and massage your spine. First, inhale deeply, and as you exhale gently, drop your head toward your chest; repeat three times. Next, gently tilt your head backward three times, going no farther than is comfortable. Gently tilt your head three times toward your right shoulder; then three times toward the left shoulder (or vice versa, as you prefer). Roll your head and neck around three times clockwise and then counter–clockwise three times.

Use this modified yogic breathing technique to relax your body and balance your brain. Place the index and middle fingers of your dominant hand on each side of your nose. Using one finger to close your left nostril, breathe in slowly and deeply through the right nostril and breathe out slowly through your mouth, silently voicing the affirmation, "Strength." Repeat three times. Next, close your right nostril and breathe in through your left nostril, slowly and evenly; breathe out of your right nostril with the affirmation, "Source of life." Repeat three times.

Open with a prayer of protection—something like "I surround myself with the white light of protection"—and read an inspirational passage or poem. The Cayce readings suggest reciting the Lord's Prayer, which activates the spiritual centers that comprise the chakra system. If you listen to music, it should be unstructured so as not to engage your mind.

The Stages of Meditation

Once you have prepared for meditation—with the above rituals or none at all except for the protection of a high spiritual intention—close your eyes and relax them, and then fix your attention on your third eye to withdraw from the outer world. The Heart Breath and/or the brainwave mastery techniques presented in the last chapter, such as slowing the breath and relaxing the tongue, will help to discipline your thoughts.

The key to meditation is to become fully present to yourself in the now-moment. For most people, resting in the present moment is a process and a skill to be learned. At first, as you relax and center your awareness inside yourself, your thoughts will vacillate between internal and external awareness. Body awareness increases at first as you become more conscious of your breath, heartbeat, or the itch on your toe. Fixing your attention on your third eye, you drift below the level of thoughts and sensations and gradually lose all sense of body boundaries. Everything fades away except your fixed attention on your third eye.

Subtle energies rising in your chakra system through the kundalini coalesce as sensations of light in your third eye and crown, and these sensations may increase as you drift down into your subconscious. Find that still point in your mind and rest in this awake and alert state of awareness, in your pure mind or pure spirit.

If creative ideas or spiritual insights well up, store them in symbolic "keys" and send them up to a chest or file cabinet in your conscious mind to be unlocked after meditation. Stay in the magic silence for as long as you like, and end your meditation with healing prayers for others. Undirected prayers work best. Simply picture people as happy, and pray for the earth and people in need. At some point you will notice that the currents of light flowing in your body–mind intensify when you pray for those who need help the most. Even if your meditation has not been what you wanted, praying for others will intensify it, since the spiritual light you are sending to others arises in you first.

After your healing prayers, draw the light that has coalesced in your head, neck, and shoulders—even if you can't feel it—into every part of your body including your organs and all the way into your fingers and toes. Close with a prayer or words of gratitude, wiggle your fingers and toes, and take a full-body stretch to completely arouse your nervous system and come back to the outside space.

After each practice, check the table of Subjective Landmarks located at the end of this chapter to measure the depth that you reached. This table, a biofeedback device, will help you pinpoint which practices support your meditations and which ones do not.

See Appendix B for an overview of the meditation techniques presented above. This overview also includes the "Circulation of Light," a Taoist practice presented near the end of this chapter, as well as techniques that the Cayce readings suggested for the intuitive passage through dimensions of consciousness into the superconscious realm of the higher self. These techniques for rising into the superconscious are presented in the next chapter.

You may wish to copy or cut out the meditation overview in Appendix B to keep it handy in your meditation space as a guide for your practice. Pick and choose the rituals that feel best to you.

Meditation, the art of becoming present to the inner self, is like moving into self-alignment in the "now" moment. If you can move into the present moment, you can meditate. All good things will come out of exchanging ordinary "absent-mindedness" for meditative mindfulness.

Emerging from meditation, you will notice a feeling of peace and unity that will keep you in "flow" with life, surfing the waves of change with grace and ease. When you lose the self–unity that creates this outer flow, you can easily regain it by returning to meditation.

When you are tempted to skip meditation for days or weeks at a time, remember this rule of thumb given by St. Francis de Sales: "Half an hour's meditation each day is essential, except when you are busy. Then a full hour is needed."

With practice, you will be able to enter meditation in minutes or moments and will want to spend an hour or more in deep subconscious meditation to revitalize your body, mind, and spirit. You will notice the difference and so will other people, who may ask you to teach them to meditate.

Deep Subconscious Trance

Some meditations are more profound than others, even for long-term meditators. Sometimes I slip down into a theta–delta trance so quickly that it's impossible to halt the slide. I don't quibble. I just accept what happens and know that at these times my body is getting the deep, healing rest that it needs. Or perhaps it's sliding down into yoga nidra's higher consciousness, which is always a good thing.

If you awaken from meditation feeling groggy, you fell asleep. If you awaken feeling lucid and energized, you slipped into a deep subconscious trance or the still–lower frequencies of psychic sleep.

The Cayce readings urged one man, Edwin Blumenthal, to stop fighting the loss of consciousness: " . . . through this we will find the first action of the psychic making the physical manifestation to the conscious mind . . . This is the correct way to develop the forces . . . " (137-5)

So don't be hard on yourself when you trance out. Deep trance is what stimulated superconscious awareness in Cayce himself, as explained in the last chapter's sections on delta and epsilon brainwaves. If you trance out repeatedly and want to stay awake, try holding a glass of water in your hand; this activity is guaranteed to keep your responsible ego awake and alert.

Of all the benefits that come out of meditation, the most important one to me is the awareness of my spirit. Connected to my spirit, I feel whole. Trusting and believing in my wholeness, I know that I can do virtually anything. In years past, when I skipped meditation for weeks at a time, I began to lose my self–confidence, accomplished nothing that was good, and sometimes brought unhappiness to the people around me. (Everyone supports my meditation practice.)

The brilliant and unlimited soul can heal any mental–emotional issue in your life by taking it to the superconscious for insights and solutions. Consider trusting your spirit to be your therapist in meditation. It will comfort, reassure, and enlighten you in silent meditation and in the working, awakened–mind meditation practices described below.

The Awakened Mind of the Masters

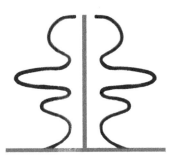 Everyone has experienced the amplified brainwaves of the awakened mind. Perhaps you were daydreaming when suddenly an "aha" insight flashed into your mind and you exclaimed, "Oh! I *get* it!" During these peak moments of awareness, beta, alpha, theta, and delta united in the high–amplitude, open flow of consciousness that is experienced in meditation. When this peak state of awareness generalizes to the outer world in a lasting way, it is the awakened mind of the masters.

We can also call it the mind of the soul, as the awakened–mind pattern flares onto the Mind Mirror screen during active, working meditations when the conscious mind awakens to and utilizes the guiding insights provided by the subconscious soul. In outer life, the awakened mind of the now–conscious soul operates through beta's intellect, alpha's sensory awareness, theta's subconscious creativity, insight, and healing, and delta's unconscious empathy, intuition, and universal awareness.

In this brainwave pattern, self–separation has disappeared enough for the soul to become conscious.

The awakened mind, writes Cade on page 116 in his book with the same title, " . . . is, perhaps, like gradually awakening from sleep and becoming more and more vividly aware of everyday reality."

The awakened mind, a higher state of awareness, is so much more awake that it finds new meaning in the flow of everyday events. This elevation in consciousness is also known as "the zone," a "flow" state of creativity and happiness, peak performance, and the high-performance mind. Athletes enter this peak-performance zone to reach the top of their game, as do business people, artists, and performers. You may have experienced this highly creative state of mind while focusing so intently on a task that time seemed to slow or stop altogether.

Becoming Numinous

Extraordinary things happen when the soul becomes conscious. Just as beta, alpha, theta, and delta unite to form the awakened mind, so does this inner unity project outward to connect us with others and our own spirit. The release of separation into an open flow of consciousness generates a high-amplitude signal, a numinosity or luminosity, which reverberates into physical reality and attracts and manifests synchronicity, defined as the meaningful coincidence of inner and outer events.

Where synchronicities seemed random before, now everyday life is filled with impossibly meaningful coincidences in which people and events seem to magically come together. Each synchronicity brings "aha" insights and revelations that further expand the mind's boundaries. It's as if some divine hand is arranging life for the awakened mind's benefit—and indeed it is because beta's intellect has surrendered its control to the higher awareness of the soul. You can see its active cooperation with its subconscious and unconscious mind in its quiet, inward curve, the first indication of the awakening of awareness.

Today, more people are awake than ever before due to global challenges that are opening so many people's minds and hearts to their souls. Spiritual teachers are stepping onto the world stage to guide people inward for intuitive answers and help.

Who are these awakened people? Look around. You can recognize them by their thoughts, intentions, words, and deeds, and by the light-filled truthfulness, compassion, love, and forbearance they radiate out to the world. As Jesus said, we can know them by their fruits.

Characteristics of the Awakened Mind

Max Cade's successor, humanistic psychologist and consciousness pioneer, Anna Wise, spent thirty years using the Mind Mirror to guide people into meditation, the awakened mind, and the evolved mind of spiritual illumination. In her first book, *The High-Performance Mind*, she writes that awakened people—without regard to any religion, philosophy, or mission in life—are warm, kind, compassionate, empathetic and helpful. Peaceful, balanced, and perceptive, they do not criticize, judge, or blame, nor do they attempt to control the thoughts and actions of other people.

Awakened people are usually self-actualized, meaning that they have reached a pinnacle of success in their personal relationships and work life. Consequently, they are able to devote their lives to love and service due to a deep, heartfelt devotion to humanity and divine consciousness.

The awakened mind is moral, creative, and accepting as it lives a life of meaning and purpose. Continually seeking the spiritual source that informs and nourishes it, the awakened mind uses this guidance to serve self and others. Therefore, as I see it, he or she is a clear and accurate channel who is working co-creatively with Universal Mind.

In sleep, the awakened mind shows the brainwave pattern of lucid dreaming. There is no "sleep of ignorance" from which to awaken in this higher state. It is consistently awake, by definition. Filled with the light of consciousness, the awakened mind consciously self-heals, self-actualizes, and self-transcends in its journey toward self-realization.

While creative and spiritual endeavors gradually awaken the mind, the quickest ways to awaken awareness are silent and working meditations, as they directly involve soul guidance that consistently transforms consciousness. There is a quantum leap from awakened-mind flares during meditation to a stable and continually maintained awakened mind in outer life. Nevertheless, any dedicated meditator can take this quantum leap, and many do. All it requires is self-mastery and personal transformation assisted by inner guidance.

The reward of this inner work is inestimable, as deep and lasting happiness comes with the awakening of awareness. The subconscious soul takes charge, and life becomes immensely richer and indescribably easier.

The following two stories illustrate the benefits of awakened-mind meditations guided by the soul.

Peggy's Story: Getting in the Driver's Seat

Working meditations that draw on soul guidance and consequently unite and evolve consciousness bring life into clarity and focus. This soul guidance was the experience of one of my clients, a New York City financier with strong beta logic and delta intuition.

Peggy, a long-term meditator, attended one of my weekend group brainwave trainings and scheduled a private session for the next day. She was concerned about having veered away from her regular meditation practice. Feeling lost—as is usually the case with fallen-away meditators—she wanted to find her next best steps in life. Tired of her high-powered job, she wanted to do something else but was unable to move forward.

Guiding her into meditation, I asked questions that engaged her beta intellect in a verbal exchange and thus generated the quiet, inwardly-focused beta of the awakened-mind pattern. Her conscious mind opened to her soul's intuition, and her inner knowing revealed that the blockage was an old thought pattern: a conflict between her mind and heart. She asked for a solution and received a vision of an automobile moving toward her second career as a life coach, healer, and psychic intuitive. Her heart was driving the car, her intellect was a passenger, and her spirit was guiding the vehicle from a higher perspective.

This sharp, clear image coaxed Peggy's ego out of the driver's seat and into a comfortable home in her heart, where she wanted it to live. She was convinced by her inner certainty of higher awareness that her spiritual heart would take her to the right places. Confident in her ability to launch a new career, she proceeded to do so with reliable guidance from her daily meditations.

Peggy was careful to make this career change with good timing, using the ego's intellect to calculate her finances and make all the logical decisions that are a necessary part of a good business move. Her awakened mind enabled her to use all of her mind's resources coopera-tively—her intuition, instinct, and intellect—for her benefit and that of other people.

Grace's Story: The Paradise Garden

Grace, a gifted writer and musician, addressed childhood sexual abuse within her family in the first part of her awakened-mind medita-tion and found soulful ways to heal a wounded inner child. Walking down a corridor in her mind and finding a door, she opened it and saw a racetrack with her whole family in the bleachers cheering her on and shouting, "You are the champion of our family, working out all of our issues. We are here for you whenever you need us."

Her family looked at her with loving eyes and complete acceptance. Throughout this meditation, Grace produced high-amplitude delta, which made sense when she told me later that her entire family is de-ceased. She was working with them on the level of her soul's spirit.

Grace attended a follow-up session with the question, "What do I need to be happy, successful, prosperous, loved, and loving?" High-amplitude delta showed up again. This time, her spirit addressed her need for self-acceptance and taught her more about her worth than she ever dreamed could be true.

Once again walking into the "house" of her subconscious mind, Grace entered a room labeled The Door to the Open Heart. Behind the door was a toolshed that opened to a paradise garden. At first she could not enter the garden, as it was too brilliant with light and was filled with total and unconditional love.

Retreating to the toolshed, she heard a voice say, "Grace, you have all the tools you will ever need." Encouraged, she walked into the garden through a heart-shaped archway and sat on a beautiful bench sur-rounded by flowers. To the far left of the paradise garden was a veil behind which were millions of beings, everyone who had ever existed. They communicated to Grace that she has always been a part of every-thing: past, present, and future. She realized that she will always be part of this group consciousness—accepted and loved—and there is no rea-son to be afraid of anything.

In the second room of the house, she found a Mardi Gras scene where everyone was dancing in celebration of her "fun" self and the good work she has done and will do. A map legend in the room read: "Pure intentions and goodness of heart." The happy, loving people asked her, "How could you not know you have been so totally accepted?"

Strengthened by their loving encouragement, Grace felt that she could go out into the world with these "friends" by her side and continue to do what was earning so much approval from them. She said after the meditation, "They are like my family, reminding me that this is my true essence, regardless of what other people see and say. I feel a lightness of heart that I haven't experienced for so long, a lightness in my chest."

Grace's judgment of her heart, split in half during open heart surgery, shifted to her soul's unconditional love and her now fearless extension of it to the world. Today, she visits the Open Heart Room and the flower garden often in meditation. She sits on the bench, the voice welcomes her back, and she feels the unconditional love and universal consciousness of everyone in the garden, knowing that she will return to this, her spirit's home, at the end of her physical journey, still wide awake to her true self.

Silent or Active Meditation?

What awakens awareness is making conscious what was not known or understood and using that information to refine the mind into a work of art. This awakening can be done passively in silent meditation in which insights emerge on their own, or during active, working meditations that involve the conscious mind and are geared to self-discovery, healing, and transformation.

My rule of thumb is: use silent meditation without an agenda most of the time. The deeper mind presents what we need to know, and consciousness rises higher in silent meditation, as experienced by this writer and as shown on the Mind Mirror in others.

Use working meditations such as "Gifts of Insight" and "The Inner Temple," as well as any other of your companion meditations, when you have an agenda like inner discovery, healing an issue, or finding a solution to a personal problem or work project. (*See* Resources at the end of this chapter.)

Silent meditation gradually conditions the brainwaves of meditation so that, at some point, we emerge from meditation and maintain that pattern in the outer world as the awakened mind. Working meditations, with their ability to proactively heal and transform internal issues, develop this brainwave pattern even faster.

The best approach to personal transformation and spiritual union is to do both.

Strategies for Working with Internal Issues

Some people believe that others can just "get over" a psychospiritual issue and that will be the end of it. Reality doesn't work that way. If people could simply declare a problem to be solved, no one would have any problems. Emotional traumas are imprinted on consciousness and plague us until we address them. Hiding from them separates the mind from the heart (beta from alpha–theta) and the soul from the body (theta from delta). Self-separation creates blocks in consciousness that project outward into our lives and separate us from others.

Removing inner blocks and releasing suppressed creativity is surprisingly easy to do. Remember, you *are* a soul and thus are *bigger* than the content of your subconscious. Since you are in charge of your consciousness, you can observe any and all content in the same way a playwright directs a staged production—in other words, it is as if you are watching a dream. Viewing subconscious material with the greater awareness of your soul will create little to no disturbance in your emotions. There is nothing to be afraid of because whatever you encounter is part of you.

There are many ways to effect inner healing. Reframing a painful issue works wonders. To reframe an issue, you need only carry that intention into a scene in your mind; the creative spirit takes over and changes the story in convincing ways that make all the difference.

Spiritualizing the issue with higher light during meditation is just as beneficial: simply radiate light into the issue to dissipate and clear it. Remember, thoughts are waves of light held together by a memory or belief that creates a pattern in consciousness; using the energy of light to dissipate that pattern is what happens in any kind of therapy.

However, it's possible that clearing a devastating emotional trauma will require professional guidance. If you come in contact with an issue that you feel you cannot handle, find someone to help you with it. Professional counselors and healers guide people into the alpha–theta crossover frequencies of 7.83 hertz, where trauma resides and meditation takes place. With courage and commitment, you can clear anything from the past that you do not want in your present and future.

Like Grace and Peggy, you will grow lighter with every release. Removing old issues purifies the soul, normalizes brain function, and opens the careworn heart to the loving guidance of its spirit. Or perhaps you will prefer to let healing take place in the spiritualizing light of silent meditation.

How can you measure your progress? If you emerge from silent or working meditation feeling clearer, calmer, and stronger, and you project this serenity out into the world, then you are succeeding. If you systematically remove any obstacles to your awakening, then you will systematically awaken to peace.

Unblocking the Mind

Everyone with a high spiritual ideal or intention who believes in his or her ability to access inner imagery is able to do so. Even when the protective ego tries to interfere, if you are persistent and use the unblocking meditation presented below, the content will yield itself up in imagery that you will grasp, understand, and use to resolve issues. In the end, your inner imagery will power up your intuitive connection with your psychic soul.

The following personal-transformation meditation demonstrates how to clear obstacles in order to open the mind to its content and soul. Personal-transformation meditations are based on the idea in Gestalt therapy that each and every part of us, even a misguided part that has an issue (and causes one), has a positive purpose. Once that part divulges its positive purpose, you can address its concerns and promise that you—your essential being, the soul—can take over the part's role so it will reintegrate into the wholeness of your being. The part being addressed might be anything: an area of your body that feels unloved, addiction, sadness, a pattern of consciousness that separates you from your spirit, or even a disbelief in this process or the existence of the soul.

This stunningly simple dialogue with the issue resolves problems quickly and effectively. Once we shed light on parts of us that meant well but in their separation got lonely and lost, they want to let go and return to wholeness. Harmony is easily restored when the discordant part is given a voice that is listened to and honored.

Awakened Mind Meditation: Personal Transformation

First, decide on a question, issue, or challenge that you want to heal. Once you have this question in mind, set it aside and relax into an alpha–theta meditation by the usual means: withdraw from the outside environment and relax the back of your tongue. Breathe deeply and evenly, and progressively relax your body from head to toe.

Take plenty of time to relax, mentally explore a natural landscape that stimulates your alpha waves, and drift down into the depths of your subconscious until you reach a still point of light, peace, and wisdom inside yourself. Expand outward to activate delta. Reach out to your Source, embrace it, and ask for its help with this work.

Once you are deeply relaxed, bring to mind what you want to work on, and allow the part to manifest as an image, symbol, sound, feeling, body sensation, voice in your head, or simply a sense of knowing that the part is present. Bring in your beta by asking verbal questions such as the following, but adjust the questions as needed. Remember to trust what you are experiencing in your subconscious.

First, ask this part of yourself that needs healing if it is willing to talk to you. If it is uncertain, ask what needs to happen to make it more willing. If it feels threatened, reassure it that you are doing this work for the benefit of your whole being—to heal and not to hurt.

Now ask the part how it is feeling. Listen to what it says and reassure it that it will soon feel better. When ready, begin the dialogue:

Ask the part how long it has been there? Is this a new issue or a very old one?

How did it get there? What does it need or want from you?

What role does this part play in your life? What is its positive purpose? If it gives an answer that is negative or obscure, ask again until you get an answer showing how the part has been serving you.

If the part is no longer playing a role that benefits you, ask if it is willing to allow you to fulfill the role it has been playing so that it can reintegrate with the whole of your being. Gently and decisively inform the part that integration is your desire.

Ask the part what needs to happen for the transformation that you are seeking to occur. Is the part willing to let this change take place? If not, what needs to happen for it to become willing? Remind the part that you are doing this exercise for its own good, too.

Use all of your senses to imagine the change taking place. Experience the transformation or healing. Live the experience with all of your senses. When you feel that the transformation is complete, sensualize yourself in the future after the transformation has taken place.

Take a few moments to give your appreciation to the part for all the hard work it has done for you. Check to see if any other parts need attention. If so, promise that part or parts your future attention. Repeat the process as needed.

Find a landmark—a word, symbol, concept, or body sensation—that represents the feeling of your awakened state of mind.

Last, find a closure for your meditation. Make a record of your experience so that you don't forget it. Consider it in conscious beta to make the transformation more real.

If you had any difficulty following these instructions, listen to the "Journey of Transformation" meditation on my CD *The Meditation Experience: Listening to Your Psychic Soul*. This personal-transformation meditation will gently clear blockages and guide you into closer alignment with First Cause.

Aligning with the Soul's First Cause

In this chapter you have heard stories of people who used insights from their psychic souls to heal and transform issues. People who consistently turn to others to heal them and never look inside themselves for solutions are missing the most enlivening and evolutionary experience in life: the soul's purpose, which Edgar Cayce called First Cause.

The Cayce readings say that First Cause is the soul's ability to cleanse itself in order to be a companion to its Creator. Resolving personal issues in the subconscious gives the soul room to grow in that relationship with the Creative Forces.

Each time we clear an issue, we are spiritualized, as Cayce put it. Max Cade unwittingly agreed with Cayce in this idea. Cade noticed while guiding people into EEG-monitored meditation that "before any pupil entered a very deep meditative state, and remained in that state for any length of time at all, this transformation was almost invariably preceded by a number of very transient appearances of the pattern of some higher state." (*The Awakened Mind*, p. 55)

Cade was essentially saying that the person was "spiritualized" by higher insights prior to entering a meditation or higher state of consciousness. These epiphanies are gifts from the psychic soul and God.

Despite the joys of First Cause, some awakened people go back to sleep, at least temporarily. The development of self-mastery as a means to enlightenment is a choice that we make day by day. Some of us slip back down into our lower natures and are ensnared for a while, but the soul's pull toward First Cause is irresistible. It's a feeling that something is missing, that something has been lost. No matter what kinds of addictive substances or material possessions we use to feed that hunger, only spiritual love can satisfy it.

Eventually we find our way back home. The light of the soul calls us back through little awakenings—spontaneous surges of light, if you will—that lift us into the transcendent perspectives of the evolved-mind's brainwave pattern.

The Evolved Mind of Illumination

The evolved mind is an expansion of the awakened mind. In experiencing this state of consciousness, even if only for seconds at a time, people feel a sense of warmth and happiness. They may feel that they are being filled with spiritual love. Some weep in awe, joy, and gratitude. Such was Joanie's experience of rediscovering her true home in the spirit—and Grace's, too, as she sat in her paradise garden with God and the millions of spirits who loved her.

Personal and universal insights flowing up from the Field into the unconscious mind cause delta to curve upward, as information that was unconscious lifts up into higher frequencies and becomes known. The surge of this inflow of insight unites delta, theta, alpha, and beta into a circle of oneness with itself and all that is. The separation between subject and object disappears into nonduality and unity-consciousness.

From this experience of Pure Spirit, there is no turning back. We will never feel alone again, for we know that the web of spiritual light interpenetrating all things is part of us. Our perceptions of reality change profoundly, as this infinite love and light, imprinted into every atom and cell of memory, fcalls us home.

Formation of the Evolved Mind

Cade wrote on page 123 of his book that the evolved mind of Creativity—curiously akin to Cayce's term, Creative Forces—"feels unified with something far vaster" than itself.

The person who experiences this brainwave pattern is typically on some kind of spiritual path that unites it with what feels like the essence of life. This essence of life transmits pictures, words, complex patterns, and sensations that travel from universal awareness into the evolved mind in a fully-developed way. Higher knowledge flows in as the psyche is held in the grip of a loving power that exists in this earth and beyond it, as Cade so brilliantly put it.

I would add that the mind and heart, receiving this inflow of love, are illuminated. The body, touched by spiritual light, raises the kundalini life force, which bathes the entire being in light. If you have experienced this illumination, you know how wonderful it feels. Floating in the formless, resonating with the infinite, the psyche can only weep with joy as it rejoins what was unconsciously longed for, yet was consciously missing and lost.

Guiding Yourself into the Evolved Mind of Light

The key to the evolved mind is whatever stirs the senses with joy and feelings of connection to something greater than self. The brainwaves of meditation and the awakened mind naturally expand into the evolved mind—the next stage of consciousness. The meditator and spiritual practitioner can expect occasional experiences of illumination and transcendence to grow more frequent, until the mind can "plug in" to Source at any time and feel the subtle energies that amplify brainwaves with the pure light of consciousness.

The spiritual intention and desire for oneness easily connect meditators, psychics, and healers with these vibrant energies, which are often experienced as light and sound manifesting in or as an electrical hum or vibration. As Cayce noted, the kundalini energy rising through the chakra system and vibrating against the crown and third eye causes the body to sway and rock from side to side or back and forth. Less common experiences of these moving currents of energy—stimulated as the body's life force resonates with higher spiritual vibrations—are indigo pulsations of the third eye and inner pitches that expand into the sounds of bees, cascading water, or roaring wind, described in the Christian New Testament as the "holy spirit."

Since time immemorial, spiritual adepts have retreated to mountains and caves to see and hear this light and sound of God, a kind of celestial music that amplifies as we shift into still-higher levels of awareness. Powerful flows of kundalini cause some people to involuntarily contort into yoga postures, called asanas, and some even levitate a few inches above the ground. (*See* the chapter entitled "The Light of Consciousness" for more information on these energetic and intuitive effects on the brain and body.)

You can connect to these spiritual energies, which are always available, simply by lovingly reaching out with your delta waves and auric field. You simply open up and plug in! The light will meet you more than halfway, whether you feel it yet or not. Repeated practice will develop your sensitivity to it.

It may help to chant "HU," the Sufi name for the divine, which opened up my third eye some years ago when I heard an Eckankar devotee singing that pure, high note in a heartfelt song to God. Soon after that, I stood in front of an immense amethyst crystal in the Natural History Museum in Washington, DC, and instinctively placed a quartz crystal on my third eye. Suddenly, I heard every crystal in the museum singing. Since then, I've used these high pitches to guide me into meditation and God–consciousness.

Perhaps you will want to sing the chants suggested by Edgar Cayce: the AAREEOM, sounded in the base of the abdomen and rising up into the head in a single, resonant pitch: ahhh–reee–ommm. Closing the mouth on the ending Om sound vibrates the sound throughout the head and lifts brainwaves into higher frequencies, as I have observed on the Mind Mirror. Or you could sing Cayce's vowel chant, aaaaa–eeeee–iiiii–ooooo–uuuuu, in a rising pitch that reverberates through your entire being; simply flow with these sound currents with your heart wide open to raise your consciousness.

Several of this book's companion meditations, especially "Breathing Light," "Woods and Water," and "The Illuminated Door," are direct experiences of universal light. "Breathing Light" is a conscious breathing and chanting meditation featuring the Om and Edgar Cayce's AAREEOM. (*See* Resources at the end of this chapter.)

Here is a simple and very powerful technique that I use in meditation to connect to a higher vibration. Called the "Circulation of Light," this practice is the subject of the rather cryptic book, *The Secret of the Golden Flower,* an esoteric Taoist and Buddhist text written by spiritual masters for their meditation students. Taoism is a Chinese philosophy referring to "the way" or "the path" through the natural order of the universe into primordial essence. Practitioners use the "Circulation of Light" in meditation to seek nirvana, attain psychic experiences, transform the self, rejuvenate life processes, and transmute to a *conscious* spirit in life and death.

This ascent through the breath into the conscious spirit rests on the premise that the golden flower—that is, light—when circulated through the chakra system, lifts the inner self into Empty Infinity. Interestingly, the text describes Empty Infinity as the state of illumination and pictures it as a circle—precisely the same as our evolved–mind circle.

Evolved-Mind Meditation: The Circulation of Light

Sit comfortably, close your eyes, and once you feel deeply relaxed, silently voice your intention to merge with Universal Mind. Think, feel, and experience this intention. Next, take a full breath, and in the quiet of your mind draw the inhalation up from the base of your spine to the crown of your head and then along the inside of your skull down to the third eye chakra in your forehead (in the shape of a shepherd's crook). Pause briefly to allow spiritual light to stream into the crown of your head; on the exhalation, bathe your chakras in this light. Allow light to flow down from the crown into your throat, heart, solar plexus, and pelvis back to the root chakra at the base of your spine.

Repeat this cycle seven times, and then let go of conscious breathing. Lift into the presence of divine light with a prayer phrased something like this: "Arise my soul and enter the Oneness, the mind and heart of God." Rest in the light of oneness and feel the love in it. When you are ready to close your meditation, be sure to distribute the energies in your head throughout your organs and systems, and all the way into your fingers and toes.

Practice this circulation of light as often as possible in meditation and in daily life as a means of relaxation, as advised by John Van Auken in his book *Toward a Deeper Meditation*. Each practice will sensitize you to the flow of subtle energy. Soon you will be able to connect with it at any time, in both meditation and waking life.

A Personal Story: A Revelation at Esalen

I discovered what evolves consciousness the most while attending a week-long meditation retreat led by Anna Wise at the Esalen Institute in Big Sur, California, in early September of 2001. Serendipitously, I'd been forced by a dentally-related flare-up of the trigeminal nerve in my brain to sit absolutely still for two weeks before the retreat, and as my writings predicted, the inner work I did in meditation and inspired writing served me well. I arrived at Esalen in a very high state of consciousness, and events conspired to keep me spiraling higher and higher.

I was greeted warmly by a pleasantly surprised Anna Wise, with whom I'd been corresponding for a year. Her kindly welcome elated me, as did the exquisite beauty of Esalen, the oldest human-potential center in America and one of the loveliest places on earth. So when Anna led the class into a kundalini meditation, I was already so high in consciousness that I spent the entire meditation blissed out in what I call the "luminous field." Reporting this experience after the meditation, as did everyone else in turn, I said to Anna that this luminous field was a familiar place. She looked down at her drawings of my brainwaves— a sustained, partial evolved-mind pattern—and suggested that I find out why this pattern is a familiar place in consciousness.

That night I walked down to the meditation sanctuary, a round stone structure located at the base of a wooded mountain at the edge of an ocean inlet. The room was filled with high-frequency vibrations so that I easily slipped into deep meditation, after which I sent healing light out to other people as the Cayce style of meditation taught me to do. The luminous field intensified, and suddenly I realized that what *always* lifts me into it is the transmission of healing light to others.

It was indeed a familiar place, and now I knew, thanks to Anna's genius, that what evolves the mind is healing prayer. I began to test this idea in EEG studies on other people, and the link proved infallible. Over the past seven years, I have studied the brainwaves of several hundred meditators, psychics, mediums, and healers experiencing or sending out spiritual light. Not once has the reception or transmission of spiritual light failed to produce a partial or full circle of the evolved mind during EEG-led meditation.

What this discovery means is pretty extraordinary. Sending out spiritual light to others raises our own and draws more into us, and that's what creates the upturned delta of the evolved mind: the inflow of spiritual energy and its infusion into conscious awareness. We feel the luminous light, and it spiritualizes and transforms us, just as Cayce and Cade said.

Form and substance, as always, are the same. In the circle of the evolved mind, the more we open up, the more light we receive; the more light we receive, the more we transmit; the more we transmit, the more we receive. To enter the circle, all we need to do is open up.

Evolved-Mind Meditation: Transmitting Light

Begin by bringing to mind a spiritual experience of some kind: a profound meditation, spiritual revelation, spontaneous healing, or a sense of oneness with nature or the universe. Relax deeply and for several minutes relive this memory with all of your senses. Immerse yourself in the experience and become aware of sensations of light. Let this light build up, and when you are ready, transmit it to several of the people you love, one at a time. See each person happy and whole. You will know how to send this light.

Be sure to notice the increasing sensations of light in your mind and body as you send out light. Find a landmark for the feeling of spiritual light in and around your head, neck, and shoulders. When you close this meditation, be sure to distribute these energies throughout your internal organs and evenly throughout your body, all the way into your fingertips and toes.

Enlightenment and Shaktipat

Cases of spontaneous enlightenment are rare; and as the late Anna Wise was fond of saying, "Enlightenment doesn't come in a box." Consciousness development takes time and dedication, as in the case of Phyllis Vorhauer, who produced a significant number of evolved-mind flares with her eyes open during a weekend group brainwave training in my home. She might have continued to do so if the meditation had not come to a close. Phyllis is a dedicated meditator and has been an active member of an Edgar Cayce "A Search for God" study group for more than forty years. She is the only person I have seen hold on to an evolved-mind pattern for any length of time with her eyes open.

Despite the spiritual dedication required to develop the evolved mind, advanced meditators, intuitives, and healers commonly flare into evolved-mind patterns for a few seconds at a time during meditation. Evolved-mind patterns show up more often today than in years past, and so does a diamond–shaped brainwave pattern wherein the soul reaches up to its higher self .

These higher–state patterns are clearly the result of people awakening each other to new possibilities. I witnessed an extraordinary proof of this evolved–mind resonance in a woman named Cindy, who was connected to the Mind Mirror while sitting in a chair on the spacious stage of an octagonal wood–and–glass auditorium at a beautiful spiritual retreat center in the Blue Ridge Mountains of North Carolina.

I was onstage tuning up my lap harp as approximately eighty people were settling into their seats after the lunch break. Suddenly, I glanced up at Cindy's brainwaves, which were playing across a huge, overhead projection screen. I was not surprised to see a quiet, calm mind in this musician and meditator, but when a friend of hers walked onstage and began a detailed recounting of an out–of–body experience in which she had visions about the future, Cindy's brainwave patterns shifted dramatically.

Cindy, listening with her psychic empathy, began to entrain with her friend's brainwave–memory of this spiritual experience. She closed her eyes and entered a meditative listening state, an awakened–mind pattern, and then an evolved–mind pattern. Resonance carried Cindy into her friend's universal awareness.

Surprised that this pattern could happen in a room full of people, I walked over and stood next to Cindy's friend so that her voice could be heard through my lapel microphone. A hush fell over the audience, which already understood the rudiments of brainwaves and quickly realized what was happening. We watched in open–mouthed astonishment as this wonderful display of synchronicity demonstrated the power of delta empathy and psychic resonance.

Extremely high energies began to reverberate through the audience, which consisted of a spiritual group of old friends who share an admiration for the Cayce work and a high degree of empathy with one another. Everyone sensed a powerful field of energy forming in the auditorium, and wonderful experiences resulted for each person. Dozens of people told me afterward about intuitive insights and little healings that occurred that day. Some of these happened during a spontaneous musical improvisation session with Cindy, a pianist, and her husband, a trombonist, as I played my lap harp while all of us, the audience included, lifted up through the beauty and power of spiritually-connected music into a very high state of consciousness.

Listening deeply, we resonated together on waves of music in a sea of love. Glancing out of the tall windows of the auditorium at the smoky blue mountains topped by white, fluffy clouds in clear, blue skies, I wondered if I had died and gone to heaven.

The point of this story is our connection by resonant fields of light, whether we are aware of them or not. It doesn't take a spiritual master to lift us up, only a person with a high spiritual intention who is reliving a story about light and love. I believe that the sharing of stories such as these, in spiritual groups and psychic circles, is what has shifted us into and beyond the evolved-mind pattern to the still higher states of consciousness featured in the next chapter.

Like everything worth having, the experience of transcendence comes out of personal transformation, spiritual connection, time, and patience. The evolution occurs as psycho-spiritual change flows through neurons, neural pathways, and brain layers to lift the mind into the superconscious higher self that illuminates and enlightens us.

Perhaps you agree that this adventure in consciousness is the most exciting journey that we could ever take. We are the only ones who can walk it, yet we never walk alone.

David's Story: Love Conquers All

David's story illustrates that even when we separate from spiritual awareness, God is ever-present and available to comfort, guide, and call us home. David did not ask me for help; instead, I visited his home in Louisiana to offer him an EEG-led awakened-mind session. I was concerned about him because of an unexpected and unwelcome life change that had robbed him of happiness, hope, and his sense of direction. For a year and a half, he had searched for the light that I assured him was somewhere in what had happened to him. He had yet to find it, and I knew that he considered my "new age" reassurances empty and less than sane.

Despite his disbelief in spirituality and my work, I brought my equipment to his home and was hoping for the best. I was surprised when he accepted my offer—and a little nervous, as I'd never worked with a nonbeliever before. When I connected him to the Mind Mirror, I immediately saw a full-blown awakened mind, a rare event even for a calm, focused, creative, and intelligent person like David. But when I saw a near-perfect evolved-mind circle show up early in the session, I checked my equipment to make sure it was working properly!

What I saw in David's brainwaves made no sense. He was a nonmeditator, and he didn't even *believe* in the existence of higher states of consciousness! How could this be?

Setting aside my questions, I led him through a five-minute relaxation and then asked him to see himself in a safe place. His psyche ushered him into a cane field with the wind blowing and birds singing. At first, no one else was there, but he had a sense of comfort, recognition, and peace—the signs of a higher state of awareness. I asked him to look for a gift, and suddenly the spirit of his sweet Cajun mother appeared.

She told him that she loved him and was proud of him and that, "We all have trials in our lives." She urged him to "hold on tight." These words touched his core, as she had passed away two years before and he missed her very much. I asked him what she, as his gift, had given him. Love, education, and his sense of right and wrong, he replied. She told him that she would be with him always.

The second gift in the cane field was David's husband, Drew, whose contributions to his life included compassion, love, peace, and the goals and impetus to always be better. David realized that his relationship with Drew would change when he struck out into a new career; he needed to articulate some things to Drew. In the cane field of his psychic soul, he clarified what was vitally important to him and voiced his feelings to Drew.

"I love you, want to walk by your side, share the burden, and help you understand who I am," he told Drew (in spirit and later in person). "But I also want to be equal. I want to pursue a separate life and for us to be supportive of that for each other."

The loving encouragement from his mother and his clarity about what he needed to say to Drew were very helpful to David, who entered nursing school two months later with a lighter heart and Drew's full support. David will work with sick children and no doubt will be a smart, funny character who laughs his little patients back to health.

The session was a real eye-opener for me, as it proved what I had only hoped was true: that even if the ego resists belief in its spirit, when we bypass the ego, the spirit is manifest.

What I didn't know until I looked at David's brainwaves was that his spiritual disbelief was losing traction. The next morning, I walked downstairs and found him cooking a hearty breakfast for us. Sitting at the kitchen counter, I quietly asked if he knew why higher-state brainwaves had showed up in his session. I carefully explained why I was asking: "These states of consciousness relate to the spirit. I know that you were raised as a Catholic, but now have no interest in spirituality."

He grew still, gazed into my eyes, and said deliberately, "That's been changing."

In his words was an acknowledgment of having found light in the tempestuous events that changed his life. Like the Beatles' song says, we can't hide our love away, especially from ourselves.

I was deeply touched by my beloved friend's confirmation that the open, loving heart cannot be kept down by the mind's disbelief. Given an opportunity, the heart opens to its spirit—the spirit that is a hair's breadth away, whose whispers call us to awaken to its presence, especially when our hearts are broken by life.

The sudden change in David's life had given him time to open up his heart and listen—and after all, that's what we *really* came here to do, isn't it?

Drew's Story: "They Are with Us Always"

The hostile corporate takeover that unseated David from his beautiful life's work also changed the course of Drew's life. Drew, the visionary dreamer in the relationship, was eager to explore his mind. So, honoring what I intuited was his need to relax and enjoy himself, I connected him to the Mind Mirror and asked him to imagine piloting a boat through the Mediterranean Sea (he chose a yacht filled with his friends) and then go for a swim in the water. Next, I asked him to find a beautiful ray of light on the bottom of the sea and to get in touch with his spirit. He did so, and this guided imagery lifted him into a higher state of awareness that would serve him well.

Returning to his yacht and docking it at a Greek marina, Drew left his friends dining at a café on the coast and followed my guidance to a room in a nearby house. There he found his father and grandmother, the two most important people in his life, both of whom had died in his youth and had left him feeling abandoned and alone.

"I'm daddy's boy!" Drew laughed exultantly as his smiling father materialized and hugged and held him, speaking words of wisdom that Drew repeated out loud: "It's for the good. It's going to be okay. My dreams will come true. I just need to be happy." These loving words of comfort soothed Drew's pain and gave him hope.

Sensing that he needed uninterrupted time with his father, I asked him to speak only when he pleased. His comments came sporadically. "It's heaven. It's love," he said happily, followed by the exclamation, "Live for the angels!" After a pause he said quietly, "They're inside us, the memories of who they are and what they believe in. Laugh. Smile. Love. It doesn't matter what I do. I just have to live and be happy."

Drew trusted these words completely because they were so unexpected and clearly emanated from some other world. "I was there!" he laughed after the session. "I was really there and saw everything! It was real!" Trusting in his experience—and some profound insights that he did not speak aloud—enabled him to release a great deal of his grief.

In every session with people, I learn something new about consciousness and the cosmos. Sometimes the insights are big and sometimes small. These sessions with David and Drew were paradigm shifters.

Drew's awakened- and evolved-mind patterns indicated communication with his psychic soul. During the session, he recognized on a very deep level that the spirits of our ancestors live on in us—in their love and morality and courage and compassion—and because we manifest their traits, we keep them alive in everyone whose lives we touch.

Standing in front of a crackling fire in his wood stove, he shared his epiphanies. "They (our ancestors) don't die and we don't either," he said in an awed voice. "The best of them lives on in us, and we carry that into the future, passing it on to other people."

With our minds flowing together, we imagined how this idea works in space and time. First, we saw that ancestral wisdom comes down to us through the millennia in memories held in our cellular DNA and the body's energy field. Our ancestors' bodies pass away, but the energy of their consciousness remains in us so that we can draw on it constantly. In a very real way, we *are* the people who came before us, until we consciously transmute these energies.

When we concentrate on our ancestors' goodness and beauty, as well as what is good and beautiful in the world, we shift into a higher vibration that dissipates what is not love. Loving energy rewires our brains, auric fields, and lives to a higher awareness, which we then pass down to our children and everyone whose lives they touch.

Drew and I realized that our essence energetically ripples into the future to create our destiny in every moment, meaning that every moment is a choice point. Reality, as I understood from remote-viewing research, can be changed not only in the present and future, but also in the past. When we reframe the past, the new story echoes into the lives of those ancestors to reconstruct events and heal them; this energy simultaneously reverberates into our minds and energy fields to refresh the present and future, allowing all realities to vibrate in harmony as one.

Deep in the psyche, the only reality is the reality we choose to hold in mind.

The Love in the Light

Looking back through the history of humankind, we can see that change does not come easily to most people, if it occurs at all. The conscious mind's ego, in its drive to defend and protect itself, struggles to maintain its control and domination. In doing so, the ego overrules the heart, which closes up in despair until there is unity and harmony again.

Such is the battleground of competing values on which we find ourselves and our world.

What can a body do? In my experience, we can only listen until the higher self communicates with the soul, the soul speaks to the spiritual heart, and the spiritual heart—with images of love, comfort, and reassurance—whispers guidance to the human heart, mind, and body. This inner reconciliation creates peace, compassion, and spiritual light that touches people and reverberates through the cosmos.

Such is the law of Love. The lower nature is not allowed to stand in Love's way. In the light of Love, all else collapses and becomes extinct. As the Beatles' song says, "All you need is love."

A Word from Our Sponsor

When we say that conscious evolution is a matter of the heart, what we are really saying is that the heart enables us to *feel and experience* the light of the soul and its spirit. It is the heart which inspires us to lift the mind into the enlightened perspectives of the psychic soul and the love, joy, compassion, and generosity of spirit that we radiate to others.

Born to a loving, open-hearted family, I felt the presence of spiritual light in early childhood. Even though I lost my belief in God by age fifteen, at age twenty-five, when radiant light poured into my body and healed it, my heart searched for what was ineffable until I found it again. In inspired writing and meditation, I opened my heart joyfully, expecting to meet the greatest love I'd ever known, and I did. I feel and know that I am blessed.

However, it's not this way for everyone. Many people have deep-seated issues involving anger, guilt, shame, or blame and are unable to relax and surrender to their spirit. It helps to know that spirituality is about the light and goodness in us and all things. Even if you don't believe this idea at first, just open up and surrender to the light in your pure and perfect spiritual heart. When you meet your spirit, you will believe in it.

If you believe in nothing else, believe in love. Love will meet you with open arms and carry you deep into yourself, where you will find everything you seek. Your inner spirit will call you to a richer and more meaningful life, and it will be everything you ever dreamed of and hoped for.

If you sense that your heart is closed right now, you can re-open it by simply asking, "Who's running my life: my mind or my heart?" If the answer is your mind, arouse sensations of love and bathe your mind in them. This will shift your awareness (and modus operandi) into your heart.

Keeping our hearts open is a lifelong surrender to the loving higher self. Opening the heart is our most effective entry into meditation, psychic readings, and all else that is good in life.

Meditation on Love

Close your eyes and remember what it feels like to be relaxed. Use one of your landmarks to invoke a deep sense of relaxation.

In your mind's eye, become aware of your spiritual heart and use all of your senses to experience it. See it, feel it, touch it, even taste and smell it.

Now place your human heart inside your spiritual heart, and place your mind inside the human heart. What does this image look like?

If you notice light flowing in and around your spiritual heart, human heart, and mind, search in this light for the people you care the most about. What did each one give you? What do you value most about each person? Do you live these qualities yourself? What are your qualities, and which ones, if any, do you want to release?

Rest in feelings of love for a while, and then send out the light of your spiritual heart to anyone or anything that needs it.

When you complete this meditation, be sure to journal about what you learned. Come back to this practice when you feel out of harmony. Bring each part back into harmony for an open flow of love—and intuition.

Personal and Planetary Evolution

Every time we open-heartedly meditate in the presence of the psychic soul, we expand into the higher state of awareness known as nonduality or unity-consciousness. Each effort brings us closer to a self-actualized life of creative expression that is entirely free of judgment, separation, and self-interest.

Look into your mind's eye to review this evolutionary journey as presented so far:

The awakened heart, mind, and body set out together as equal partners on a soul journey and consciously open up to new experiences. The soul encounters stumbling blocks, but in a systematic, orderly fashion clears them from the path. Each day brings "aha" insights filled with exciting revelations that lead to still greater insights causing the awakened mind to *fill* with Light and *become more as-Light*, achieving the brainwave patterns of the evolved mind, the superconscious mind, and the godlike, angelic higher self.

Feel yourself reaching into these higher states in this very moment to develop a superconscious intelligence that is growing new nerve cells in the creativity and intelligence centers of your brain. Imagine yourself as a new human—a smarter and more creative you—born out of the psychic soul.

Looking through the soul's eyes, we can see signs of this new human and this new reality being born today. If we are sensitive enough to subtle energies, we may feel the birth of a new reality. Even if we do not sense the light, we can allow our hearts to break open and *be* it.

You are the light of the world when the energy of your psychic soul emanates through your auric field to uplift All That Is. On a quantum, subatomic level, your mental coherence and emotional equanimity bring the whole world into balance—intuitively.

Mapping Your Progress

In the absence of a Mind Mirror of your own, the Table of Subjective Landmarks at the end of this chapter will help you map the quality of your meditations. This table correlates subjective descriptions of the descent into meditation, as mapped by University of Oregon researcher Terry Lesh, with associated EEG states as measured by Cade. You may wish to use the Subjective Landmarks chart after each meditation or psychic reading to check the state of consciousness you reached.

Your connection with your psychic soul is of course the best indicator of your progress. The Table of Subjective Landmarks is for your intellect's use and enjoyment.

Stage 0 is an ordinary, thinking mind. Stages 1 and 2 are preludes to meditation; 3 is a light meditation state; 4 is a stable meditation; 5 is a deep, profound meditation or awakened mind; and 6 is an awakened-mind, evolved–mind, yoga–nidra pattern, or out–of–body experience. Stage 6 also describes the superconscious mind and the godlike, higher self's brainwave patterns introduced in the next chapter.

Defining your progress in meditation will help you attain the highest possible states of awareness for psychic practice.

Resources:
"The Inner Temple," *a journey along the river of life to a temple for self-discovery and insight.*

"Creative Light," *a meditation opening with light and the chakras that guides listeners into the subconscious to retrieve ideas and insights regarding a question, issue, or challenge in one's work or life.*

"Gifts of Insight," *a journey into a redwood forest for gifts you can use in everyday life.*

"Journey of Transformation," *an awakened-mind meditation used to address a question, issue, challenge, or block.*

"Breathing Light" *features conscious breathing, chanting of the Om and Cayce's AAREEOM, and meditative connection with superconscious light.*

"Woods and Water," *an awakened-mind meditation that deepens into the psychic soul for personal discovery and self-realization.*

(For the above meditations, *see* Selected Bibliography for track information regarding: Pennington, Judith. *The Meditation Experience: Listening to Your Psychic Soul.* A.R.E. Press, 2011, CDs.)

Table of Subjective Landmarks

#	Descriptions	EEG
0	May have difficulty stilling the mind or mind racing out of control Itchy, distractible, inattentive state A feeling of "Why am I doing this?" Just beginning to relax A feeling of "settling down"	◆ Continuous beta, often with some flares of other waves ◆ Possibly intermittent alpha
1	Foggy state • Feeling dizzy • Sensations of going under an anesthetic Occasional feeling of nausea Mind filled with everyday affairs—almost as an avoidance of inner stillness A feeling of scattered energies A sensation of drifting off to sleep or being pulled back from the edge of sleep	◆ Somewhat reduced beta, but still present ◆ Intermittent but stronger alpha
2	Scattered energies beginning to collect Childhood flashbacks Beginning to feel calmness and relaxation Uninvited vivid flashes of imagery Images from distant to immediate past Attention not very sustained A feeling of being in-between states Transitional state	◆ Reduced beta ◆ Stronger alpha could be continuous ◆ Intermittent low-frequency theta
3	Greater sense of stability Well-defined state Pleasant bodily sensations of floating, lightness, swaying, or rocking Occasional slight rhythmical movement Concentration easier and stronger Increased and clearer imagery Increased ability to follow guided imagery	◆ Highly reduced beta ◆ Continuous alpha ◆ Possibly more continuous theta with increased frequency and/or amplitude
4	Extremely vivid awareness of breathing, heartbeat, blood flow, or other body sensations Feeling of loss of body boundaries Sensation of numbness in limbs or of being full of air Sensation of growing to great size or becoming very small Sensation of great heaviness or lightness Sometimes alternating between external and internal awareness	◆ Highly reduced beta ◆ Continuous alpha ◆ Increased theta
5	Very lucid state of consciousness Feeling of deep satisfaction Intense alertness, calmness, and detachment Sensation of spacing out or disappearing from environment and/or body Extremely vivid imagery when desired Feeling of altered state lacking in previous levels, 0-4 Sense of peak experience, "ah-ha" moment, intuitive insight High performance	Best meditation (alpha, theta, delta) Awakened mind (beta, alpha, theta, delta) ◆ Strong beta mastery, ranging from no thoughts to creative thoughts ◆ Continuous alpha ◆ Continuous theta
6	New way of feeling Intuitive insight into old problems, as though seen from a more aware level Synthesis of opposites into a higher union Sensation of being surrounded in light A feeling of higher spiritual awareness A sensation that nothing matters other than just being The experience of bliss or of indefinable peace	Five possible patterns: 1. Awakened mind (beta, alpha, theta, delta) 2. Evolved mind (circular pattern) 3. Occasional flares of delta (yoga nidra) 4. Little to no brain activity (out of body pattern) 5. Superconscious mind or higher self

6

The Superconscious Mind
and the Angelic Higher Self

" . . . Turn thy face to the light and the shadows fall behind."
Edgar Cayce reading 987-4

The most accurate psychic readings come out of attunement to the soul's higher self, which resides alongside helping spirits in the superconscious realm near the formless energy of Universal Consciousness, according to Edgar Cayce. The sleeping prophet once described to an audience a recurring dream in which he ascended through dimensions in consciousness to the highest realms of Light:

> . . . I see myself as a tiny dot out of my physical body, which lies inert before me. I find myself oppressed by darkness and there is a feeling of terrific loneliness. Suddenly I am conscious of a beam of white light. I move upward in the light, knowing that I must follow it or be lost.
>
> As I move along this path of light, I gradually become conscious of various levels upon which there is movement. Upon the first levels there

are vague, horrible shapes, grotesque forms such as one sees in night-mares. Passing on, there begin to appear on either side misshapen forms of human beings with some part of the body magnified. Again there is change and I become conscious of gray-hooded forms moving down-ward. Gradually, these become lighter in color. Then the direction changes and these forms move upward and the color of their robes grows rapidly lighter.

Next, there begin to appear on either side vague outlines of houses, walls, trees, etc., but everything is motionless. As I pass on, there is more light and movement in what appear to be normal cities and towns. With the growth of movement I become conscious of sounds, at first indistinct rumblings, then music, laughter, and singing of birds. There is more and more light, the colors become very beautiful, and there is only a blending of sound and color. Quite suddenly, I come upon a hall of records. It is a hall without walls, without a ceiling, but I am conscious of seeing an old man who hands me a large book, a record of the individual for whom I seek information.   294-19, Report #12

The Community of Saints

Propelled by his spiritual ideal, Cayce's soul traveled beyond the realms of discarnate entities and even the superconscious to reach Universal Consciousness. Sometimes he lingered along the way to receive and pass on messages from departed souls who wanted to communicate with his own family or the person for whom he was giving the reading; at other times he received information from helpers residing higher than the soul realm in a superconscious, spiritual realm that is well described as a community of saints.

The community of saints is a descriptor extrapolated by Cayce expert, John Van Auken, from reading 262–87, in which Cayce said, " . . . Thus, the communion of saints means that all who have one purpose, whose thoughts and motivative forces are one, may communicate; whether those in the material plane, in the borderland, or those that may be upon the shores of the other side of life . . . " The Archangel Michael, whose booming voice Cayce channeled on occasion, would be one example of a helping entity or angelic guide inhabiting the community of saints in the superconscious realm next to the throne of God. Other angelic beings and master teachers of an equally high vibration coexist in this realm with the higher self, a godlike ideal variously described by

Cayce as the higher consciousness, individuality, or spiritual essence of the soul. (5754-2)

While this spiritual essence is " . . . That self that has been builded, that that is as the companion, that must be presented—that *is* presented—*is* before the Throne itself . . . " we are not left to fend for ourselves in the earth plane. Cayce went on to explain in 5754-3, " . . . for has it not been said, 'He has given his angels charge concerning thee, lest at any time thou dashest thy foot against a stone?' . . . " Protected by angels while incarnate, we ourselves are angelic beings on the spiritual level of the community of saints. If only we could conceive and know this to be true!

It was in the community of saints that Cayce met an old man, the Keeper of the Records, who either handed him a Book of Life or directed him to the volume containing the information on the recipient of the reading. Sometimes other spirit helpers contributed their perspectives and advice.

Readings on his psychic process informed Cayce that these records of life, which he sometimes referred to as God's book of remembrance (1650-1), were formulations of his mind intended to symbolically show each soul its ability to ascend into the infinite. How the infinite is perceived—whether as books or "many mansions"—does not matter. What matters, he said, is the soul's understanding that it makes a record containing information that it can read and use for its growth.

Interestingly, Cayce's readings explain that these "visions and expressions" in Universal Consciousness " . . . go upon the waves of light, upon that of space. And those instruments that are *attuned* to same may hear, may experience, that which is being transmitted . . . " (3976-16)

Cayce's description of "waves of light" closely matches that of modern quantum scientists who perceive existence as a quantum field of energy composed of oscillating waves of light that encode and resonate information. Somewhere in the unconscious mind, recounted Cayce, is a mechanism for picking up this information, and it attunes minds telepathically. This mechanism is undoubtedly the radar-like brainwaves of delta's unconscious mind, which works like a sender and receiver to tune in and transmit information psychically.

While resting in these lowest and slowest brainwaves of his unconscious mind, Edgar Cayce was an ideal receiver and transmitter of the light-waves of information in Universal Consciousness. His utterly still mind was easily able to attune with this formless realm of pure energy from which he drew information.

Out of Universal Consciousness, through Cayce, emanated what is undoubtedly the most important message of these times: that our development depends on our ability to *release spiritual energy from the superconscious and bring it into conscious expression.*

Occult, Mystic, or Psychic?

In his book *Understand and Develop Your ESP,* author Mark Thurston explains the differences between the occult, mystic, and psychic. He writes that the occult is limited to psychic phenomena and therefore experiences higher-dimensional realities without necessarily accessing their origin in Universal Consciousness. Examples would be channeling the voices of dead spirits by a trance medium, or psychokinesis, in which a person's mental energy moves an object across a surface.

In contrast, the mystic attuned to the superconscious or the still-higher vibration of Universal Consciousness engages in a trance-like spiritual ecstasy that is not necessarily expressed in the physical world. The brainwave pattern of the practiced mystic is most likely to be the evolved mind of bliss, illumination, and spiritual oneness, which dissipates with the return to external awareness.

While spiritual energies might certainly emanate from the mystic into the ordinary world for a period of time, the challenge for the mystic, as Thurston points out, is to translate his or her spiritual oneness into daily life. This challenge is met by the spiritually-minded psychic who, while reading for self and others, reaches up for insights to the superconscious higher self. In still higher frequencies, the godlike, angelic nature is transformed by these energies and conveys them into the earth.

Literally and figuratively, the spiritually-intentioned psychic brings heaven to earth and earth to heaven as intuitive insights and powerful energies flow through the soul and are grounded in creative service that awakens and evolves the world.

When the psychic soul rises into the superconscious, an energy transfer takes place, and it brings that vibrant light into the physical plane in two high-frequency brainwave patterns introduced and explained here for the first time: the superconscious mind of the psychic, healer, and meditator, and the angelic, godlike nature of the higher self.

Bringing Heaven to Earth

A remarkable energy transfer takes place when the high frequencies of the superconscious cascade into the brain as super-fast gamma waves ranging in frequency from 25 to 100 hertz. These powerful gamma waves appropriate the frequencies of fast beta and at times high alpha on the Mind Mirror. Gamma masquerades as the high beta brainwaves of stress, anxiety, and panic, but the meditator's experience is exactly the opposite of those feelings.

When I work with advanced meditators, psychics, and healers who produce gamma waves, their subjective experience always includes one-pointed mental focus and calm lucidity, extraordinary insights, spiritual illumination, kundalini energy rising up the spine, astral projection, and the reception and/or transmission of high-voltage spiritual light.

Edgar Cayce's Source indicated that when he was in deep unconscious trance, high vibrations resonated through his mind and body. These were surely gamma waves and even higher frequencies, as Cayce could rise above the superconscious realm of the higher self into Universal Consciousness. Deepening into the unconscious mind, as Cayce did, is one means of producing high-frequency gamma waves: as the mind relaxes into very low frequencies, the brain compensates by arousing high frequencies that connect us with higher vibrations of spiritual light.

But as Cayce told one person, Edwin Blumenthal, people can be wide awake and in touch with these high vibrations. Today, we are seeing this awakened-mind state in advanced practitioners of compassion meditation and devotional prayer. Gamma is produced by one-pointed attention and breathing techniques used by Kriya Yoga practitioners. The rising kundalini triggers gamma, as well.

Some of the people featured below and in Chapter 10 on Healers and

Healing were awake and active in the outer world when their gamma waves showed up on the Mind Mirror. They were doing exactly what Cayce said was so important for each soul to do: *release spiritual energy from the superconscious into conscious expression.*

In the two new brainwave patterns presented here, we see the human brain/mind accessing the superconscious realm that is so close to the formless energy of Universal Consciousness. The first pattern, the superconscious mind, draws information from the higher self and/or spiritual helpers and manifests this information in the earth. The second pattern, referred to as the godlike, angelic nature, is the contemplative soul merging with its higher self.

The Brainwaves of the Superconscious Mind

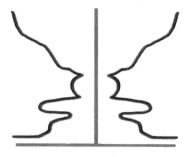 Now let's take a look at the remarkable brainwave pattern of the superconscious mind. Composed of the bottom half of an evolved-mind circle (gamma) above an awakened mind that is reduced in size, this brainwave pattern depicts superconscious energies flowing into the mind of the psychic soul that expresses them in the earth.

People who manifest this pattern in meditation, psychic inquiry, and healing work—the only three instances where I have seen it appear—draw in powerful revelations and a flood of revitalizing energy. The surge of kundalini stirs the body to arousal as it surges into the heart and brain, produces gamma waves, lifts consciousness, and at the same time forms new brain cells and circuits around the intellectual and creative centers.

If the psychic is giving a reading, the feeling of this superconscious connection is elation; if the healer is transmitting energy, the healer and recipient benefit from this surge of electromagnetic light. The meditator is carried by these powerful currents of energy into super-lucidity, super-psychic insights, or mystical transcendence.

Everyone who enters this brainwave pattern—in meditation or the outer world—experiences and manifests this flow of creative energy, making life a joy to live.

For a period of five years, I assisted Anna Wise when she presented her week-long awakened-mind seminars at Esalen Institute. She correlated the appearance of this high beta (that we now know as gamma) to the presence of kundalini and accurately said that its energetics dominated the brainwave pattern. I knew there was something very important to learn about this and soon tapped into a synchronistic flow of brain studies related to gamma and higher states of consciousness, beginning with a landmark study by radiologist Andrew Newberg.

The Mind of Transcendence

In his landmark book, *Why God Won't Go Away: Brain Science and the Biology of Belief*, published in 2001, University of Pennsylvania professor of nuclear medicine Andrew Newberg, MD, discovered that our brains are built for mystical states of transcendence. When Tibetan Buddhist monks and Franciscan nuns pulled a length of cotton twine in Newberg's laboratory to signify that they had attained spiritual ecstasy, Dr. Newberg wheeled their gurneys into a radiology lab where he injected a radioactive dye that enabled him to view their brain activity.

Newberg brought to light the brain physiology of heart-centered meditation coupled with mindful focus. The steady deepening of relaxation in the body causes the body to compensate by streaming neural impulses into the arousal center of the involuntary nervous system at the base of the brain. The double streams of neural impulses cancel each other out, suspending the flow of energy to the superior parietal lobe located toward the top and at the rear of the head, precisely where mystics place the crown chakra.

Newberg explains in his book that the superior parietal lobe, or orientation association area (OAA) of the brain, provides our sense of self in time and space. When the OAA is inactive, the meditator is unable to find any boundaries between the self and the outside world; consequently, the brain perceives "that the self is endless and intimately interwoven with everyone and everything the mind senses." (p. 6) Human beings yearn for this Absolute Unitary Being—the ultimate unitary state—as Newberg describes it on page 120. This longing is why God won't go away. On some level, we know that the brain is easily able to provide us with access to this sea of pure consciousness, which is ultimately who we are.

Years of scientific study convinced Newberg and his co-researcher, the late Dr. Eugene D'Aquili, that the brain's neurological processes "evolved to allow us humans to transcend material existence and acknowledge and connect with a deeper, more spiritual part of ourselves perceived of as an absolute, universal reality that connects us to all that is." (p. 9)

Newberg and D'Aquili not only discovered the brain physiognomy of mystical transcendence but also touched on what occurs as we deepen into lower and slower brainwave frequencies of the brain/mind. Newberg writes on page 155, "Mystical reality holds, and the neurology does not contradict it, that beneath the mind's perception of thoughts, memories, emotions, and objects, beneath the subjective awareness we think of as the self, there is a deeper self, a state of pure awareness that sees beyond the limits of subject and object, and rests in a universe where all things are one."

Newberg did not measure the brainwave frequencies involved in a phenomenon that occurs when the parietal lobes (crown chakra) release their sense of separation and shift brain activity to the prefrontal cortex in the frontal lobes (third eye), the seat of beta's reason, logic, and higher brain function located in and above the forehead. But a neuroscientist at the University of Wisconsin, Richard Davidson, PhD, did measure this frequency shift. Together, the findings of these two scientists explain how connecting with all that is shifts the brain into higher states of consciousness and evolves it into higher functioning.

Davidson's research corroborated Newberg's findings in a study of eight accomplished meditators chosen by the Dalai Lama of Tibet, that country's exiled spiritual leader. Richardson used EEG and functional magnetic resonance to measure brainwaves and see which parts of the brain were active. His study showed that the monks' single-minded focus on compassion and unconditional love produced extremely powerful gamma waves in the brain's left prefrontal cortex, which

Davidson's previous studies had associated with joy, compassion, happiness, and other positive feelings like love. In an interview, Richardson said he had never seen brain activation on such a scale before.

The high attentional activity in the frontal lobes of Davidson's Buddhist meditators stimulated heightened awareness, higher mental function, coherence, and brain/nervous system coordination. Their mental fluency enabled them to easily shift brain states on command.

Another study performed by an investigator in Copenhagen identified gamma frequencies with spiritually awakened awareness, kundalini, thankfulness, and the shaktipat transmission of light.

This preliminary study was carried out by Erik Hoffman, PhD, formerly a psychologist at Copenhagen University, who specialized in EEG biofeedback and psychophysiology. Hoffman used multiple electrodes (QEEG) to map the brainwaves of Maneka Philipson, a spiritually awakened woman from Sweden who is a disciple of two spiritual leaders in Southern India. During maximum energy transfer, referred to in this study as *deeksha*, Maneka's beta and gamma waves increased by a factor of twenty. Gamma activity increased in her left and right prefrontal cortex (the third eye area), which hyper–synchronized when she raised her kundalini energy on command. The same thing happened when she meditated on thankfulness or gratitude.

Hoffman conducted a complementary study on spiritually advanced people over a twenty–one day period in Golden City, India, home to Philipson's gurus, Amma and Bhagavan. The research team consisted of Hoffman, assisted by Stockholm University professor Harald Kjellin, and Inger Spindler, a neurotherapist working with New Brain–New World. This research organization, formed by Hoffman and Spindler, uses EEG to study meditation, altered states, the awakened brain, and the transformation of consciousness.

Once again, Hoffman found marked increases in gamma waves and brain symmetry during meditation and other exercises performed by spiritually advanced people. But this time he detected gamma wave activity in their frontal lobes *after* the experiments, meaning that their brains were *conditioning* gamma brainwaves and higher states.

This result is no surprise, since gamma is typically present when the brain is making new circuits. The same continuation of gamma waves has been found in Buddhist monks after their meditations have ended.

Gamma Synchrony: A Quantum Leap in Evolution

The superconscious mind is a quantum leap in evolution for several reasons. Most importantly, its gamma brainwaves lift awareness into *spiritual* states including divine union, heightened sensory perception, profound intuitive and healing abilities, out-of-body experiences, and cosmic consciousness. These states of consciousness, stimulated by gamma, arise in the brain's prefrontal cortex, the seat of human intelligence—meaning that *the evolutionary movement of the brain's intelligence is in the direction of the spirit.*

Research by a German neuroscientist, Wolf Singer, MD, confirms that gamma powers up the brain into a higher state of consciousness. Like Richard Davidson, Singer conducted studies with Tibetan monks chosen by Tibet's Dalai Lama under the auspices of the Mind and Life Institute. In EEG studies, Singer found that the monks' sustained meditative attention produced gamma brainwaves that organized their brains into a high level of mental coherence called whole-brain synchrony.

In most people, the brain uses some eighty percent of its potential. For most tasks, the brain activates only one or two regions at a time. If you are describing a work of art, for example, the visual cortex at the back of your brain, the emotional amygdala in the midbrain, and the frontal lobes of the intellect work together to formulate the description. Gamma changes the game. If you interpret a work of art during a deep, highly focused meditation or a creative flow of universal insight, the brain arouses gamma waves that synchronize its frequencies, layers, and regions into the single-minded attention needed to perform a higher level of processing.

The synchronized brain operates in a highly coherent, cohesive way. The two hemispheres balance for a better flow of information accessed from all parts of the mind. Instinct, intuition, and intelligence integrate to produce the higher level of intelligence that we know as creative genius. Exponentially increased brainpower is the well-known result of gamma synchrony.

It's no wonder that Edgar Cayce believed that meditation is the path to the superconscious! In meditation, the gamma frequencies cascading into the advanced meditator's mind, *from the superconscious*, power up and rewire the brain to higher states of consciousness that are the hope of humankind. The seat of this superconscious awareness is the conscious mind's intellect, which uses gamma to contact a higher form of intelligence: its spirit.

Whether you develop superconscious awareness in meditation, creative endeavors, psychic readings, healing, spiritual study, or a mixture of these activities, you will ultimately generate the high-voltage brainpower of the *spiritual* superconscious mind. The spiritual superconscious mind contains our potential to evolve human consciousness and create a finer reality on Earth.

As mentioned earlier, while the evolved mind is rarely functional in the outer world (it's too blissed out), the superconscious mind does operate in physical reality. Like the Magician on his card in the tarot deck, the superconscious mind reaches up to bring the higher self's heaven to earth and at the same time, lifts the earth into that light-filled heaven. It is active in the world, for the sake of the world.

Superconscious Energies in Reiki Healers

I've seen the brainwave pattern of the superconscious mind at least once in every Mind Mirror study that I've conducted on advanced meditators, psychics, and healers over the past two years. Proof for this book's claims about higher states and intuition shows up most clearly in the psychic resonance of healers as they perform group healings. In one such study, intuitive messages flew around like little birds—amusingly, in the form of pigeons.

I conducted two studies on Reiki healers in an artist's beautiful apartment in New York City on a snowy February afternoon in early 2011. After the first thirty-minute session, I asked the five Reiki practitioners, who were healing a single recipient lying on a massage table, to report their experiences. One woman, Meryl, mentioned having had visions of looking out a window at a beach; Agnes, the recipient, had been relaxing on the massage table by imagining the "nice, warm, blue waters and white sands" of Hawaii.

Agnes, who had argued with her identical twin sister, Angela, the night before, got the impression that Meryl had argued with her son. Questioning showed this information to be true.

Still more convincing were the healers' reports of seeing green, indigo, and purple colors behind their closed eyes. These colors confirmed that they were in an optimal alpha–theta meditation: green and yellow are the frequencies of alpha; blues and purples are theta; and white and gold are delta.

Each healer had his or her own distinctive brainwave pattern to begin with. But as the group tuned in to universal light to transmit healing energy, everyone shifted from occasional awakened-mind flares into surprisingly stable awakened-mind patterns—and all at the same time!

Then suddenly, at 3:24 p.m., Dennis' brainwaves flared into a superconscious pattern that downloaded gamma waves into the group's energy field. After that, everyone flared into partial evolved-mind patterns until, at 3:47 p.m., Sylvia experienced a "dancing purple–indigo light" that produced a beautiful evolved-mind circle with high-amplitude alpha that resonated through the rest of the group: Meryl, Kristin, Dennis, Angela, and Agnes.

Resonance and entrainment are always the governing principles in group healings. Investigator James L. Oschman, PhD, notes in his book, *Energy Medicine: The Scientific Basis*, that when two electromagnetic (light) waves of the same frequency move into phase with each other, their amplitudes add together to create still higher amplitudes (power) through what is called constructive interference.

In other words, each person's energy field locks into phase synchrony with everyone else's field to produce higher-amplitude frequencies of healing light. By entrainment, the weaker frequencies—the compromised energy field of a recipient—are raised to the higher vibration of the group. The recipient and healers must be on the same wavelength for healing to occur. This synchrony of energy is achieved by their common intention to heal, which enables the healers to "plug in" to universal light and transmit it to the recipient.

Working together in a group amplifies the energies running through the healers and creates a powerful field of light that remains in place until someone dissipates it. I saw evidence of this state in the second study, which was held soon after the first one in the same location.

Psychic flashes and healing energy also flowed through the second group of healers, but at a much higher vibration and with greater power. Agnes was once again the recipient. All of the healers were different except for Sylvia, who was a good control for the study, as I was already familiar with her advanced brainwave patterns.

There was a tangibly higher vibration in the second session—the room fairly crackled with energy. After the thirty-minute session, I asked the healers and the recipient for feedback. This time, each person saw the white and gold colors of delta frequencies behind closed eyes and felt a great deal of heat in the room. Everyone was uncomfortable with the heat level, but after the lights were turned back on, each person was surprised to find that the air felt quite cool.

Lora reported that throughout this session, she was struggling to find inner balance due to the room's intense heat. At one point, she had a vision of Cleopatra and then saw a white triangle containing a large black cross suspended over Agnes' head. About that same time, Agnes saw in her mind's eye three male entities standing around and asking, "How do we find balance?" Agnes said that she didn't know the meaning of that vision, nor did Lora understand what the appearance of Cleopatra meant.

Others in the group shared psychic visions. Lora reported having felt a transient pain in her left side, as did Albert, who also saw pigeons in his mind's eye. Sylvia was thinking about pigeons, also.

Leaving the apartment after the session, Agnes, who had not intuitively seen any pigeons, suddenly spotted a large number of pigeons hopping around in the white snow. Perhaps the other people's visions of pigeons presaged the amusement and pleasure that Agnes took in them.

Oschman notes in his book that animals sometimes move into resonant fields of healing, presumably to contribute their helpful energies, which may also explain why Agnes' three entities and Lora's Cleopatra showed up. Perhaps visions arising during meditation are transporting specific energies in symbolic messages. Shamans would certainly agree.

What impressed me most was the correlation of the second group's more advanced brainwaves to their more pronounced psychic phenomena. Where I had seen only one flare of a diamond-shaped brainwave pattern in the first group, everyone in the second group produced diamond flares throughout the session. The diamond is an interim pattern between the awakened and evolved mind that occurs as the soul reaches into the infinite.

Less than five minutes into the session, Lora, Sylvia, and Arthur connected with the infinite as their diamond patterns shifted into partial evolved-mind patterns. Shortly afterward, Arthur, who was holding quartz crystals in his hands, flared into the superconscious mind and downloaded gamma waves into the group's field. The appearance of gamma seemed to anchor the group's field to a higher state: now, partial and strongly circular evolved-mind patterns flowed through the group, alternating with diamonds that consistently flared in every person.

Albert produced the delta-only pattern of yoga nidra, a doorway to Universal Consciousness, and Arthur nearly went out-of-body (shown as a flat pattern with no electrical activity). Michelle's brainwaves literally shook with the power of kundalini and incoming energies. (No wonder it was so hot in the room! These healers could have dried seven layers of frozen sheets!)

Sylvia's near-perfect evolved-mind pattern reached such high amplitudes sixteen minutes into the session that I later asked her what she was experiencing. This Kundalini Yoga practitioner replied, "It was like being in Shavasana (a yoga posture). I felt the heart-centered energy of the group and our openness to Reiki's divine energy. It felt like the space changed, as if there were a loving, special presence. The Divine was more present."

The first group's residual energy field helped the second group of Reiki healers rise higher in consciousness. Both groups, connected with a New York City network of Reiki healers, reported that they practice meditation daily and regularly heal other people. It's no surprise that they manifested kundalini heat, white and gold light, and visions of entities. They were releasing superconscious energies into the earth—energies so powerful that I was having some difficulty staying grounded enough to properly work the equipment and draw their brainwaves. Later on, I studied their brainwave patterns frame by frame to check my analysis.

Brainwaves, as mentioned earlier, are not confined to the brain but instead cascade in waves through the circulatory and nervous systems into every atom and cell. As these energies reverberated through this field-coupled group, I and anyone who passed by outside also received good vibes from them. (I guess that included the pigeons!)

Energies emitted by healers continue into infinity, according to Oschman, and only lose their power over great distances. The energies aroused in healers stay strong within them and radiate into the world, wherever they go.

Their Reiki techniques helped these healers' minds to ascend through Cayce's described passages into the superconscious. In the process, they were also supercharging their brains, bodies, auric fields, and psychic powers.

Rising into the Superconscious

How can the reader pass through dimensions in consciousness to reach the superconscious realm and higher self? It takes a bit of practice, unless you are a natural—which you are! This passage is made every night by your soul, as your conscious mind goes to sleep and the soul rises into the superconscious to connect with its godlike, angelic nature—the higher self—to measure its progress in body, mind, and heart.

Practiced meditators, intuitives, and healers will find this superconscious journey an easy one to make, as they will already be familiar with the feeling of spiritual energies. Others with a spiritual practice that connects them with soul and spiritual awareness will also enjoy making this passage to the realm of the higher self.

Cayce's passages through dimensions in consciousness are highlighted in John Van Auken's book, *Toward a Deeper Meditation: Rejuvenating the Body, Illuminating the Mind, Experiencing the Spirit*, from pages 213 to 217. Van Auken is a devoted meditator whose brainwave patterns perfectly demonstrate his mastery of Cayce's passages, which he has been practicing for some forty years. I wired up John to the Mind Mirror in November of 2011 and witnessed the expansion of his awakened mind into Universal Consciousness, whereupon he produced an evolved-mind pattern. When he "brought heaven to earth," as he labeled this stage of his meditation, he produced the gamma-driven brainwave pattern of the superconscious mind.

To practice Cayce's passages through dimensions in consciousness, find a quiet, comfortable place and begin with the meditation practices presented in the last chapter, including stretching exercises and head-and-neck rolls. Then sit in a comfortable position and do the alternate-nostril breathing that brings the body, mind, and spirit into harmony. If you lie down for your practice, said Cayce, cover your solar plexus with your hands to prevent soul travel and imbalances in the body.

To the following steps chronicled by Van Auken, I have added brain states. If you find that your thinking mind is not quieting down, use the brainwave mastery/meditation techniques presented in previous chapters to clear your thoughts and stay focused.

- *Set Your Earthly Self Aside.* Closing your eyes, imagine grasping your earthly self and setting it outside of your body. Just take all of your cares and concerns and place them outside of you. Hold them there. (Reduce beta.)

- *Subjugate Control to Your Soul and Subconscious Mind.* See, feel, and know that your soul and subconscious mind are taking control of your system. (Generate alpha.) Feel yourself turning over control to your subconscious and your soul. Your breathing will slow down and become steady. (Generate theta.)

- *Ascend and Expand into Universal Consciousness.* Once your breath is steady and you have surrendered control to your soul, ascend and expand into Universal Consciousness. State a directive like this: "Arise my soul and enter into the presence of God, the mind and spirit of God, the infinite, universal consciousness of God." Feel yourself rising up and believe that it is happening. Direct yourself to become universal and infinite. (Generate delta.)

- *Connect with the Infinite Presence of God.* Draw your head back slightly and expand upward and outward into God's infinite presence. Become part of the whole of Universal Consciousness, and when you sense God's presence, plug in, hold on, and maintain your connection. Use an affirmation like, "Not my will, but thy will be done in and through me." Feel God's spirit flowing into you and permeating your body, mind, and spirit. For ideal attunement, subdue emotion and remain still. (Epsilon)

- *Abide Silently.*   Rest in your spirit and try to remain conscious. In this state of suspended animation, flowing with high–frequency gamma waves, you may feel intensely alert and awake or you may begin to fall asleep. Try to stay conscious or semi–conscious. Your breath may cease for long periods of time without your realizing it. You will breathe again as needed. If you fall asleep, awaken slowly. Allow the magic in the silence enough time to do its work. Rest in a calm, detached state of pure awareness. (Gamma)

- *Close Your Meditation.*   When ready, come back very gradually into waking awareness. Bring your attunement and spiritual oneness back with you and slowly move back into your body, taking a deep breath to help with this awakening. Take another breath to draw the energies of your higher self into your body. Be sure to redistribute the energy that has accumulated in your head throughout your mind and body. Draw it all the way into your fingers and toes and through all of your body's organs. Close with thoughts, words, or feelings of gratitude.

Van Auken points out that living this attunement in thought, word, and deed strengthens attunement to Universal Consciousness and opens the door to a steady flow of insights in dreams and intuitive guidance. With practice—an hour at a time to begin with, advised Cayce—the meditator eventually begins to experience individuality and universality simultaneously.

In this attunement, John has perfectly described the brainwave pattern of the superconscious mind, the point of which is "to let God come through us into this dimension and into the lives of people around us," an invitation that closes his comprehensive meditation book. (p. 217)

Terri's Story: Onstage with Superconscious Kundalini

There is one caution about these superconscious energies, and that has to do with how they are handled in the earth plane.

While presenting a meditation program in Detroit, I connected a woman named Terri Lynn to the Mind Mirror in order to demonstrate live brainwaves to the audience. I had a psychic flash as I was hooking her up and asked her, "Have you ever had a brain injury?" She said no, but she *was* planning to see a neurologist about some debilitating dizziness that she had been experiencing for some time. On occasion the dizziness was so intense that she had to lie still in bed to stop the spinning sensation in her head.

Seeing in my mind's eye that it was kundalini activity, I asked her how often and how long she meditated. Once a day, she responded, for three or four hours at a time! I was stunned by her dedication and knew that her brainwaves would be very interesting.

A few minutes into the meditation I saw the gamma–driven pattern of the superconscious mind, wherein the kundalini blasts up from the lower chakras through the large resonating cavity of the heart into the brain's comparatively smaller skull, where frequencies rise from hertz to kilohertz. This sensation can give anyone a headache and often does, so in private I advised Terri to cut back her meditation time and to carefully distribute the energies in her head throughout her body, as Cayce encouraged.

Terri followed this advice. She cut back on her meditation practice and began to distribute the energies throughout her body. As a result, she did not need to see a neurologist. The dizziness decreased so much that she has not once needed to lie down to stop it since our conversation. We stay in touch by email, and at last report, she was still experiencing and enjoying kundalini symptoms: a soft ringing in her ears, head movements, levitation of her arms and hands, seeing auras, and watching moving colors and geometric patterns in her mind's eye during meditation. Sudden bursts of bliss keep her smiling.

Recently, Terri reported that during a meditation at three a.m., she heard the noise of a busy city and opened her eyes slightly, only to see a "smoky white blob" in the room. She knew it was a little girl ghost. The little ghost pulled Terri's covers up around her shoulders and then ran away.

This was Terri's first ghost but probably not her last one, as she is so regularly visiting the community of saints in the superconscious that now they are visiting her.

Other superconscious healers are featured in the chapter titled "Healers and Healing." Be sure to read more about the effects of kundalini energies and how to manage them in the chapter titled "The Light of Consciousness."

Now let's look at the highest state of consciousness seen with any regularity on the Mind Mirror.

The Godlike, Angelic Pattern of the Higher Self

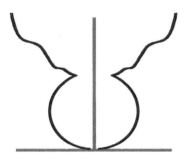

Composed of two evolved-mind circles, the brainwave pattern of the higher self is the most advanced state of consciousness that I have mapped (except for vortex-like downloads of energy from Universal Consciousness seen in several people featured in the chapter, "Healers and Healing").

The pattern of the godlike, higher self appears on the Mind Mirror screen when the meditator, psychic, or healer is in direct and profound contact with the superconscious and when there is no separation between the soul and its higher self. In other words, the person *becomes the higher self* in those moments when the pattern appears.

Occurring only in quiet communion with Source, the rounded gamma frequencies at the top of this pattern resonate into an evolved-mind pattern below them which signifies oneness with the higher self. Since this brainwave pattern does not exactly *belong* to this realm, it is probably not functional in the outer world, except in the energies the person expresses afterward. So far, I have not seen anyone bring this pattern out of meditation, psychic inquiry, or hands-on healing.

The effect on the meditator differs, but sensations of spiritual oneness, connection to Source, joy, and bliss are always involved in this brain state. It is safe to say that the person who surrenders completely to his or her angelic nature is profoundly transformed by and rapidly evolving into this ideal consciousness.

This statement closely agrees with what Edgar Cayce said about the soul and the higher self.

I have seen the godlike, angelic pattern in a few people, including professional intuitive Linda Schiller–Hanna, spiritual healers Malcolm Smith and Frans Stiene (*see* the chapter on healing), several practitioners of Stiene's Usui Reiki Ryoho healing techniques, a Polish meditator and chi kung practitioner on the edge of kundalini awakening, and a spiritual devotee with prodigious psychic powers. The latter, a woman named Rose, first recognized her angelic nature—although others can see it emanating from her—while meditating in a temple filled with angels.

Rose's first encounter with angels took place at age thirteen. While lying in a hospital bed, she crossed over to the other side. Two archangels lifted her out of her body and took her to meet God. They showed her pictures of what would happen if she stayed there. Not wanting her mother to grieve her death, she decided to live.

Since her near–death experience, Rose has been able to see spirits and angels and to predict the future, as is often the case with near–death survivors. Sitting in my library chair while I connected her to the Mind Mirror, she did not tell me about these experiences of higher consciousness, and I knew nothing about them beforehand. So I followed the routine: I asked what she wanted to accomplish in the session. She closed her eyes to consider the question and saw a quick vision of a temple. I guided her into a meditation called, "The Inner Temple." Her journey was unusual, to say the least.

Rose's brainwave patterns were surprising from the start. Closing her eyes, she showed a stable, high–amplitude awakened–mind pattern, which is rare enough. But within a minute, her awakened–mind brainwaves diffracted into screen bursts that looked like electrical disturbances of some kind. Puzzled, I checked her hookup to the Mind Mirror. After the session, which was silent on her part, she told me of having left her body right away to enter a temple of angels. The electrical "disturbances," I realized, were caused by vibrational energies flowing in from the superconscious and the adjustment of her brain to those high frequencies.

I had watched Rose slump over in her chair but knew that on some level she was conscious, as the screen diffractions soon settled into a high-amplitude evolved-mind pattern that immediately shifted into the gamma-saturated superconscious mind. The experiences that generated these higher-state patterns were extraordinary:

First, the angels in the temple telepathically told her, "You are the light. It's all about the light. You don't need anything else but the light." Rose's mind flared into the still-higher godlike, angelic pattern when the angels gave her an orb as a gift. They told her that "You are now part of the light," and gave her wings. She could not recall everything that happened, but remembered having felt the flat blade of a large sword resting first on her right shoulder then on her left, as in an initiation.

At the end of the session, she very slowly opened her eyes and said that she was getting back into her body, but it was a rough landing. "It's like astral narcolepsy," she said. "My body becomes so heavy, I have to detach."

While returning to ordinary awareness, she realized why she had come to the session—to find out if she had a higher calling. So I asked her to close her eyes again and ask the angels. At first, the same bursts of energy appeared on the screen, and then the pattern progression repeated: the awakened-mind, evolved-mind, superconscious-mind, and higher self patterns, all occurring during a series of super-ordinary events.

"You are God," the angels told her. "*I* am God?" she asked doubtfully, at which the angels laughed. Her grandparents then entered the temple along with people she knew who had passed on. "They just came by and circled around me," she recounted later. "They show up whenever I have a quiet moment."

This time, Rose's gamma waves showed up two minutes after she closed her eyes. To my delight, the godlike pattern flared repeatedly on the screen: it was the evolved-mind circle above a perfectly formed evolved-mind circle. I was astounded, as I had long predicted the musical and mathematical possibility of this pattern. I had only learned what to call it thirty-three hours before, when John Van Auken emailed to me a copy of his unpublished paper on Cayce's psychic rise into the superconscious and Universal Consciousness. (Van Auken called it the angelic, godling nature.)

I could hardly contain my excitement as Rose shifted back and forth between the superconscious and godlike pattern more times than I could count over the next twenty minutes. "I felt like we (Rose and the angels) were meshed together in the now," she commented later. "I just feel so grateful."

Her calling, according to the angels, who said they were "past the principalities" and on a council, was to write something for them. She declined, saying she wasn't smart enough to be a writer. But they said she only needed to translate what they were going to give her. They wanted to show people how to use the white light of God.

"It was about love, God, and harmonious sound," Rose explained. She had asked the angels several times if this task were really what she needed to do. She looked at her spirit family with this question in mind, and they all nodded yes in confirmation.

Other paranormal experiences of Rose's have proved credible. As she told me after the session (by now I was all ears), on one occasion a spirit dressed in blue jeans and a red flannel shirt asked if she would describe what he was wearing to her boyfriend, with whom she was walking outdoors in nature. The spirit wanted her to be sure to mention the sunglasses in his pocket.

She described the clothing to her boyfriend and the message about the sunglasses, at which point her boyfriend began to cry. He told her about standing at his father's coffin and secretly placing sunglasses in his father's pocket. His father was wearing precisely the clothing that Rose described. The confirmation of an afterlife changed her boyfriend's life and made Rose's otherworldly orientation more palatable.

"I'm like a radio," she shrugged. What channel, I wondered?

Edgar Cayce could have answered that question, since he likened psychic attunement to a radio and so easily received and transmitted himself. Edgar used a radio analogy in the Meditation chapter on page 8 of *A Search for God* to explain how to attune to the superconscious:

> Attunement {*of self to the Whole*} depends upon soul development. Physically, the radio may be an illustration. The attunement on any radio may be somewhere near the same point of another, but on no two, even when sitting side by side, will it be the same, for the position of the set alters. So in attuning our consciousness to the Divine, each of us must make the attunement according to his own development. Attunement,

like all attainments in creation, is a {*matter of*} growth.

Since her near–death experience, Rose has often been approached by angels. She pushes them away, however, if they appear when she is at work. Sometimes she forewarns people of danger and knows when family members have died. She has memories from before her birth, including a very private conversation between her parents that was about her. She asked her mother about the conversation, and her mother confirmed that it was true.

Apparently, when Rose returned from her near–death experience, she brought a good bit of her higher self's angelic nature back with her.

The rest of us will have to rise up to our higher self's godlike nature on angel's wings. Perhaps the following meditations will provide a little lift.

Superconscious Meditation: Transcendence

Using the Passages techniques in this chapter or your brainwave meditation's techniques and landmarks, drift very deeply down inside of yourself. When you reach a place of light and peace in your subconscious, become aware of the light of your soul.

Now step into your soul, as if rising into a higher dimension of yourself. Feel your awareness lift up. Sense the fullness within you now and the stirring in your chest, as your physical body begins to vibrate with love. Draw your awareness to your third eye and allow it to fill with universal light. Open up fully to this Light and take it in, through your third eye . . . your crown . . . your throat . . . and your heart.

When these higher spiritual centers are spinning quickly with vibrant light, draw the energies flowing in the core of the earth into the bottoms of your feet, the base of your spine, your navel and solar plexus, and on into your heart to join and blend with the higher energies waiting there.

Now do the "Circulation of Light" breathing: inhale up the chakra system to the third eye, pause for a moment to allow light to drift down from your crown into your head, and then exhale this light back down your chakra system to bathe each chakra in light. Repeat seven times. On the last inhalation, pause at the third eye, and fix your attention there.

Holding your attention on the third eye, become aware of a tiny light in the far distance. Let your consciousness move toward that light, farther and farther beyond your body until you begin to rise up into a tunnel leading to the light. Beams of light show you where to ascend as you continue upward. Let nothing stop you.

When you reach the top of the tunnel, you will find in front of you an evening sky filled with stars. There are stars in every, direction, twinkling celestial light. You move into the dark sky and float there. Then, expand outward to see and feel the majesty of the cosmos.

One star is brighter than all the others. You can feel its radiance. It is the star of Pure Love, and you move toward it, rising in the sky toward the heart of God. Higher and higher you go, feeling the waves of light cascading over you as you approach the most brilliant Light imaginable.

As you continue to rise up, God's light washes like golden honey into your spirit, filling you with love and gratitude. Your body opens up to the light of God, and your atoms spread apart as light fills you. You expand into the infinite and experience bliss.

Rest in this Pure Spirit, and drink it in until you are full.

* * *

Before you end this meditation, find a landmark for the way you feel—a word, image, concept, or body sensation—and crystallize it into words that you can repeat in meditation and your daily life as a mantra.

Be sure to disseminate the powerful energies in your head, neck, and shoulders at the close of your meditation. Pull them down into your organs and all the way into your fingers and toes.

To close your wide-open energy system to normal levels, take a few deep, sharp breaths and gradually settle back into your body. Wiggle your fingers and toes and carry this spiritual love into your life.

Higher Self Meditation: The Bridge of Angels

Close your eyes, relax, and silently voice a prayer of protection, something like: "I throw about myself the protecting power of spiritual light." See or sense a field of light enveloping your body. With your mind, find the outer reaches of this field of light and then expand your awareness beyond it into a realm of pure light where there is only the light of God. Connect with the love in this Light and drink it in.

Now become aware of a bridge across a river running through a landscape so beautiful that it is magical. Stand on the bridge and explore this landscape with all of your senses. Notice the radiance in the land, water, and air. Feel it and spread your awareness out into the light in all things.

You begin to sense a divine presence and hear exquisite music that is like nothing you have ever heard before. The air stirs and angels appear next to you on the bridge. There are thousands of angels, shimmering with light, their countenances radiant with love. The force of their love stirs something in you, and together, as one, you lift up into the air. The angels rise up all around you, and you soar with them in the air currents created by their movements.

Over the river and land you fly, the angels smiling at your delight as their divine energies permeate your body and soul.

You fly with them toward an immense white cloud that stretches across the sky, and together you land on it. The angels wait silently as you become aware of a magnificent structure in front of you. You notice every detail and feel drawn to enter it.

Walking inside, you hear the celestial music again. Iridescent colors flow together on the ceiling and floor. You feel drawn to the throne of God and an angelic figure that you know is your higher self and oversoul: a divine spark of God residing in this house of light.

You sit in a chair and slowly find your awareness moving into your godlike self, clothed as a radiant angel. Light floods into your consciousness like a rushing river and you overflow with love. You are home, where you have always lived. Here is where you belong. And at last you are content, as never before.

Strength and power flow into you and you move your wings slightly, knowing that now you could fly by yourself if you wanted to. Instead, you begin to explore your angelic nature. First you feel yourself as a divine spark of God. Creation is not complete without you. You complete God with your essential being.

Resting in silence, you receive a stream of information about your true nature. See, hear, feel, sense, and know who you are and what you bring to Creation. Let the truth of your being stream into your mind.

* * *

When you are ready to close your meditation, crystallize into words what you learned about your godlike, angelic nature and imprint them on your conscious awareness. Then, bidding your angelic self good-bye, join the angels waiting outside for you. Rise with them into the sky and soar above the landscape toward the bridge, where you land. Surrounded by thousands of smiling angels, you gaze at the river and countryside and meditate on how to bring your angelic qualities into your life.

While you meditate, the angels begin to vanish one by one. Behind them, they leave their loving energies for you. You remember the feeling of being surrounded by them and being in the house of God with your angelic self.

When you are ready to find a closure for your meditation, become aware of your fully extended auric field and retract it closer to your body. Open your eyes and return to the outside space, taking time to distribute the high-frequency energies in your upper body and chakras throughout the rest of your body, especially into your arms and legs.

Write about this experience in a journal to ground yourself, and return fully to consciousness with your divinity intact. Return to your angelic self as often as possible to discern what you need to know to make yourself and your life more perfect.

Manifesting the Superconscious Mind

Other chapters discuss ways to maintain higher states of awareness in daily life. For now, it's enough to say that meditative and psychic contact with the superconscious transforms us in many beautiful ways that will be clear to you by now.

Contact with the superconscious awakens our dreams to the luminous presence of the soul, a stunningly talented scriptwriter whose messages are conveyed in clever stage plays with characters vocalizing and acting out what we need to learn. The psychic soul's attunement with superconscious awareness expands our wisdom and understanding until we view earthly life as a stage play that teaches us who we want to be and who we do not want to be, as preparation for a conscious life here and in the spirit.

Viewing the world with the transcendent eyes of the soul, we ride the waves of light in the superconscious with joy and wonder. Psychic impressions flow effortlessly to us and lift us higher into Universal Consciousness for constant communion with God.

There is no greater pleasure in life than to be in and of the earth—to inhabit the spiritual dimensions of the soul with the feet firmly planted in the magnificent beauty of this blue and green planet. Flowing with the light–filled energies of love, we channel these higher energies into the earth with our loving touch, kind words, and good works.

By bringing heaven to earth, we lift earth to heaven, accomplishing an energetic integration that lifts all realities into higher dimensions of light. With that integration, we become superconscious.

Resources:
"The Illuminated Door," *an evolved mind meditation leading to the Akashic Records for insights into the meaning and purpose of your life.*

"The Heart of Meditation," *a guided meditation that deepens the mind into stillness. Includes Edgar Cayce's technique for entering psychic trance: Passages through Dimensions in Consciousness.*

(For the above meditations, *see* Selected Bibliography for track information regarding: Pennington, Judith. *The Meditation Experience: Listening to Your Psychic Soul.* A.R.E. Press, 2011, CDs.)

See Edgar Cayce readings related to Passages through Dimensions in Consciousness: 294, 254, 900, 137, and 3744 series.

7

The Awesome Power of Dreams

"Dreams are a visual language. Ignoring them and not seeking to understand their messages is like living most of your life in a foreign country without once taking a class to understand what is being said around you."
—*Silk Gypsy, message posted on an AOL board*

People have been studying their dreams since well before re-corded history. Aboriginal cultures encouraged dream sharing in families the first thing each morning as a source of personal insight and tribal guidance. The ancient Greeks consulted the Oracle of Delphi for help and waged—or did not wage—many a battle on the basis of dreams. The Egyptians studied their dreams, too, and so did the biblical Joseph with the coat of many colors, who won his passage out of prison by interpreting the pharaoh's dreams and saving the Egyptian people from a seven-year famine and starvation.

Edgar Cayce, often referred to as the "sleeping prophet" and "the beautiful dreamer," well understood the awesome power of dreams. His

Source said that every normal person dreams in the same unconscious state in which Cayce gave his readings, and that in dreams anyone can experience the same psychic phenomena that he did. The readings instructed Cayce to study his own dreams so that he could teach others about dreaming.

Why engage in dream study? Studying dreams, which always concern the body, mind, or spirit of the dreamer, strengthens soul awareness and psychic abilities. When the conscious mind falls asleep, the soul's sixth sense enacts a three-dimensional stage play that is reviewed and commented on by its higher self in Universal Consciousness. Studying our dreams shows us whether we are meeting our superconscious ideals or are in conflict with them. The sixth sense, a gifted director, declares "Lights, camera, action!" and the curtain rises on settings, characters, and brilliantly woven plots that invariably portray our life challenges and the wisdom and guidance of the soul's higher self.

Dreams occur in theta–delta frequencies, a channeling pattern in which the subconscious connects with Universal Consciousness. Dreams parade across the stage of sleep whatever the conscious mind needs to know. They show us how we can heal the body, resolve mental–emotional issues, and live in spiritual consciousness. Each insight draws the conscious mind closer to its subconscious intuitive awareness as it draws the soul closer to its higher self.

Our souls are best able to communicate with us in dreams, as this is when the pesky ego is sound asleep.

Beginning in 1924, Cayce interpreted 1,650 dreams for sixty-six people in seven hundred readings. Their needs were pressing and he willingly helped them. But his goal was to teach dreamers to interpret their own dreams in order to increase their psychic powers. He told many people, amusingly, that " . . . For every tub, yes every cup, must sit upon its own bottom, its own legs . . . " (3440-2)

What you will find in your dreams is an underground river of inspiration that will carry you, the psychic soul, wherever you need to go. Just sit in your tub and float along.

The Types of Dreams

Everyone dreams, except for people with brain and endocrine damage, and every dreamer is able to interpret and learn from his or her dreams, according to the Cayce readings. The readings named four different types of dreams—nonsense, literal, symbolic, and visionary—which provide information and insights about the body, mind, and spirit.

Every dream, Cayce believed, relates in some way to our own life. Body dreams can be frightening or entertaining. Disturbances in the body, most often from digesting food, cause *nonsensical* dreams that we need not bother to interpret. But clear and vivid dreams about the physical body provide important information about our health, as I have learned from twenty-five years of dream study.

Sometime ago I was in Scotland, feasting on fish and chips, when I dreamed about a doctor and nurse injecting a baby with poison. Not bothering to interpret this dream, I missed the message entirely until weeks later, when I was miserably ill and did a meditative writing to find out why. The *literal* interpretation of this dream was easy, once I grasped the *symbolic* meaning: I was the doctor and nurse and had poisoned myself with the fish and chips.

Easily the funniest dream I've ever had also related to the physical body. Eight or ten merry elves were dancing in a line back and forth across a stage behind a banner that read COELI in stark capital letters. I woke up laughing, told my husband about it, and then fell back asleep. The dancing elves were still there, scooting back and forth across the stage with their sign! Now I awakened entirely, went to the Oxford Dictionary, and looked up the word "coeli," which means "heaven sent" and is the root of the word celestial. A thrill of excitement shot through me, until I read further and learned that "cel-" also refers to gluten-related celiac disease. I got the message: the Celtic elves were warning me—correctly, as it turned out—about a wheat allergy. (Good-bye, fish and chips.)

Because we are multidimensional beings, so are our dreams. For example, some years ago I dreamed of a pudgy clown standing in a circle of accusing people and goofily singing, over and over again, while hopping from one foot to the other, "I am conflicted, I am conflicted!" This symbolic dream—with its literal meaning—mirrored my inner conflict, created by my self-accusation of being overweight. I did not see the solution, so I asked for help in an inspired writing. The solution was right there in the dream.

Its deeper meaning, said my inner voice, was this: the concepts in the heart and mind reach out to affect every cell in the body. Releasing self-accusation and creating a positive self-image rids self of the conflict and solves the conflict in the cell body. With this release of conflict and resistance, one can celebrate the joy in food which makes the experience of eating truly delightful.

Still no fish and chips for me, but what a consolation prize! Taking this multi-dimensional dream seriously, I wrote some spiritually-informed affirmations in meditation, posted them on my bathroom mirror, and repeatedly impressed them on my subconscious mind several times a day. Within a few weeks, I lost the offending fifteen pounds. I still enjoyed most of my favorite foods, and as much of them as I wanted.

Bizarre Elements in Dreams

People often dismiss the bizarre elements in dreams as nonsensical, such as the poisoned baby, the merry elves, or the pudgy clown. Instead, these are the dream maker's flourish! The bizarre elements in a dream startle the conscious mind awake just enough to lucidly watch the dream, at which point the dream's events are recorded in conscious memory and are more easily remembered.

When you awaken with a bizarre dream or dream element, pay special heed to it. Chances are that it also contains the key to the dream's meaning and what your soul wants you to clean up.

Why, for example, did my soul create a tableau in which a doctor and nurse were poisoning a baby, rather than, say, a tennis instructor? Because the soul works with our inner system of symbols and is multi-dimensional: it can and does address more than one issue in a single dream sequence and often works on several levels. Closer scrutiny of my killing-doctor dream revealed a destructive thought pattern in my mind. In my childhood, a family tragedy involving a physician had caused me to view them as perpetrators of evil, masquerading as help-ers. (I am still repairing that unfair generalization. A very big hypoder-mic needle was used to poison the baby, so I have a lot of clean-up work to do.)

Every single element and even the finest details in dreams contain meaning, and the meanings are entirely our own.

Visionary Dreams

The most powerful dreams are the ones that push at the edges of awareness until we remember them. These *visionary* dreams always con-tain life lessons and "quicken the dreamer to new potentials which are his to claim," writes Harmon Bro on page 11 in "Edgar Cayce on Dreams," a chapter in *The Edgar Cayce Collection*.

In these dreams, we may hear a nameless voice, experience a mysti-cal feeling, sense the presence of spiritual light, or see beyond what we know (as in ESP).

You are reading this book and listening to its companion medita-tions because in two visionary dreams, my soul encouraged me to step beyond my limited self-concept and contact this publisher.

Sometimes the soul does not resolve the problem in the dream, said the Cayce readings; instead, the dream puts the dreamer in a creative frame of mind for resolution in the waking state. Perhaps you have awakened with a solution that popped into your mind or came to you "out of the blue" during the day. This answer is the work of the soul's sixth sense.

Remote-viewing research has found that the psi dream occurs in the hour before awakening. The soul sequences its dreams so that we awaken with the most important one.

Recalling Your Dreams

Intention is the key to dream recall, as it is the key to everything else. A clear, coherent intention spoken inwardly before you go to sleep at night will help you remember your dreams. Your intention will be rein-forced by keeping a dream journal and pen next to your bed, along with a pen light in case you awaken in the dark to record a compelling dream.

When you awaken in the morning, advised Cayce, keep your eyes closed and try not to move. You are in a meditative state of quiet, inward contemplation, so the idea is to allow the dream memory to surface out of this deep, open flow of consciousness. Simply lie still with your eyes closed until a fragment of the dream floats from your theta subconscious across the alpha bridge into low beta; another fragment and then another will follow until these fragments coalesce into a conscious memory of the dream from beginning to end.

Once you have the entire dream in mind, replay it in its entirety to allow your conscious mind's beta waves to crystallize the memory into words. This practice is the equivalent of an awakened-mind meditation, wherein all parts of your mind are working together on a single task.

Recording Dreams

Even if your intuition now grasps the meaning of the dream, don't analyze it yet. Analysis might activate higher frequencies of beta that could separate you from your low-beta memory of the dream. Just stay relaxed, open your eyes, and write down in your dream journal everything you remember. Be sure to include how each event made you feel. Re-experiencing the emotional content of the dream keeps you connected with your subconscious, which may be inspired to provide new details.

While recording the dream, you may experience flashes of insight into its meaning. Jot down these insights in the left margin of your journal in a kind of shorthand that you can read later on. Once again, don't get involved in examination until every detail of the dream is recorded on paper.

Interpreting Dreams

What you now have is a record of your dream's plot, setting, and the characters' thoughts and feelings—the latter being especially important. Much of the time, each of the characters in the dream represents some aspect of you. Reading over your chronicle of the dream, write a theme statement that distills the story into one or two sentences. Every element in the dream, as in meditation and psychic inquiry, contains meanings that are specific to you. The following two examples demonstrate how to free-associate to interpret your symbolism and how to write a synopsis of events that relate to your life.

Dream Sample 1: The dreamer is driving a car very fast, unaware of her speed as her daughter, sitting next to her, tells her to slow down to make an upcoming turn. The dreamer hits the brake pedal to make the turn, but she is traveling too fast. The car skids sideways out over a huge expanse of water. The car drifts very slowly down toward the surface of the water, so slowly that the dreamer has time to tell the four or five people in the car not to worry, just relax; there's no danger as long as they move slowly and keep their wits about them. Finally the car hits the water with a splash, the occupants swim out of the open windows, and everyone stays afloat in a busy shipping lane under a bridge, where they are easily spotted and then rescued.

Synopsis: The driver is going too fast and ignores a warning until it's too late. There is an accident, but because everyone stays calm and composed, all ends well.

Once you have the synopsis, your intuitive soul will show you how the dream applies to your life in an "aha" insight. It works this way most of the time, since we know very well what's going on in our lives—once we take a moment to look at situations.

I realized after this dream that I was indeed going too fast. I was speeding to meet a deadline—working long hours and not getting enough rest—and I had unconsciously been worried about the possibility of making a mistake in my work. The dream told me that if I did choose to keep moving at this velocity, everything would be okay if I simply remained calm and self-aware.

Every detail in this dream, as always, was meaningful. My daughter represented my soul's care and concern for me. The other symbols were universal: the water of the spirit, the bridge leading upward to safety (and higher awareness), and the vehicle of my life. The strangers in the car were reminders that my actions affect others.

The bizarre element in the dream was the very slow drift of the car toward the water. The dream's message was in this slow motion and the voice of my higher self that spoke to me via its instructions to the passengers: "Just stay calm and reflective, and all will be well."

I can still feel my right foot pushing on that brake pedal and the slow careening of the car over the land's edge toward the water below. The calm detachment that I felt, as the driver and lucid dreamer, is the ultimate indicator of the higher self's presence in a dream.

Dream Sample 2. The dreamer walks into a small, plain house and looks around to see how well her belongings will fit into it. She sees a meditation nook and is very happy and relieved to find it. Next to the meditation room is a hidden wing on the first floor and stairs leading up to a hidden second floor. She is surprised to find these rooms, which have paying tenants. The house appears to be a good investment, even though it will require renovation and maintenance. The dreamer realizes that if she loses her husband, the house would generate security in her old age. Walking outside, she sees her daughter carrying a lawn chair into the neighbor's yard, where she intends to sunbathe. She watches her daughter apply sunscreen and warns her to be careful of the sun. But it's too late. Her daughter's lower legs are already sunburned.

Synopsis: Worried about her financial future should she lose her husband, the dreamer walks through her house and finds security in meditation as well as a hidden wing and upper floor. Outside, she sees her daughter getting burned despite protection.

You won't have any trouble interpreting this literal, symbolic, and visionary dream; nor did I. The universal symbol of a house, representing the subconscious and one's own life, provides the context. Relating the dream to my life, I saw that I was worrying about money, as usual; this pattern in consciousness is a leftover from my childhood. The dream maker was honest with me: I could get burned. But even if I did, there were hidden "rooms" (places in my consciousness) that would sustain me. These spiritual resources were always present and available (and they paid dividends).

I wasn't aware of my higher self in this dream, but perhaps it was the tenant of the hidden rooms in this reassuring dream constructed by my subconscious soul. The bizarre element was my daughter's (my own) sunburned legs. Logic tells us that anything can happen in this tumultuous world; the psychic soul tells us that this world is not all there is.

ESP and Past Life Recall in Dreams

The soul's extrasensory perception (ESP) can draw the dreamer's attention to the past, present, or future for insights and guidance. The common thread is that every dream is about the dreamer and usually relates to his or her *present* life. Even dreams about local or global disasters relate to one's own life; in some way, we resonate with the event.

The soul travels through time and space while we sleep, and sometimes we see glimpses of past lives. Past-life dreams are intended to shed light on the present and the future. For example, Cayce dreamed about his lifetime as Ra-Ta, a beloved Egyptian priest who was nevertheless banished for marital infidelity. A reading given on the dream said that some of those same people were in his present life. Cayce paid attention to this warning dream, and, as you will see below, his doing so may well have saved the life of his work.

When we repeatedly dream of a past life, then that's what it is, according to the readings. The soul connects us with the past-life memory, recorded in our own Book of Life in the Akashic Records, to draw attention to a pattern in consciousness that is repeating itself in our present life. The soul highlights the past to provide information that will guide us through challenges in the present. The soul's concern is not its past, but our thoughts, intentions, words, and deeds in the present.

More often, we see glimpses of our future. The Cayce readings say that every major event in one's life is first previewed in a dream—a factor that may well explain déjà vu, the revisiting of something "already seen."

Future vision was the interest of several New York City investors who went to Edgar Cayce in the 1920s for advice about their financial holdings. Cayce was morally opposed to giving readings for anyone's personal gain, and when he did so, there were physical consequences to his circulation and nervous system. But he could and did advise these stockbrokers to record and study their dreams. He said their dreams would tell them whatever they needed or wanted to know.

Cayce's dream methods proved profitable for this group of investors. Between their dream ESP and clarifications in the Cayce readings given to help them refine their interpretation skills, the dreamers made enough money to share, helping out Cayce's Virginia Beach hospital and Atlantic University.

When conflict among hospital board members arose, as several of Cayce's dreams had forewarned, the hospital had to close and was turned into a night club. As in his life as Ra-Ta, Cayce was essentially "banished" from the hospital by some of the same people he had known in Egypt thousands of years before–just as his prescient dream had suggested!

Losing the hospital was a tremendous blow to Cayce, who grew depressed as he watched people come and go in the rambling three-story building that had seemed destined for his life work, but suddenly was no longer financially sustainable. His son, Hugh Lynn, said that his father was so disappointed that he literally wanted to die. In time, however, Cayce remembered his dream of his past life as Ra-Ta. A reading on the dream had encouraged him not to respond to coming events with malice or any other attitude that would hinder his best development as a soul.

By remaining faithful to his dream and mastering his emotions, Cayce broke an ancient pattern in consciousness and reaped a well-deserved blessing. He did not grow bitter, and two years later, in February 1931, a gathering of Virginian supporters appealed to him to carry on. The Association for Research and Enlightenment was founded to support his work. What had seemed like such a blow to Cayce's dreams of a hospital turned out to be a precious gift. The founding of an association that would preserve his work and make the information available to the entire world was finally accomplished.

Nor was the hospital entirely lost. Some twenty-five years later, a decade after Cayce's death in 1945, the A.R.E. regained ownership of the old hospital building and turned it into its headquarters. The grand old structure had been used successively as a beach club, a hotel, a Shriners' clubhouse, and a summer stock theater. Today it is home to some of the A.R.E.'s administrative offices and the Health Center & Spa.

In the end, Cayce's Ra-Ta dream and faith-filled emotional restraint led to the fulfillment of what was promised to him: "new gifts of counsel that enabled him to bring his associates into greater growth than he had ever been able to foster before," writes Bro on page 114 in *The Edgar Cayce Collection*.

Spirit Guides in Dreams

The need to mind our actions in the present was the superconscious message to a man named Henry whose dream is recounted in *Edgar Cayce on the Akashic Records: The Book of Life* by Kevin J. Todeschi. Henry placed a pen and paper by his bed and asked for a dream that would guide him to personal spiritual growth. He dreamed of being in Egypt and knowing that he would meet a man with the most beautiful eyes who was surrounded by light. It would be Jesus, and he knew that Jesus had been waiting for him for a long time.

Henry's parents showed up in the dream and told him to hurry. He did so, and found Jesus waiting for him in one of the pyramids, surrounded by light and people with whom he was very much at home. Henry taught the people some dance steps he had learned from Jesus, who watched him fondly. When Henry had an unkind thought about someone, Jesus looked up at him and said that more than anything else, Henry needed to start working on his thoughts.

Spirit people (the deceased) and spirit guides (teachers and helpers) appear in dreams to provide comfort, encouragement, insights, and important messages. Urgent messages may be conveyed in a repetitive dream or different dreams with messages from different spirits.

So it was for one Nancy G., a visual artist and sculptor of three-dimensional cakes who attended my dream interpretation class at a community college. Standing in the front of the classroom, I wrote on a chalkboard each event in Nancy's dream as she recalled it.

"I was in an upstairs bedroom of a very old house with my mother," she said. "I looked outside, and rain was coming down in sheets, like in a hurricane. Water started coming into the house and the walls began to buckle. I knew the walls would collapse. The floors buckled and gave way. My mom told me to hold on to something, so I grabbed a safe—a very old and heavy safe. She was swept away in the floodwaters, down the river, and there was nothing I could do. I kept holding on to the heavy old safe, which had a combination lock on the front of it. Then I woke up."

I asked Nancy what she felt during this dream. "Fear and sadness," she answered. "I know my mother is slipping farther away. She has Alzheimer's disease and septicemia (systemic blood poisoning that can lead to death), and she's getting sicker in a nursing home." We could see from the synopsis that this was one of the dream's messages, but no amount of free association revealed the symbolic meaning of the locked safe. With persistence, Nancy was able to unlock the warnings in this ESP and spirit–guidance dream.

Nancy and I kept in touch, and over the next few months, the messages in her dreams grew increasingly urgent. In one dream, her mother stood next to Nancy's house and told her, "Don't stay near this house. It might look okay, but it's evil." In another dream, her mother was in a kitchen writing a message on a cake: "Stay . . . " Nancy knew that her mother, very ill by then, was desperately trying to write the next word and it was "away."

Nancy's deceased father appeared in several dreams. In one, she found herself standing in a long, dark, narrow hallway. A strong wind whipped through and blew open the door at the end of the hallway. Nancy's father and his mother, whom Nancy had never known, yelled at her, "Get out of that house. Leave him!" The reference was to Nancy's husband of nine years, a seemingly ordinary man, albeit with a secretive side and a mercurial temper, who had been trained as an encryption specialist in the Army.

Nancy followed my advice and began to keep a dream journal. Looking back over her dreams, she saw that the warnings were mounting up. She was being told in no uncertain terms by deceased family members and her sometimes comatose mother to leave her marriage and home. Finally, she dreamed of digging up ostrich eggs in a field. Looking to her left, she saw a large computer keyboard and in that moment realized that here was the key: her husband was hiding something in his computer.

Suddenly she understood. His computer was the "heavy old safe." She hired an encryption specialist and a private investigator. Over five months' time they cracked the safe and discovered the truth. Her husband was living a nefarious life as a gambler and sexual deviant addicted to child pornography. She asked him to leave their home, and his departure made her initial dream come true: her marital home was destroyed by a "downpour." She was kept afloat by dream telepathy and ESP that overflowed into her waking life.

For weeks, Nancy saw the number 6:11 every time she looked at a clock, and on November 16, her mother died. She later appeared to Nancy in two dreams, just as she had while in a coma. In the first dream she was healing; in the second she was young and healthy again—and still helping Nancy, as she had promised.

Nancy's story illustrates some important points about dreams. One is that keeping a journal increases the frequency and clarity of dreams. The second is that, in the dream state, the soul is in contact with helping spirits in the superconscious and calls on them as necessary to get the message to the dreamer.

The third point is that the soul guards us and does not let us suffer. Clairvoyants tell us that the souls of the people killed in the 9/11 terrorist attacks left their bodies before the planes crashed into the World Trade Center buildings. Many other people did not go to work that day as the result of dreams and a gut instinct that something just felt wrong.

Were Nancy's messages sent by her soul or spirit guides? According to Edgar Cayce, these differences dissolve in the realm of the superconscious, where the higher self, spirit guides, and angels all dwell together in a community of saints. There are no differences at all in the formless energy of Universal Consciousness, where everything expresses oneness.

It's comforting to think that the higher self, spirit guides, and angels are looking out for us and perhaps pulling a few strings on our behalf. We can use a little help from our friends.

Dream Telepathy for Healing

Psychologist Henry Reed discovered the awesome power of dreams in 1968, after an artist friend who dreamed for life guidance told him about the Edgar Cayce work. Reed, who was preparing for his PhD research examinations at UCLA, handcrafted a dream journal, covered it with attractive material, and wrote a dedication prayer asking to see through the fog of his life. By then twenty-five years old, he had been an alcoholic for seven years and at first did not realize that his drinking was affecting his dream recall. He was persistent, and three months later, he had an extraordinary dream that set him on his life's journey as a beautiful dreamer.

Reed dreamed of camping in a tent on the land of an Old Wise Man who held his gaze in a compelling way. Behind the Old Wise Man was a flying goat whose presence conveyed that this was a special and magical place. Beside a haystack was an empty wine bottle. Reed grew upset and told the Old Man that they needed to kick the drunk out, but the Old Man said that he had put the wine bottle there to lure the drunk in so that he could feed him. Reed saw an empty jar of mayonnaise and an empty bag of potato chips near the haystack. He was ashamed of his judgment of the drunk and could not look the Old Man in the eye. So he wandered back to his little round tent.

Where did Reed's dream come from? The reader will know by now that the source of this dream was Reed's psychic soul, represented by his higher self, the Wise Old Man. The Wise Old Man made himself visible in order to show Henry his pure and perfect nature. The symbols in the dream eluded him for quite some time, but he was deeply touched by and never forgot the *feeling* of the kind, accepting Old Man, who made him feel kinder toward himself.

Cayce said that, during sleep, the soul connects with the higher self and thereby measures its progress—and, of course, the personality's progress as well. Reed was so affected by his memory of the Wise Old Man that after accepting a position at Princeton University as a professor of psychology, he began to attend Alcoholics Anonymous meetings. His dreams grew ever more brilliant: in one, a dove flew into his heart and he felt deeply loved. It was this feeling that helped him quit drinking—quite abruptly and without having made a conscious decision to do so.

Referred to these days as the Father of the Modern Dream Movement, Reed works with individuals to help them recall and interpret their dreams, as he knows firsthand that all dreams are about personal healing. He lives on a farm in Virginia, the Flying Goat Ranch (where there are non–flying goats), and offers visitors a residential Dream Therapy Chamber, along with personal guidance, books, and at–home dream development programs.

Reed worked with Robert Van de Castle, former director of the Sleep and Dream Laboratory at the University of Virginia and a professor in the Department of Behavioral Medicine, to develop a dream–helper ceremony. Van de Castle was already conducting experiments in dream telepathy wherein people were asked to dream about pictures they were not shown beforehand. After his son's death, Van de Castle visited the A.R.E., met Reed, and the two collaborated on the creation of a dream telepathy project geared toward service.

The idea of these dream–helper ceremonies is to assist one person who is the target to gain a better understanding of a self-selected issue that might be placed in a new perspective. The dreamers are told nothing about the target person's issue, but there is a meditative bonding with the target person. Sometimes the target person gives each dreamer a personal object to keep overnight.

This spiritual and energetic bonding proves to be enough to establish a telepathic link in study after study. The next morning, the dream helpers awaken with insights that provide healing to the target person. People who have experienced the Dream Helper Ceremony say that it takes dreams out of the therapy room and enables non–experts to assist other people.

Henry's research into how people can dream about solutions to the undisclosed problems of strangers led him to create—for the Edgar Cayce Institute for Intuitive Studies—the Intuitive Heart Discovery Tools program, now taught by teachers around the world who are certified in this system.

What extraordinary gifts came out of Reed's visionary dream of a drunk, some potato chips, a wise old man, and a flying goat!

The Role of Emotions

The real genius of the dream maker is the emotions we feel in dreams. While experiencing a dream in the depths of the subconscious and unconscious mind—in the soul's undistorted resonance with the superconscious higher self—we feel the events in dreams on every level of our being. We feel how our thoughts and actions affect other people, what it is that we want and do not want in our lives, and the unconditional love of the soul and higher self.

Edgar Cayce pointed out that dreams give us more than life-enhancing guidance; they give us powerful physical experiences that we can remember and use to create change. In one of his own dreams, Cayce saw the floor of a house cave in to a cemetery below. His feeling about the dead and useless floor and the cemetery was repugnance. At the time he was building an effort on a shaky foundation. Remembering the feeling of disgust helped him let go of that effort.

In another dream he saw a stubborn bull. The unsettling feeling of its blind energy prompted inner change.

Feelings also profoundly affect the dreamer's ability to dream. When Cayce was ill, he could not give readings at all. When he was tired, his readings were less expansive and detailed. Cayce also found that a disturbed state of mind may cause dreams and psychic readings to be inaccurate. Inaccuracy may also be produced by the presence of disturbed or doubting people. Rest and physical fitness improve the depth, scope, recall, and clarity of intuitive readings and dreams, which in turn heighten our psychic powers in waking life.

If you want to be a "beautiful dreamer," dine early and lightly, sleep in a comfortable bed, and keep your dream journal by your side. Good night, sleep tight, and don't let the bugs bite!

Interpreting Dreams in Higher Consciousness

Some twenty percent of dream symbolism is universal, according to the Cayce readings, and the rest is unique and personal to the dreamer. Some dream symbols have universal meanings because of their repeated use in myth and art. For example, fire may relate to anger. Light might mean insight and help from the divine or an upward movement. A child often signifies helpful beginnings or might refer to the inner child. A horse and rider might be a message from higher realms of consciousness, whereas a key in a lock might be about unlocking something within the dreamer.

The book, *Dream Images and Symbols: A Dictionary*, by Kevin J. Todeschi, contains 2,500 dream images and many helpful ways to interpret and understand dreams.

Henry Reed's book, *Getting Help from Your Dreams*, may also give your dream studies a boost.

Your best dream interpreter, however, is the dream maker—your psychic soul. Even when you grasp the basic meaning of a dream, it's always beneficial to take your dream to higher consciousness for deeper understanding, as I did with the pudgy clown.

Begin with relaxation techniques and deepen into your subconscious in the usual ways: relax your eyes to access inner awareness, and drift deep down inside yourself. As your mind drifts down toward a meditative dream state, insights may arise. Send these intuitive ideas to your conscious mind in keys—words, images, concepts, or body sensations. Receiving this intuition is an awakened-mind activity. Let your psychic impressions lead you to deeper and deeper levels of the dream's meaning.

Continue with this process until you feel a click of understanding. If complete understanding does not come, expand your awareness up and out the top of your head, asking for help from your higher self. Stay in this higher awareness until answers ensue.

If you still do not grasp the meaning of your dream, turn to the next chapter on inspired writing. Putting pen to paper activates the unconscious mind in which all things are known and understood.

8

Writing the Voice of Your Soul

"You must have a place to which you can go in your heart, your mind, or your house, almost every day, where you do not owe anyone and where no one owes you—a place that simply allows for the blossoming of something new and promising."
—*Joseph Campbell*

Inspired writing is one of the most touching and beautiful ways to evolve consciousness. The infinite awareness of the psychic soul flows through the pen onto paper in words and images that connect us with its essential being and lift us into its transcendent perspectives. The feeling heart opens to the peace and joy of unconditional love, the mind sees how to direct its life, and the body absorbs the revitalizing currents of energy in Universal Consciousness.

Some twenty-five years ago, I picked up pen and paper and listened deeply to an inner voice that lifted my entire being into unity and the light of higher consciousness. Since then, many hundreds of inspired writings have enlivened my life in countless ways.

Anyone can do inspired writing, although learning to listen deeply may take a little practice. Inspired writing is very different from ordinary writing, which is usually a matter of getting thoughts down on paper and arranging them until they make the most sense. The conscious mind, moderating the flow of creative ideas, crafts them into an orderly, logical presentation.

In inspired writing, the thinking mind takes a back seat: it is entirely passive, except for transcribing what it hears. Ideas from the subconscious and unconscious, resonating with the superconscious, rise into the thinking mind in its language and punctuation. But the thinking mind does not choose the words or add the punctuation. The subconscious soul *becomes* the conscious mind and takes care of these mechanics.

The challenge in inspired writing is to concentrate on deep inner listening without thinking, analyzing, or trying to find words for the impulses rising into conscious awareness. The only way to keep your thinking mind quiet is to listen very deeply to the whisper of wisdom in your psychic soul and not for one second waver from listening to that inner voice. This is where the practice comes in.

Early in my practice of inspired writing, I expected a jumble of nonsensical foolishness to flow from listening inwardly, as I assumed that only my conscious mind was truly conscious. Instead, I discovered that by comparison the conscious mind is like a toddler who has not yet learned to walk. The subconscious soul is ancient and knows how to fly.

You simply allow it to do so, by listening to and trusting in the Infinite Mind that is holding your pen.

Tuning in to the Still, Small Voice

Sit or partially recline in a comfortable place that is free of noise and distraction. At first, you may find it easier to practice deep inner listening late at night when people are asleep and the earth's atmosphere is still. Late night is a good time to get started for another reason: sleepiness relaxes the mind into the alpha–theta–delta brainwaves of meditation. Continued practice with inspired writing conditions these brainwaves, at which point you can tune in at any time of the night or day to ask specific questions in an inner dialogue.

Begin with a spiritual intention or a prayer. I always ask to speak with "the higher beings of light." Your intention sets the level of your attunement.

Once you are comfortable, relax your body and mind. If you feel any pulling on the back of your tongue, your conscious mind is still active. Relax your tongue so you can't talk to yourself, and thoughts will drift away. Once your mind and body are relaxed, simply listen and wait patiently for the flow of words to begin.

One way to distinguish the voice of your ego from the voice of your soul is to allow the first few words to repeat themselves; when they do, you have adjusted to the right signal. (The ego changes words around.) Write as fast as the words arise, without thinking, analyzing, or judging: being in the channel means allowing the flow to carry you along. Just listen and write what you hear.

If you find yourself changing a single word, your ego is interfering. Stop writing, listen deeply again, and start over. Pick up where you left off, but read only the last few words so that your deeper mind can take over from there. Just keep pen to paper and write what you hear until nothing else flows. Then, read what you have channeled.

Listening and writing without knowing what is coming next opens and widens the channel. The need to release control and surrender the stronghold (we might say stranglehold) of the ego is where faith comes into play. The words will surface. Just trust that one will follow the other. Stay tuned until the flow is steady. With each practice session, you will find greater ease and faith in your own deeper self's connection with a higher source of wisdom and knowledge.

If you have tuned in to the voice of your soul, the writing will be universally applicable to everyone—that is, transcendent in its perspectives—yet will also relate to your present needs, consciousness, and life. Its multidimensional content will be more than you knew before and of a goodness that is much greater than your own.

The Rise in Consciousness

The second time I picked up pen and paper, my inner voice said, "We cannot perceive more than we are" and claimed that Medjugorje (now Bosnia and Herzegovina) "intensifies what we are. This is the nature of God. He is energy in its purest form." The implication was that if I went to Medjugorje, I would experience a change in consciousness that would enlarge my perceptions in some way.

I had just heard about Medjugorje, where six young missionaries had been receiving telepathic messages from the Virgin Mary, the mother of Jesus, since June of 1981, and although I was not sure that God existed, did not believe in the historical Jesus, and despised organized religion (I had a few issues), I felt the truth of this message.

I would never have trusted this guidance enough to act on it—trust was not my strong point—but I did not need to. My soul knew what was going to happen to me. Soon after the writing took place, two violent attacks on my body, mind, and spirit by loved ones sent me to my knees and changed the course of my life. (I recount this story for a higher purpose.)

A few days later, I was sent by the Sunday newspaper to interview the daughter of a world-famous sculptor for a feature article, and to my astonishment, conversation arose about Medjugorje, which turned out to have been her father's home. Sensing my hurt and despair, Maria Mestrovic insisted on contacting a friend of hers, a Catholic priest leading a spiritual pilgrimage to Medjugorje, and all doors flew open—relating to finances, work, and family—for me to go there.

In the tiny village of Medjugorje, nestled in the meadows and craggy mountains of western Bosnia and Herzegovina (it was Yugoslavia when I visited), everything conspired to help me release a heavy burden of guilt, shame, and self-hatred that had closed my heart, confused my mind, and crippled my body over the previous two decades.

The energies in this spiritually-charged community transformed me in countless ways. I felt clear and peaceful in my mind and heart, and the consequent rise in consciousness was tangible. I saw the world through new eyes that perceived nature, people, and events as patterns in consciousness that I could read and understand. Life awakened for me, as if spring had blossomed in my mind. The voice in my meditative writings grew more eloquent and profound, also, as if my shift in perception had attuned my soul to a higher vibration (as promised).

Through inspired writing, your soul will provide omniscient guidance that will always lead you to a higher path. The higher path is the soul's purpose. It wants to become conscious, and it does not want to suffer. Listening to soul guidance night and day makes it unnecessary for us to attract and suffer people and events that cause pain. Karma dissipates in the light of the spiritual life. When difficult things must happen, the soul helps us see the higher purpose in the challenges so that we can stay afloat.

The soul teaches us that everything in life—every person and every event—exists because it is needed for our personal and spiritual growth and that there are no accidents. Everything in life is following a higher purpose. The path set out before our incarnation is the path designed by the soul for it to become conscious and bring earth to heaven and heaven to earth.

With this understanding, I have hardly made a decision in the past twenty-five years without consulting the voice of my soul. I rely on it every day to reveal what my conscious mind cannot or will not see. I can't imagine what life would be like without its genius.

The soul is endlessly patient, as you will see in the deeply personal writings that I will share with you in this chapter for the sake of their messages.

In the early days of my inspired writings, their lyrical beauty and wisdom carried me into self-love, truthfulness, forgiveness, inner peace, tolerance, and an energetic concept of God as universal light—a Source that I could love and praise. That Source led me back to nature, the practice of meditation, a spiritual study group, the science of spirituality, peace in my family, and a self-actualized life of joy, fulfillment, and oneness.

As a watchful journalist, I observed each rise in consciousness. For me, inspired writing has been a wonderful tool for transformation, and I know it will inspire you in equally magnificent ways.

The universal truths and lessons conveyed by your soul will pertain to your unique needs and level of soul development. Your soul will always guide you to greater love and compassion for yourself and others in order to release separation in favor of wholeness. Rereading your writings, especially when dated and timed as in a diary, will reveal their precognitive nature and the synchronicities that occur to motivate and support your journey.

You will feel the effects of soul attunement: the sensation is uplifting, peaceful, and calming, like a deep meditation. I was moved to connect myself to the Mind Mirror to see what the brainwaves of inspired writing look like. There is a definite inflow of intuition into delta's unconscious mind, which curves upward into the subconscious as we enjoy the transcendent perspectives of the higher self and the illumination of the evolved mind.

Everyone who takes up inspired writing develops these brainwaves. No other result is possible, since these are the brainwave patterns of the soul in direct communion with the higher self and Universal Consciousness. These brainwaves improve our psychic abilities in waking life, meditation, and dreams.

Edgar Cayce urged everyone to try this form of soul guidance, which comes easier to some but can be developed by anyone. The most quoted reading says, " . . . turn to the voice within! If this then finds expression in that which may be given to the self in hand, by writing, it is well; but not that the hand be guided by an influence outside of itself. For the universe, God, is within . . . " (1297-1)

If you hear a single unkind word in your inspired writings, then the source is your ego or a discarnate spirit. Should this error happen, re-attune with a higher spiritual intention. The soul's angelic higher self does not criticize or judge. Nor does it insist on a specific course of action. It suggests and encourages with words, images, metaphors, parables, and natural laws that we recognize, deep inside, as universal truth.

In every case, we decide what is best for us to think, say, and do. Free will is everything to the soul, which comes here to blossom in its own time and way.

Uniting the Mind, Heart, and Body

Every aspect of the soul—the heart, mind, and body—possesses the free will that enables it to make mistakes and learn from them. If you engage in dialogue with these parts of yourself, your still, small voice will help you satisfy the needs of each. The heart, mind, and body can then integrate with each other in the unity and wholeness of higher consciousness.

Here is such an inner dialogue, dated August 27, 2006 (time not recorded).

Q: What is the meaning of the inner message, "Things are not even in here"? Of what is this spoken? What does it refer to?
A: Seek within self for the truth of this: how the body suffers from what is being done to it by the mind: the ingestion of foods causing difficulties, the lack of rest when the mind is busy with a task. All of these contribute to difficulties needing to be remitted by other, more self-strengthening ways of being.

Q: What role does my heart play in this?
A: Ask the heart.

Q to heart: What are your needs at this time?
Heart: I seek to be released from the hold of the mind, which squeezes me out of the picture and brings me such turmoil with its thoughts of despair and desolation. I seek to be free of these thoughts.

Q to mind: What is the reason for these thoughts? Where do they come from? What do they refer to?
Mind: I am justified in these by deeper fears of inadequacy and incompetence. Rid me of these fears and I will not voice them to the heart.

Q to subconscious beliefs: Why do you hold such thoughts? Are they necessary for some reason? Why do these still hold, and why are they not lifted by the work already done?
Subconscious: I see lifetimes of victimization and despair, times when the best intentions were not good enough and times when there were no good intentions held in heart and mind. These must be faced and expunged with care to understand why this despair was so.

Q to soul: Past life regression? Is that the suggestion?
Soul: It is, for in seeing what occurred, one can account for the presence of left-over patterns in the current life. These patterns disappear in the light of understanding.

Q to soul: Is health unattainable by me if I do not complete this past-life work?
Soul: Do it in self, dear one, working out the memories with sessions such as these.

Q to soul: I ask, then, for a past-life memory to be worked on for the sake of my body, mind, heart, and soul.
Luckily, I was in my meditation room with pen and paper at hand.

Deepening into meditation, I saw cinematic visions of three past lives. After viewing each one, I wrote down the details of that life. First, there appeared the story of an abused, shrill, and aggressive maid. Next, there was a superior, harsh, and unattractive priest. The third vision depicted a terrified young soldier skulking below a line of bunkers in World War II. The maid's unhappy life played through my mind first, and I asked my soul what to do. "Change the picture and reframe it to set her free," said my soul.

I had never heard of reframing before, yet I intuitively knew what to do. Simply infusing the thought of love into each of these personalities changed them completely. I injected into the maid's life the thought of love, and the beatings stopped. Blankets warmed her, along with long johns. Her employers took her upstairs into a spacious room with a white bedspread. She married the butler and died of old age with her Bible and rosary in her hands. The family was proud of her, considered her a triumph, and loved her. Her name was Ella.

The priest prayed to God for the ability to love, grew the close-cut hair on his lizard-like head into long, black curls, and found love by helping a little boy who was holding an injured bird. The priest picked up the boy and took him home. His mother opened the door and said he was like Jesus, taking care of little children. The priest watched innocent children play and felt more like Jesus. He began to speak of Jesus's love in his sermons. People congregated, and he loved them for the kind things they said to him. He learned to love, his church grew, and he was promoted to the office of bishop. He ruled with love and generosity until his death from an embolism. He died instantly in full regalia, his hair and beard long and dignified.

The terrified soldier, as a boy, listened to his parents and realized the need to overcome his fears. He sat outside on the porch, listening to loud sounds and watching children play. One day, a little girl played on the porch with him, and he eventually dared to go out to play with other children. He attended school, always retreating to quiet at every opportunity, but he was no longer afraid. When he and the little girl grew up, they married, and he became the president of a bank. The couple lived happily and tenderly together. He wore a cravat. Edgar Robinson was his name. He died of old age, peacefully, in his bed, surrounded by his family and employers who loved and respected him. No one knew of his fears but thought of him as courageous and strong. So he was.

Were these past lives real? I can't say, but I do know that aspects of these people lived in me as stubborn willfulness. Willfulness was the pattern of consciousness that I needed to change, as it was making my present life "uneven." Years later, I learned that reframing is a central technique in hypnosis, and in this practice, too, providing love to the past life resolves present-life issues.

Once these lives were reframed, I turned back to my writing:

Q to heart: This is enough for now. My heart?
A from heart: I see love for the broken and why so many have created occupations as soldiers, bankers, and the like: to remediate their lack of courage and stature. I am in awe of this and love people more. What counts is their love, the motivating factor in all self-healing. With love, there is no need to be angry, frightened, or aggressive. It gives us what we need, in direct and positive ways.

Q to body and mind: Body and mind?
Mind: I am more at peace.

Body: I relax, as fear dissipates in the mind and heart. Treat me well and I will be free.

By the end of this lengthy writing, I felt inwardly united, calm, and clear. The present-life issues created by my stubborn willfulness so completely disappeared that I could not remember what they were. Stubborn willfulness creeps back into my life at times but with nowhere near the original power and force.

By listening inwardly, I am usually able to keep my heart, mind, and body happy with each other. My soul is lighter, as a result, and I am able to perceive more. This is the result for everyone willing to do the mind-expanding work of inner reconciliation.

Dream Interpretation by the Higher Self

Inspired writing is the perfect way to get insight into puzzling or complex dreams and, particularly, visionary soul dreams that deserve extra attention. Life-altering lessons can result from dream writings, as in the example at nine a.m. on September 29, 1999, shared below. I included the full transcript of this writing in my *Voice of the Soul* book, as its universal insights made such a difference in my life. Perhaps this wisdom and encouragement will be of use to you, too.

Q: What was the meaning of the dream last night, in which a child was hit by a truck while coming toward the driver's side of a car I was sitting in? The blame assigned by the hospital? The missing insurance card?
A: It is your decision, dear one, as to whether you follow the dictates of heart or mind, but know that nothing can be done to help your child at this time. There is a point at which all souls feel helpless and yet are not, for prayer, hope, and belief in ultimate good are like unto weapons of old and do bring forward victory in battle. See this as a battle and know that your child cannot help but engage in it at this time.

Q: What if my child dies, as she now appears to be on the verge of doing? And how do I know that this message is not being given by a part of me that fears or refuses to help her?
A: It is for thee to decide the rightness of these words, as always, but know that the universe aligns itself to give thee indications of outcomes regardless of the path chosen.

See in the dream the mother separated from the child and how the child, moving toward the mother, is injured greatly and may die. The accuser in the hospital did accuse thee, dear one, of interference with the child's return. The damage occurred when you called the child to thee. The outcome was uncertain.

Q: The insurance card?
A: There is no insurance against death, beloved, no matter what is said or done, for this decision belongs to each soul, at each moment, and may not be made by another, even if in love or fear.

Q: Why does this hurt so terribly?
A: Thou hast taken this as a message of helplessness and hopelessness, while it is solely one of love. Look within self for the power necessary to bring thee into consciousness of strengths, such as faith in the Father and faith in the soul's reach toward the Father's love. All is for learning. All is for love.

Each soul journeys toward enlightenment, out of the darkness, in answering this call. It is known to all and heard by all, but denied, until the pain brings us to cry out and the cry is answered. Thus begins the journey, a response to the soul's aching desperation for knowledge and enlightenment.

Q: How can I release the pain and fear?
A: Come back to this connection often, and spend time in prayer. Know that this learning and doing is part of thy path, too, and out of these tools develops a magnificent sculpture of love and understanding, compassion, and forgiveness. For not one but many suffer as you suffer now, refusing to allow the heart to be hurt and attempting to stop the hurt by taking control of another's learning. This cannot be, for love allows all souls to be free to exercise choice, out of which comes the sense of self-love, self-faith, and all the gifts of understanding that bring us ever closer to the Father.

Thy daughter is not alone in these works and is carried by the Light no matter how deep her darkness. Have faith in this and know that every outcome is the right one for her soul, as long as the outcome is her choice.

Unburden thyself and go forth freely into thine own destiny, for the two will meet again, in time. They are inseparably intertwined, in love, and cannot be severed from each other or the Source . . .

Other words of comfort followed in this writing, which exhorted me to allow my daughter to suffer her own mistakes. Up until this point, I had suffered along with her. But finally I let go of my imprisonment in the fate of another, as my writing put it, and I began to trust that God is in everything, "no matter how deep is the pain cloaking the beauty that is the reality inside the illusion."

Two years passed before my daughter turned away from her self-destructive life. Had it not been for meditation, dreams, and inspired writings like this one, I do not know how I would have survived the pain and fear of watching her slowly kill herself. Inspired writing and daily meditation kept me sane and well. Later, my daughter told me that my peace and faith gave her the hope she needed to change her life. She is happy and healthy today.

The Peace That Passes Understanding

The tragedy of Hurricane Katrina in August 2005, which affected so many of my loved ones and the people of New Orleans, stirred in the depths of my mind many hidden issues that needed attention such as the past-life reframing shared above. For more than a year after Hurricane Katrina and the previous Southeast Asia tsunami, I was beset with sadness about people's suffering. My soul spoke of these times as being long-expected and as the reason it had prepared me for these difficulties over the previous two decades.

Nevertheless, inner peace eluded me, so I turned to a meditative writing. I received what was needed, as always. Learning more than we know is ultimately why we listen to our inner oracle, which sees into the past, present, and future and never fails us.

Perhaps you have already learned to love unconditionally, as the soul's higher self does. If not, you may find the following meditative writing to be as profound as I did. It taught me how to attain, at least most of the time, the "peace that passes understanding," not only in meditation, but in waking life as well. This meditative writing is dated June 2006.

Q: I feel that the beast (of evil) walks the Earth right now, conjuring war, death, and destruction. Everything in me wants to rise in opposition to stop him, and yet these writings teach me to oppose nothing. I see how it is possible to speak in the language of love and call people to a finer way of being, but is this enough? What would you have me do? What can be done?

A: What comes to thee now emerges from the depths of thy being, sought and given in the depths of love, where inspiration lives. Seek always here for thy directions, for in this non-essential place of being is the essence of being, and nowhere else does it lie. For all else stems from here as well: the peace of mind and body, the hope of humankind.

What stirs thee to movement and protest is the lack of oneness within, for in this there is no reason to protest, for all is understood. The lessons of old come to bear in the heart, as love rules with All That Is. So it was in the beginning, so is it still today.

Allow the heart to resonate with these words and feel them, for it is the lack of love which creates and participates in opposition. Rather, allow self to lead with only love in the heart.

Can a way be found to do this? Rather, many ways.

Speak of what can be and will be in time to come: a place of brotherhood in which all are equally respected and honored. A place of engagement in the beginnings of new ways of being in the world, which is no longer ruled by fear, control, and domination, and instead is known to be safe and free.

How will this come about? See the ways:

The old struggles will give way to higher ways of being, as young and old perceive that peace is the way. Those who hold these beliefs will shout them from the rooftops until they are heard and will pray for the beginnings of these ways forever predicted and beheld.

These will lead the world into its new beginnings, and the world will gladly follow.

How to bring this era about?

By living it now, without lapse or participation in anything that is other than love. Any opposition, any ill word spoken in defense or offense of another creates the opposition that undermines the possibility of peace.

Speak, then, of these possibilities. Shout them from the rooftops and go back into the heart repeatedly to find strength and connection to do so. Waver not. Be whole and free in this and peace will result.

Encourage, urge, strengthen, and build peace—with only peace. All else must fall away for peace to reign.

Q: And the threat to Iran? Am I to watch more people killed, more destruction of cultures and lives, without saying a word?

A: Say the words of peace, dear one. Shout them from the rooftops and be heard. Speak of love's way, in the language of love: to hurt no other, to encourage and support, to give what is needed by another, to serve and be served by love. Out of these ways flows peace.

Call the world to a higher way of being—and do so now.

It is thy time to soar on the wings of love. In the winds of time, life has prepared thee for these moments. Speak what is known and felt to be true—and none else.

Call the world to its heart and the love in the heart. That is all.

Q: Speak no opposition, hatred, or disgust?

A: Speak and feel none, for these separate thee from the higher self of love. Speak only of peace. Be love. Call these forth in each person and know them to be true—the only truth. Set each and all free.

This meditative writing did set me free. I drove to a local Congressman's office with two freshly baked pies and talked to him about love and the need for peace in the Middle East. What I said did not sway him, but I felt immensely better for having done something positive. I wrote about this event and surrounding lessons in my international newsletter, "The Still, Small Voice," found online at TheStillSmallVoice.org.

This writing and my positive actions brought about a distinct (and sorely needed) rise in my consciousness. Shortly after this experience, I emerged from meditation one day with the clear understanding that everything in this world—from loving and hateful relationships, to professions, institutions, and even poverty and war—exists because some soul created it to learn from. Without these lessons, souls cannot grow. This realization, more than anything else, gives me the peace that passes understanding.

Opening to Inspiration

I asked my still, small voice what most needed to be expressed here. It gets the last word, as is fitting.

> For each person, the journey into inspired writing will differ. Some people will listen inwardly and rejoice in this ready source of guidance, in which all things can be addressed and brought to consciousness. Others will hear nothing at all, as doubt and disbelief will intervene and prevent the flow of awareness from the soul.
>
> Still others will find self at a loss, unable to reach the level of consciousness needed to do this work. Listening inwardly at every turn and watching the thoughts held in mind will reveal what needs to be addressed and corrected in order for thoughtfulness to open the mind to the soul. For it is not the purpose of the mind to correct itself; this work belongs to the realm of the soul. When inner change is the goal, the soul is able to speak and be heard. All rests with the mind's purpose and willingness to listen and hear.
>
> Going deeper and deeper into self's patterns of consciousness requires commitment and courage. It is all too easy to live in the mind of the ego, in the judgment and separation that is the way of living in the earth. Turning to a higher reality disempowers the ego's hold on the mind and soul. Self-awareness, in every moment, will unlock the mind and open it to the voice within. Hearing the voice in daily life, through intention, makes it easier to hear the voice in inspired writing, as the writing increases daily intuition.
>
> Each soul will guide the mind to what it needs to know, when it is ready for the information.

9

The Light of Consciousness:
The Body's Subtle Energy System

" . . . If thine eye is single, thy whole body also shall be filled with light . . . "—Jesus, in Luke 11:34

The most startling demonstration I have ever seen of the resonant power of light and sound to raise consciousness took place in a small class held at the A.R.E. Center in New York City a few years ago. During a discussion on the body's subtle energy system, each of four women took turns holding a pendulum over the chakras of one person who was lying down on a massage table. The idea was to gauge by the pendulum's swing which energy centers were wide open and which were partially closed and needed to be unblocked. Each of the women had one or more chakras spinning at slow speeds or hardly spinning at all, as indicated by the listless swing or stillness of the pendulum.

I knew that hands-on healing and intuitive dialogue can restore energy to chakras, but as an experiment, I asked the group to sit together and chant a series of ancient tones discovered by the Sufi mystics of Islam. The women sang the seven tones in three or four rounds, with one of them raising the highest pitch into harmonics. After the chanting, everyone felt very much expanded in consciousness. On the next diagnosis, the pendulum swung out above each woman's chakras with so much power and force that it nearly got away from the hand holding it!

This occurrence of raised consciousness was a remarkable display of the power of sound and intention to shift reality. Because subtle energies are so powerful, this chapter explores the chakras, kundalini life force, auric field, and their interaction with meditation, intuition, hands-on healing, and the Field itself.

The Chakra System

The chakras, meaning wheels of light in Sanskrit, consist of seven subtle energy centers located along the spine at the intersection of bone curves, nerve ganglia, and the major endocrine glands. These energy centers are the most active ones in the human body at the present time, but many others exist in and above the body to carry energy to and from higher dimensions.

The Cayce readings speak of seven primary energy centers but note that we have twelve or more centers that we will use someday to communicate with God. (1861-11)

God meets us more than halfway in the chakra system, where the electromagnetic currents of light that we were born with in the three lower chakras instantaneously rise into the higher frequencies of the three upper chakras in meditation or with spiritual intention, thus raising us into spiritual consciousness.

The chakra system is composed of 1) three physical chakras located near the base of the spine and at the navel and solar plexus, 2) the heart which serves as a bridge, and 3) three spiritual chakras at the throat, third eye, and crown of the head. The chakras are energy reservoirs interpenetrated by meridian lines that transport their subtle energies to every part of the body.

Scientific measurements of the chakras verify that they vibrate at the frequencies and in the colors reported by mystics and medical intuitives. Beginning at the base of the spine and moving upward, their frequency-produced colors are red, orange, yellow, green, blue, and indigo, with violet at the top, or crown, of the head, just as in a prismatic rainbow.

CHAKRA	COLOR		ELEMENT	REALM
Crown	Violet		Spirit	Prophetic knowing
Third Eye	Indigo		Spirit	Clairvoyance
Throat	Blue		Spirit	Clairaudience
Heart	Green		Air	Love
Solar Plexus	Yellow		Fire	Will/Clairsentience
Navel	Orange		Water	Emotional feelings
Root	Red		Earth	Physical being

Valerie V. Hunt, formerly a kinesiology professor and chair of the Physiological Science department at UCLA, has conducted credible research into the chakras and the body's auric field. In 1974, she used several different laboratory instruments to map changes in the chakras and auric fields of four subjects during a series of eight Rolfing sessions. The Rolfers were deeply massaging the subjects' neuromuscular systems in order to release physical tensions and associated mental–emotional traumas in their bodies.

Hunt's instruments detected a dynamic, rhythmically pulsating field of electromagnetic energy that surrounds the human body. Her instrument readings agreed perfectly with color changes in the chakras and auric fields of the subjects, as independently observed and recorded by clairvoyant Rosalyn Bruyere, who took part in this landmark study.

In other studies, Dr. Hunt mapped changes in the body's electromagnetic field using a special telemetry device, designed by her, that reads from 0 to 250,000 hertz. Placing sensors on the chakras of her subjects to measure their energetic output, she found that the energy field of a person anchored in the ordinary physical world registers in the range of 250 hertz. The sick body's frequencies are lower.

Psychics and healers, while actively visioning and healing, register between 400 and 800 hertz. People in trance and trance channelers read from 800 to 900 hertz. From 900 hertz upward are the readings for what Hunt terms "mystical personalities." Those who possess psychic and healing abilities can enter deep trance states, and while being anchored in reality, they are able to remain in cosmic consciousness.

Hunt's studies confirm that rising frequencies in the chakras correlate to higher states of consciousness. Still more interesting is the fact that her highest–mapped frequencies describe the superconscious minds of the psychic and healer. Chief characteristics are the ability to enter deep trance states, as Cayce did, and in waking states, the superconscious ability to integrate earthly awareness and Infinite Mind.

Altogether, her scientific measurements confirm that super–ordinary states of consciousness flow from and/or produce higher than normal frequencies of vibrations and that these states of awareness are a rise up the evolutionary ladder.

The Cayce readings and yogic science are mostly consistent with each other in correlating the root chakra to the health and survival of the physical body, the navel chakra to the emotions, and the solar plexus to the mind and its will. The heart is a bridge that unites the three lower physical chakras and the three upper spiritual chakras, serving as a kind of transducer that steps up and steps down the frequency streams between the upper and lower chakras.

The three upper chakras are attuned to the higher frequencies of the spiritual realm. Cayce did not specifically correlate the upper chakras to spiritual dimensions, so you will see in the chart that I have assigned them to their high–sense functions. Medical intuitives say that the fifth, sixth, and seventh chakras are etheric templates that respectively correlate with the spiritual body, emotions, and mind. Use your psychic senses to decide for yourself.

Naturally enough, the fifth chakra, located at the throat and taking in the ears, relates to the clairaudient ability to hear and speak your own truth and to perceive that of others. The sixth chakra, located at the third eye between the eyebrows, relates to the clear seeing of clairvoyance. The seventh chakra, located at the top and slightly to the rear of the head (where monarchs once perched crowns), is the crown chakra of psychic knowing.

Some believe that the seventh chakra is where spiritual light comes into the physical body. Whether or not this is true, the seventh chakra is where we experience divine union since it is the location of the brain's parietal lobes, as noted in previous chapters. When this center in the brain suspends activity, we lose our sense of physical time and space and merge with infinite Light.

Cayce perceived the kundalini life force as rising not from the root chakra, as most people think today, but from the navel/solar plexus chakra to the crown and then over and down to the third eye in the shape of a shepherd's crook or a raised cobra poised to strike. The most ancient Hindu texts also perceived this same origin and path followed by the kundalini (meaning coiled). I have retained the classical numbering of the chakras here for the sake of simplicity, and I want to point out that the area of the third eye is where light and imagery form the best point of focus during meditation.

Personally, I have found that in deep, profound meditation, the kundalini light that coalesces in the head vibrates equally as powerfully in the crown and third eye chakras. Distinctions of every kind disappear in the presence of this potent, radiant spiritual light.

Cayce's perception of how the chakras interface with organs and systems also differs from that of other intuitives, who usually differ with each other. For example, the Cayce readings relate the root chakra at the base of the spine to the gonads (testes and ovaries) and the hormones they produce. Others place the sexual organs at the second chakra.

Once again, it's best to rely on your intuition to sort out these distinctions, if you care about them at all. (I don't.) The differences may exist because of internal resonance. Just as brainwave frequencies resonate throughout the head, so do physical and subtle energies resonate throughout the body, which makes it hard for the seer to be precise.

Medical intuitives and energy practitioners have written prolifically about the chakras: most notably Barbara Ann Brennan, Rosalyn Bruyere, Donna Eden, Anodea Judith, and Caroline Myss. Each agrees on the importance of keeping the chakras open and balanced for an unimpeded flow of energy and information for the body, mind, and spirit.

When the chakras are blocked—just as in the brainwave categories of beta, alpha, theta, and delta—we feel as disconnected as we are since the information flow between the body and soul is impeded, and consciousness is also inhibited. What's most important is keeping the brain and subtle energy system flowing with the energies that are needed to power up all of the organs and systems in the body.

Before we leave this section, you may wish to tune up your chakras and raise your kundalini (like a snake charmer) with the following Sufi tones, which musician and sound healer Jonathan Goldman teaches on his recordings.

Sound Toning: Tuning up the Chakras

Sing out very strongly, from your diaphragm, the chakra tones listed below so that each sound vibrates the associated chakra and produces resonant overtones that energize the chakras and expand consciousness. To hear these harmonic overtones, slightly cup one hand and hold your fingers close to your ear, but not touching it, and your palm near the side of your mouth. While singing each tone, move your jaw backward and forward a little and slightly purse your lips to bounce the tone and its harmonics into the cupped palm of your hand for easier hearing.

The bass pitch is for the root chakra; go up the scale until you reach the highest and seventh pitch, the eeeee (as in we) at the crown. Now sing the closing sound of ooooo (moo) in a still higher pitch and slide it back down the scale, as if in a sigh, so you end up on a low pitch at the root chakra.

Sing these tones for four to seven rounds. If even one chakra sounds wavy or scratchy, take a pure chakra tone above it and quickly slide down the musical scale to bring the pure sound into the wavy or scratchy one. Soon the wavy or scratchy tone will clear and normalize, which signifies that its chakra is now tuned up.

Oooooo (as in moo)—closing sound,
dropped in pitch back to the root
Eeeeee (as in we)—7th chakra
Aaaaaa (as in say)—6th chakra
Iiiiii (as in high)—5th chakra
Ahhhhh (as in ma)—4th chakra
Ohhhhh (as in so)—3rd chakra
Oooooo (as in moo)—2nd chakra
Uhhhhh (as in mud)—1st chakra

You may wish to adopt chakra toning as a daily practice. I sing these tones while sitting in my tub or while driving a car to relieve boredom. Chakra toning benefits the physical body just as much as the energy body. I have cured severe allergic congestion, cleared my mind, and sharpened my vision in mere minutes by singing these tones. This quick fix opens the chakras to the kundalini flow that harmonizes the entire being.

The Kundalini Experience

Psychiatrist Lee Sannella, MD writes in *The Kundalini Experience: Psychosis or Transcendence?* that the kundalini is a natural force which arises from deep within the body to therapeutically remove stress from the system. This force is electromagnetic in nature, according to research by the scientist Itzhak Bentov, whose findings are featured in Sannella's book.

Bentov explains that the kundalini arouses in a 7–hertz (alpha–theta) standing wave generated in meditation. It resonates waves of energy through several oscillators in the upper body, most notably the brain's ventricles, where these currents of energy rise up into kilohertz frequencies. The kundalini force pummels the brain's sensory-motor cortex, a narrow strip composed of nerve endings that travel to every part of the body.

As these electromagnetic waves oscillate, their fields of energy are responsible for the kundalini symptoms experienced by meditators, from the super-high frequencies of the inner light and sound, to the swaying and rocking of the body and shifts and transformations in consciousness.

Because these powerful energies arise in meditators, psychics, and healers, this section takes a look at kundalini symptoms and how to handle them.

Kundalini awakenings typically occur gradually and over time without causing much distress in people who meditate no more than an hour or two each day and who do not try to control or resist the flow of these energies. Even gentle awakenings, notes Bentov, can involve experiences of visionary light and occasional feelings of vibration, fluttering, tingling, and itching that move in definite patterns over the body.

Energetic awakenings can cause sensations of heat, especially in the hands. Equally common are emotional swings from doubt and despair to sensations of bliss, harmony, and peace. Sexual desire may increase as the kundalini works its way through the first and second chakras.

Kundalini symptoms do not occur in everyone, but when they do, it's good to know that they are positive signs of normalization in the body.

Kundalini symptoms that follow the outlay of the brain's sensory-motor cortex, the terminus of nerve endings travelling to every part of the body, are experienced first as a tingling, prickling sensation in the bottoms of the feet, toes, or ankles, and sometimes as a vague sense of itching on the inside of the soles of the feet. Sensations may move up the left side of the leg sequentially to the hip, where a throbbing, rhythmic rumbling sensation travels to the lower lumbar and sacral spine. Then, the energy is felt as a sensation rising up the spine to the cervical and occipital regions of the head.

In some people, transient occipital headaches and neck aches accompany this kundalini movement, along with pressure in the eyes and ears, which may produce various auditory tones, high-pitched ringing, and a temporary decrease or loss of vision. Symptoms travel from the head into the lower abdomen and legs. The pattern repeats on the right side of the body.

The spiritual practitioner may experience only a few or none of these symptoms. Kundalini awakening may occur spontaneously or it might take years or decades before it reaches completion. It is smoother and quicker when we are deeply engaged in psycho-spiritual healing and transformation.

During meditation, the raised kundalini can manifest as sensations of light that concentrate in the crown chakra and third eye. When kundalini opens the third eye, the meditator may see a pulsing indigo light opening to a white screen embedded with geometric figures that coalesce into images and/or movie-like visions.

Swamis and yogis have reported seeing a tiny seed of white light or a blue pearl in the third eye that may remain visible with the eyes open. Sometimes the inner eye opens to a cosmic landscape of stars and planets experienced as pure mind and blissful union with the cosmos.

Intense kundalini flows can produce high pitches of sound that rise in frequency and grow louder in volume, as in the sound of buzzing bees, cascading water, or roaring wind. Spiritual adepts seek the solitude of caves and temples in order to hear this "music of life." The early Christians called it the "holy spirit."

Sannella's patients—some of whom he sought out for study—experienced intense kundalini symptoms. Over the course of a year, a female psychologist endured prickly itching heat all over her body. After experiencing painful feet and headaches, she felt sensations of light in her skull, intense heat, insomnia, rippling sensations, and shaking in her body before these disturbances suddenly ceased. Later, the psychologist opened a personal growth center to help others through the kundalini process.

A male artist lost consciousness when white light exploded in the back of his head, stimulating hissing and roaring sounds in his head during meditation. Psychic surgery relieved some of his symptoms, and he subsequently became a psychic healer. Another man, a writer and wood sculptor, experienced intense heat in his body and spontaneous trance states during which he received accurate psychic information. When he learned to enter a lighter trance, his difficulties abated.

In all of Sannella's cases, kundalini symptoms decreased or disappeared when the person reduced the length of time spent in meditation and embraced a more disciplined and balanced lifestyle.

The symptoms of kundalini arousal are easier to tolerate and even welcome when people understand that these currents of light are clearing blockages in the mind, body, and emotions to bring about healing and wholeness. The best response to these energy flows is surrendering to the movement of kundalini. It is helpful to try not to control or force its arousal to bring about enlightenment, as some aspirants do. Attempts to resist or control the kundalini may stimulate negative symptoms. Kundalini needs to awaken in her own time and way, as a natural progression of practicing meditation and cultivating a spiritual life.

Should you become concerned about the sudden appearance of symptoms, take time in meditation to intuit whether the symptoms are related to a kundalini awakening rather than an illness. If inner guidance tells you that kundalini energy is responsible, then do everything possible to ground yourself—especially by spending time in nature—so that your frequencies of vibration will decrease to levels that suit your constitution.

Balancing personal, family, social, work, and spiritual endeavors also calms kundalini symptoms. If you are like most people, your kundalini flow will decrease and symptoms will disappear in a timely manner so that there is no need to seek medical help after all.

What's important is your experience and how you relate to the kundalini serpent. Over time, she stimulates psychic awareness and the *siddhi* powers of intuition, such as clairvoyance, clairaudience, clairsentience, prophetic knowing, telepathy, teleportation, telekinesis, precognition, levitation, invisibility, bilocation, materialization, and healing.

These natural spiritual gifts make her the psychic's best friend.

Gail's Experience: Receiving Shaktipat from Sai Baba

Not every kundalini awakening is gradual, since some people wish to reach divine consciousness as soon as possible. Shaktipat initiation by an enlightened teacher instantly shifts the mundane kundalini—the human life force—into the cosmic kundalini that awakens the initiate to divine consciousness.

Gail G., a psychotherapist and Holotropic Breathwork teacher, experienced a total kundalini awakening via the transmission of light to her by her spiritual teacher, the late Sai Baba. He was an enlightened master who lived in India and was best known for his ability to bilocate, materialize ash out of thin air, and heal people by appearing in their dreams.

While she was visiting his ashram, Gail felt Sai Baba's eyes lock on hers. It was not until a year later in 1999, when she was visiting the ashram during the Diwali festival of lights, that kundalini blasted up her spine, and light poured in through the crown of her head. Since then, she has felt that kundalini is burning away her past-life karma and battering at her ego, which has been steadily losing its hold on her concepts of reality.

As a psychotherapist, spiritual practitioner, and teacher of breath work developed by Stanislav Grof (an expert in spiritual emergencies), Gail was prepared for her kundalini awakening. Even so, her kundalini awakening has proved to be quite a ride. One day she is filled with bliss and cosmic awareness; the next day she feels insignificant and "like the scum of the earth," she reported.

Releasing the mind's power over her spirit has diminished these emotional swings, which ended after the first year and a half as she came into the realization that, "We are all embodiments of the divine, or God. There is no doer of any experience. There is experiencing but no experiencer. I would not say I have awakened," she said in a later interview, "but I have had glimpses of truth through the kundalini.

"The truth is that there is only One, and we are all part of the automatic functioning of the One, while living in a society that believes we are actually doing something."

The benefits of Gail's kundalini awakening have been well worth the effects. She has become increasingly psychic, especially in terms of synchronicity, and is now developing the medical intuition that enables healers to see the chakras and auric field in order to diagnose imbalances and illness in others.

Happily, Gail lives at the Findhorn Foundation, a spiritual intentional community in Northeast Scotland. Findhorn's very advanced level of consciousness radiates an auric field that will continue to stimulate and support her kundalini process in every possible way.

The Auric Field

People once believed the aura to be a figment of the psychic's imagination. Over the past few decades, science has proved that the auric field is real.

Researcher James L. Oschman, PhD, a leading authority on energy and complementary medicine, explains in his book, *Energy Medicine: The Scientific Basis*, that the human energy field is now understood to be a high-speed communication network that enables the body-mind to communicate with itself and with environmental fields.

Yale professor and scientist, Harold Saxton Burr, PhD, investigated these "fields of life" from 1932 to 1956 and believed them to be basic blueprints of all living beings. Because these fields reflect physical and mental conditions, said Burr, they can be used for diagnostic purposes.

Edgar Cayce gave precisely the same information about the auric field, first mentioned in a 1924 reading for an oil prospector. Looking at the man's aura, the sleeping Cayce noted that, " . . . All is not good . . . " but due to planetary influences, the man would climb high in terms of material success. (221-2)

Cayce wrote in a little book entitled *Auras: An Essay on the Meaning of Colors* that the auric field is "the weathervane of the soul." Like a weathervane, it shows which way "the winds of destiny are blowing" and shifts its colors and composition in the winds of our moods and life changes. (*See* Resources at the end of this chapter.)

Cayce recounted several interesting stories in *Auras*, one of only two books that he wrote. (The other book, *What I Believe*, contains his philosophy of life.) One story was told to him by a friend who was shopping for sweaters on the sixth floor of a department store in a large city. She rang for the elevator, and when it arrived, it was filled with people. However, the well-lighted interior of the elevator appeared dark to her. Feeling that something was amiss, the woman impulsively stepped back and said, "Go ahead" to the operator.

Returning to a display of red sweaters, she realized what was wrong: no one in the elevator had an aura. Moments later, the elevator cable snapped, the car fell to the basement, and all of the occupants were killed. She concluded that when one is marked for death, the soul withdraws and the aura naturally fades.

"An aura is an effect, not a cause," said Cayce. "Thus at any time, in any world, a soul will give off through vibrations the story of itself and the condition in which it now exists." This quotation is on page 121 of *Edgar Cayce on Auras & Colors* by Kevin J. Todeschi and Carol Ann Liaros.

How to See the Aura

Some clairvoyants, including Cayce, are born with "aura vision" and are surprised to discover that not everyone has it. Gradual attunement to subtle energies and psychic perception may adjust the senses to the light, color, and sound sensitivity that develop aura vision.

Cayce said, and biology agrees, that as human consciousness evolves, the eye will be able to see more colors. Someday, everyone will be able to see and read the auric fields of every living thing in existence. In the *Auras* booklet, on page 120 of *Edgar Cayce on Auras & Colors*, Cayce wrote: "But in the fact of these colors we cannot see, these sounds we cannot hear, these thoughts we cannot apprehend, lies the hope of evolution and the promise of eternity."

Even now, many people can perceive at least the closest layer of light around the body. Edgar Cayce wrote on page 121 that the aura is "most easily seen around the shoulders and head," probably because of the many glandular and nervous centers located in those parts of the body.

The best way to see an aura is to look through soft, relaxed eyes at someone seated in front of a white or black wall. At first you may see a transparent field of energy extending from one to three inches from the body; with practice, this image may expand into the rich and beautiful colors of all seven layers of the auric field. Practiced observers see this multi-layered field around living organisms and a less complex field around rocks and minerals.

Most medical intuitives and energy healers see the auric field as a projection of the seven major chakras, while Cayce perceived it as an emanation of each atom and cell in the body. It is likely both a projection and an emanation: it is a cell-generated field that conjoins the chakras and projects into the aura.

Biophotons and the Auric Field

I am delighted when science proves the claims of mystics like Edgar Cayce, as this confluence draws science and spirituality closer together. Such is the case in the 1970s research of Fritz–Albert Popp, PhD, a theoretical biophysicist whose credible research proved that, on a cellular level, the body generates light.

While searching for a cure for cancer at the University of Marburg in Germany, Popp discovered that the consumption of food causes subatomic photons of light to concentrate in the DNA/RNA double helix at the center of every cell. Everything we take in contains photons of light—food, water, sunlight, thoughts, and emotions, and even the energies in environmental fields. This fundamental principle tells us that if we want to live in light, we must seek, absorb, and circulate the purest light possible in the body, mind, heart, and spirit.

The biophotonic light concentrated in the DNA/RNA helix at the center of every cell serves as a master tuning fork that turns cellular activities on and off in a conscious orchestration of bodily processes, reports Popp. These cellular waves of light link together to form a common electromagnetic field in which cells resonate together, communicate, and know about each other.

Performing different functions at different frequencies, biophotons emit a weak biophotonic field that we call the aura. Streaming a constant current of photons, this wave–field of light is a colorful, multilayered biofeedback system saturated with information about the body, mind, heart, and spirit.

Cayce said that the auric field, vibrating with rainbow colors, can be raised into the highest frequencies of pure white light. This high vibration occurs with attunement to Universal Consciousness. The body-mind takes in high–frequency white light and radiates it out into the world. When we see this white light in others, we should "follow it as if it were a star. It is," wrote Cayce in his *Auras* book. (p. 124)

Rising into the white light of Universal Consciousness involves spiritualizing the body's energy system through psychophysical healing, soul guidance, and constant intuitive connection with Source. Until that process is complete, Cayce advised, we can "draw comfort from blue, get strength from red and be happy in the laughter and sunshine of golden yellow." (p. 124)

Resonant Fields of Light

Over the past decade, several dozen pioneering scientists have conceived some fascinating theories about how intuition works. These theories revolve around the essential nature of the light of consciousness.

Physicist, psychologist and psi investigator Dean Radin, PhD, senior scientist at the Institute of Noetic Sciences (IONS), has developed an overarching theory that explains the dynamics of the intuitive Field and the telepathic people in it. Radin speculates that psi information is exchanged by way of a subatomic phenomenon called entanglement. Everything was entangled at the time of the Big Bang and still is, he says, and this entanglement explains why information is most easily exchanged among people who are highly entangled with one another, like family members, loved ones, friends, and colleagues.

Remote-viewing research has also found that emotional connection is conducive to psychic ability. Likewise, Edgar Cayce was best able to read the auras of people he knew. Common sense tells us that being on the same "wavelength" with a person who shares our history, interests, and talents would naturally establish an intuitive mind-link.

But exactly how does this connection work, and what does it mean to us?

The new reality in physics, says Radin, is nonlocality, a term referring to the theory that all of reality is interconnected in a subatomic, quantum field. In this nonlocal field, entangled minds are already in unconscious communication with one another. Radin states on page 263 in his acclaimed book, *Entangled Mind: Extrasensory Experiences in a Quantum Reality*, that the field is like a "gigantic bowl of clear jello" in which every movement, event, and thought is felt throughout the entire bowl. But unlike a localized bowl of jello, the entangled quantum field extends beyond the bounds of ordinary space-time, making it nonlocal. Because we are embedded in this nonlocal "substance," for lack of a better word, "we can get glimpses of information about other people's minds, distant objects, or the future or past," Radin writes on page 264. At some level, he explains on the same page: "Our mind/brain is *already coexistent* with other people's minds, distant objects, and everything else. To navigate through this space, we use attention and intention. From this perspective, psychic experiences are reframed not as mysterious 'powers of the mind' but as momentary glimpses of the entangled fabric of reality."

While the unconscious mind is continually scanning the field for pertinent data, the conscious mind's preoccupation with tasks drowns out the information in the field, Radin points out, except when a loved one is in danger. This "spooky telepathy" might seem to be an information transfer, but in fact, he notes on page 265, "within a holistic medium we are *always connected.* No information transfer need take place, because there are no separate parts. Navigation through this reality occurs through our attention, and nonsensory perception takes place through our activated memory and imagination."

Unconscious communication is possible, Radin explains, because photons of light comprising the entire universe are entangled with our biophotonic fields and the environmental fields that surround us. The interconnection of these interpenetrating fields enables us to gain information from a distance without the use of the ordinary senses; the information simply flows into the unconscious mind. Radin and Popp agree that the nonlocal quantum field provides the medium for information to transfer virtually instantaneously.

Other scientists investigating psi phenomena have developed theories involving information transfer and have found that it occurs in harmonic resonance, referring to the alignment of two sources with the same frequency pattern, wherein atoms and molecules resonate with and "speak" to each other.

Theories highlighted in the book, *The Field: The Quest for the Secret Force of the Universe,* by Lynne McTaggart, speculate that the Zero Point Field—a quantum sea of coherent light—is consciousness itself. As such, it interpenetrates the brain and body of every living organism, placing the unconscious minds of all living creatures in constant communication with the unconscious mind of the Zero Point Field. This field is constantly interacting with all subatomic matter and cannot be eliminated by any known law in physics, writes McTaggart.

Imprinted in its waves of light is an (Akashic) record of everything that ever was. We connect with this Field, adds this writer, through the very slow brainwaves of delta's unconscious mind.

In other words, as Cayce believed and brainwave science agrees, the unconscious mind of every living being is constantly communicating with the mind of God. Scientific evidence resides in the fact that, at the molecular level, the Zero Point Field is constantly absorbing and reemitting photons of light. Popp's research noted the same process in the human body on a cellular level. Like the holograms that we are, we take in light as well as emit it, and so does the Field.

What these theories tell us is what mystics have always known and Edgar Cayce believed: on the quantum level of pure light, we *are* God. In one of his readings, he said: "And what is life? God manifested in the material plane. For it is still in Him that we live and move and have our being. Thus life as a material manifestation is the expression of that Universal Force or Energy we call God." (3590-1)

The only separation is our disbelief in our own divine nature. We begin to know our divine nature in the silence of pure mind resonating with the brilliant light that entangled us at the beginning of time. In this infinite field of intelligence, we find all knowledge, wisdom, and energy; and in soul-deep praise and gratitude, we unite with it.

Quantum Transformation

What all of this means to us is profound and far-reaching. If we accept these scientific studies and theories, then we must believe that all sentient beings, from plants and animals to humans and the earth, are communicating unconsciously with each other and the Field. As Buddhists believe, there is only one mind and thus only one of us. And as Jesus said, "The Father and I are one."

The concept of our intimate connection with cosmic fields of light leaves us with a pivotal question that we can use to measure our evolutionary progress: are we facilitating our psychic and spiritual experience in the earth or blocking our evolution?

Using the information from a research paper on intuition published by the Institute of HeartMath, you can answer this question for yourself.

HeartMath's research shows that when we focus our attention around the area of the heart and breathe in feelings of love and appreciation (*see* the Heart Breath in Chapter 5), this heart feeling ripples out into environmental fields. The coherent field of energy emanating from the heart—the largest electromagnetic field generated by the body—carries a wave of focused energy that resonates harmonically with the incoming wave of energy generated by the person you are reading, healing, or simply loving.

Harmonic resonance between two wave-fields creates an optimal channel for communication of nonlocal information that operates instantly at superluminal speeds, according to HeartMath's researchers.

When many people resonate love, peace, and coherence into the Zero Point Field at the same time, their amplified energies transmit these traits over infinite distances and *change the Field itself!* Peace, love, and harmony prevail, at least more than before, in a resonating field that is available to everyone.

With one thought, one word, one action at a time, we change the very fabric of reality. Thanks to the marriage of quantum science and mystical spirituality, this transformative shift in consciousness is well underway. The consciousness is shifting not just globally but in every interconnected dimension of reality we touch—from earth creatures and our planet to spirit people, to the higher self's angelic nature, and finally to Universal Consciousness itself.

What connects us is the resonant power of love. Love is contained in each photon of light and is the driving force of all creation. Each soul comes here to learn how to love, for it is love that streams the psychic force into the field of creation to be experienced and embodied.

Each soul incarnates for this purpose alone: to learn to love. The greater the love, the greater the connection with the Field, whose Heart is love.

Resources:
Todeschi, Kevin J. and Carol Ann Liaros. *Edgar Cayce on Auras & Colors.* A.R.E. Press, 2012, pp. 107-124 (Cayce's booklet on Auras).

10

Healers and Healing

"We never know how high we are / Till we are called to rise."
—*Emily Dickinson*

I knew almost nothing about Malcolm Smith, an English healer,
when I travelled to the A.R.E. of New York's Edgar Cayce Center in 2003
to write an article on him for my online newsletter, "The Still, Small
Voice." People were raving about him, so I thought it prudent, before
the interview, to test his abilities on my chronic back pain.

I was greeted by a merry, blue-eyed man with a ruddy complexion
and bowl-cut red hair. Following Malcolm into a small healing room, I
sat down on a chair without a back. He sat on a chair behind mine and
gently placed his hands on my shoulders, moving them from spot to
spot. Warm, golden light flowed into my body and lifted me into bliss.
Malcolm rocked me back and forth, as if opening my spine to the flow
of healing light. I leaned against him "bonelessly," like the lifeless body
of Jesus, resting in the lap of his mother in the Pietà. Everything disappeared but the golden light, which carried me home to my soul.

When the thirty-minute session ended, I floated out of my chair and the room. Where had the time gone? I sat down on a sofa to wait for our interview, and Malcolm handed me a worn book of handwritten testimonials. Reading them startled me back to earth.

The most exciting to me was this one: "Malcolm asked me if I were aware of a terrorist attack coming to the US from men whose hearts were full of evil. He said he felt it was very, very near, but I should not be frightened and that it would be good to have extra water and food on hand." The man wrote this note two days before the terrorist attacks of September 11, 2001. Weeks later he added a comment that this warning helped alleviate "terror that has consumed my life." Cured of his paralyzing fear in a single session, he spoke of Malcolm as an "earth angel" and of how, during his healing, he couldn't tell if he were sitting in the chair or floating above it. (I could relate.)

I read on. A woman wrote about crying for no apparent reason during her session. She reported feeling surrounded by a white light that was so beautiful and full of love that she almost couldn't bear it; this light opened her "closed, hard heart," she recounted.

A Jewish woman went to Malcolm for a healing of tinnitus (ringing in the ears) and was surprised when he asked about a pain in her hand. She had cut three fingers to the bone with a circular saw twenty-five years before. After the healing, she felt relaxed and nauseous. At home, she vomited for hours; afterward, all of the pain in her hand was gone. Smith cured the tinnitus during her next session.

Other people wrote of healings that resolved multiple complaints within a single session. For one woman, a ruptured disk, frozen shoulder, and emotional pain were "healed below the surface, never to be seen (again). Words are insufficient," she wrote. An AIDS patient was thankful for the healing of a chronic pain in his shoulder, diminished asthma, and an improved T cell count enabling him to refuse "toxic medications." A woman with aggressive breast cancer wrote that she needed no more surgery, after all. A man who was depressed about being jobless saw a vision of his mother during his healing. She told him not to worry; afterward, Malcolm said he'd seen her, too. Malcolm said that his client would have a good job within two weeks and would learn about it within two days. He did.

People's stories of animal healings by Malcolm ruled out the power of suggestion. One entry concerned a twelve-year-old poodle with congestive heart failure, kidney failure, and a year-long illness. After four visits, Ginger rallied and is the "longest living dog" known to her veterinarian. Someone recently told me that Malcolm healed another dog of a deadly tumor that simply disappeared.

During my session with Malcolm, my back pain disappeared. I suspected that it would return later on, and it did, due to busy haste and a lack of consideration for my body's basic needs. Still, the pain was never again as intense as it had been for more than thirty years. Other changes did last. The energy flowing through my body had increased and now enlivened my meditations, stimulated psychic visions, and stirred energy in my hands and feet. I gave "the healing energy," as I called it, to my little grandson after he tripped down the stairs and suffered a serious blow to his head. Inexplicably, there was no subsequent bruising.

The next time I saw Malcolm Smith was eleven years later. I arrived early at a hotel near Philadelphia where he was conducting healings, and I wired up each of us to a Mind Mirror. By then, I was sensitive enough to feel streams of golden light flowing out of each of Malcolm's fingers even before he touched me. The same golden warmth spread through my body, accompanied by feelings of ecstasy so intense that I floated in bliss and could open my eyes only a few times to watch my brainwaves on the Mind Mirror.

Due to a computer glitch, my brainwaves did not record into a computer file. But when I looked at the Mind Mirror console, which has its own screen, I was producing exclusively a high-amplitude delta wave, the yoga-nidra pattern that appears when only unconscious brainwaves are present and are reaching out to the Field for healing.

Malcolm's brainwave patterns recorded successfully. Quick scrutiny after the session revealed high-amplitude, awakened-mind patterns as well as the most perfect evolved-mind circle I have ever seen.

Later on, a frame-by-frame study of his brainwave patterns revealed much more: a superconscious-mind pattern two minutes into the session, followed two seconds later by the godlike, angelic nature of the higher self and a steady alternation of these two patterns throughout the session. Interspersed with these patterns were vortex-shaped downloads of powerful energies that may be the next and final Mind Mirror pattern: direct connection with the formless energy of Universal Consciousness.

After the session, I asked Malcolm what he experienced while healing people. "I just open up and let God come through," he said.

Smith, a descendent of Yorkshire coal miners, was born with the gift of healing and says that everyone has it, if we would simply practice using it. Everything in his life conspired to make sure that he used his gift. At age eight, he held the hand of his dying grandmother for thirty minutes in the middle of the night. She took a deep breath, slipped into a trance, and woke up twelve hours later, fully recovered.

Later on, a psychic told him that he was a healer and could heal his wife of a kidney condition. He did so in five minutes. When he gave healing to his seven-year-old daughter, Adele, for bronchitis, she awakened from sleep to see a glowing spirit who put burning-hot hands on her chest. This same glowing spirit appeared to thirteen other people who were healed by Malcolm around that time.

Perhaps it was this same helpful spirit who terrified his family with poltergeist activity. Ghostly knocks, loud footsteps, pictures flying off walls, giggles, and icy blasts of air drove him to a Spiritualist church in search of an exorcist. Hearing his story, a member of the church went into meditation and pronounced that the "spirit people" had succeeded in getting him to the church and would not bother the family anymore. And they did not.

The members of the Spiritualist church had only minor aches and pains; it was their encouragement that caused Smith to become a healer. For the next eighteen years, people went to his house to be healed. There, he charged fifteen dollars per session, except for children, invalids, and cancer patients, who received his healing at no cost.

Today, he travels from England to various cities in the United States several times a year. In Virginia Beach, VA, he does his healing work through A.R.E. volunteers who host and locally promote him. In this writer's opinion—and that of the Mind Mirror—Malcolm Smith deserves recognition as one of the most powerful healers in the world.

Frans Stiene's Bright White Light

Internationally known healer Frans Stiene says that everyone possesses the ability to heal, if we are willing to develop the focused attention and sustained awareness that connects us with the inflow of universal light.

Frans' own healing from the pain of spinal scoliosis began in India, when he was serendipitously guided in the village of Ladakh to a female healer named Lha–mo. She went into a trance, put her hands on his shoulders, and used a wooden tube to suck out a dark, greasy red material from his lower body. Frans felt tremendous heat, and his body awareness disappeared into a profound connection with what he calls his "true self," his soul. In this awareness, his pain began to fade away, and he cried in relief.

Frans did not realize it then, but Lha–mo had charged up his body with energy and had changed his vibrational rate and patterns. Formerly a drinker and partygoer, he awakened the next morning with a desire to read about spirituality. He bought books on Buddhism, Hinduism, and Ayurveda in the hope of learning more about his true self and healing his soul along with the back trouble that had caused so much pain since the age of sixteen.

Stiene, a Dutchman, and his wife Bronwyn, an Australian, found themselves on a light–filled, spiritual journey from that point forward. They studied Western Reiki in Nepal and then visited Darjeeling, India, where they felt that they had found their home. Settling there for the next year, they lived in a house filled with the energies of high Tibetan lamas. Soon, they found themselves at tea plantations giving free Reiki treatments to local people with polio, open wounds, and eye diseases.

During this year, Frans experienced a strange series of visions. For weeks at a time, while in bed at night and neither awake nor asleep, he saw clear visions of himself pulling splinters and then chunks of wood from his hands. Next came weeks of dreams in which he pulled metals and then liquid out of his hands and body parts. Each morning, he awakened feeling massive amounts of energy in his hands. It was a purification process, a Buddhist teacher explained, which seemed to be true. Frans felt more vibration in his body, and his healing powers grew stronger. His back pain began to disappear, and his mind and emotions cleared.

In Darjeeling, all of the healers had spiritual practices, and soon Frans followed suit. He traveled to Japan to study with a traditional Japanese Reiki healer and a Tendai Buddhist martial arts expert. Returning to Australia, he studied with a Chinese Daoist healer. Each of these teachers emphasized the importance of a spiritual practice and self-development, so Frans devoted himself to meditation and to mantras that built up his capacity to hold and sustain healing energy. He explains that these practices help people "unlock what is inside of them—their true selves—so that they can connect with the bright, white light."

Some thirteen years ago, Frans and Bronwyn founded their Australian-based International House of Reiki and through it have taught many thousands of people worldwide to connect with the bright, white light of healing. Their traditional style of Japanese Reiki, called Usui Reiki Ryoho, teaches students to connect with their true selves and hold the higher vibrations without being physically impacted by them.

I traveled to Washington, DC, in April of 2011 to monitor Frans' brainwaves. Setting up in his spacious hotel room, I connected one Mind Mirror to Frans and a second one to his recipient, psychic medium Deborah Harrigan. To my astonishment, whether Frans was telling a joke or healing Deborah, he produced the yoga–nidra "psychic sleep" brainwave pattern wherein only the lowest and slowest delta waves of the unconscious mind are present to receive and transmit energy from the Field. Chi kung healers produce high–amplitude delta waves, too, but presumably not while talking and joking!

"When I am in this state," Frans explained later, "I feel my physical body collapsing, and my sense of separation disappears." Remaining in what he calls the witness consciousness, he enters the "formless," in which he is aware only of energetic impulses moving through his body.

During our EEG study, Frans surprised me further by shifting into the out-of-body pattern of virtually flat brainwaves, meaning that his mind dissociated from his body to merge with the Field. This shift happened just before a huge vortex-like download of, as in Malcolm Smith's brainwaves, what seemed to be a connection with the formless energy of Universal Consciousness.

Deborah, a psychic empath, was able to "mind walk" with Frans into his yoga–nidra and out–of–body patterns. When he knelt down a few feet away from her to send distance healing, within three minutes his brainwaves flared into a high–amplitude, delta–only, yoga–nidra pattern and a near–perfect, godlike, angelic pattern, which caused Deborah's brainwaves to flare into a succession of superconscious–mind patterns.

Later on, she reported a sensation of energy moving into her feet and "blue lightning" moving up her legs. Paula Michal–Johnson, a Usui Reiki Ryoho teacher in Pennsylvania who facilitated this study, saw a blue arc of energy enter Deborah's feet and had privately mentioned this image to me well before Deborah said anything about it.

Frans explained that huge energy downloads are common during a practice like Shinpiden, the third level of the style of Reiki that he has formulated and teaches. I witnessed this energy in a series of group EEG–monitored studies involving five of his students, most of whom had the same series of advanced brainwave patterns as their teacher. There were tornado–like downloads of high–voltage energy followed by the superconscious–mind and godlike, higher–self brainwave patterns.

It's important to say more about these powerful gamma waves. While gamma frequencies are momentarily generated in the brain by people engaged in creative "aha" insights, focused attention, and the bliss of spiritual ecstasy—all of which produce whole–brain synchrony—the body is not constructed to operate on these super–fast frequencies. One must learn how to build a "body of light" that can sustain him or her. This practice is the genius of Frans Stiene's style of Reiki.

While Western Reiki teaches how to draw energy from the Field during healing and then disconnect from it, Frans states that the meditations and mantras used in traditional Japanese Reiki enable people to build up the current and sustain it in their bodies. They are super-charged by these high gamma frequencies, which surge into and through the brain to form new brain cells and circuits in intellectual, creative, and memory centers.

Western Reiki healers experience the same energetic surge when they tap into these high energies. Gamma frequencies magnify everything in consciousness, positive and negative, until the brain–mind manifests the evolutionary body of light. (*See* the section on kundalini in the last chapter for the importance of managing the subtle energy system.)

By teaching his students how to connect with the soul and the great, bright light as well as how to hold and transmit these energies, Frans is conveying what Lha-mo transmitted to him: the enlightened master's shaktipat.

Stiene's trainer in the United States, Heather Alexander, produced the same superconscious patterns while healing Irene Gubrud, an opera and concert singer, during an EEG-monitored session in New York City in early 2011. Heather almost held this pattern constant during the half-hour healing session, and Irene resonated with it nearly the whole time. At one point, Heather flared into the vortex download of energy, and two seconds later, Irene flared into the godlike, angelic brainwave pattern.

The superconscious brainwave patterns of healers affect recipients in special ways. According to vibrational biophysics, the higher the frequencies (most safely under 50 hertz) and the stronger their amplitudes, the fewer the photons and the more light they contain, which amounts to a "supercharge" from gamma-producing healers. On the other hand, most healing takes place between the frequencies of 1 and 30 hertz, where there are more photons containing less light in each one. Healers working in these frequencies provide a steady current where most recipients need them.

Studies have shown that healers intuitively "sweep" the recipient's energy field to concentrate light where it is most needed. I saw this concentration occur when Heather transmitted a protracted, high-amplitude delta band at 2 hertz, the frequency that heals the nervous system. This transmission was right where Irene needed healing. As a teenager, she had been thrown from an amusement park ride and had sustained spinal injuries that left her on crutches for the rest of her life.

In this session, Irene's superconscious mind, flowing with light, applied to her body the frequencies needed for healing and repair. Harmonics to the fundamental frequency of 2 hertz resonated through her body at 4, 8, 16, 32, and 64-hertz frequencies in delta, theta, alpha, beta, and gamma, all united in a single, super-awakened-mind pattern open to healing on every level. Irene reported feeling that her body and mind were vibrating at higher frequencies.

Irene is well acquainted with higher frequencies of light and sound. She and her husband, choral conductor Steven Finch, founders of Sound–Mind Connections, are sound clinicians who teach people across the United States how music influences brainwave frequencies, energetically heals the body, and rewires and evolves the brain.

The first time I wired Irene to the Mind Mirror, she had just listened to a gamma brainwave entrainment recording by neuro–acoustic guru, Dr. Jeffrey Thompson. She immediately produced the brainwave pattern that I have introduced in this book as the superconscious–mind pattern.

For Irene and everyone else, the challenge is to attune to the higher frequencies of the superconscious and carry its godlike pattern of perfection into the earth.

The Soul of Healing

Studies show that healing most often takes place in a narrow band of frequencies involving both alpha and theta at 7.8– to 8.0–hertz. These meditation frequencies lead us deeply inward to emotional healing and the sixth sense of the psychic soul, or outward to resonate with nature at 7 to 10 hertz, the average resonant frequencies of the earth. These "brainwave" frequencies of the earth, created by lightning strikes that pump energy into the cavity between the earth and her protective shield, the ionosphere, create standing waves that travel around the globe, according to a scientific measurement called the Schumann resonance.

It was always clear to me that healers, through their alpha–theta brainwaves, meditatively synchronize with the earth to tap into her energies of healing and growth. But it's not enough to say that nature *contains* divine energy. The truth is more profound than that.

Mother Earth, *the living heart of God*, is divine energy. Like the heart chakra in the human body, she conducts us by harmonic resonance into superconscious waves of light, and in turn, steps down the Field's frequencies into her frequencies. Life is all about the heart.

Emptying the Cup

During our interview, Malcolm Smith told two stories of instantaneous healing. In one case, a teenager paralyzed from the neck down by a car wreck emerged from a coma and began to move his arms and legs after twenty minutes of energy healing. The other case involved a woman who had been blinded by retinitis pigmentosa twenty-five years before and regained her sight during the session.

Yet sometimes, Smith mused, "You can cure a blind woman and not a person with floaters in the eyes." Frans Stiene has had this same experience. The cancer disappears but not the wart on the thumb.

When does energy healing fail to work and why? First, these two healers say, the spirit must be open to receive the healing. Sometimes it is not. The illness or injury may be karmic, or perhaps there is some secondary benefit. For instance, a woman once told me that being in a wheelchair had given her "personal power" for the first time in her life. Consciously, she wanted to be healed, but unconsciously, she did not.

Stiene uses an analogy to explain this problem. "The Sanskrit word for initiation means pouring," he said. "The cup needs to be empty. If the client is not empty of attachment, fear, and worry, then you can pour only a little bit into it."

In the end, though, why energy healing works for certain people and not for others is still a mystery. In one Reiki class conducted by Stiene, he sent out energy that caused an amazing reaction in an Indian woman. Her mouth locked up, and when it opened, she fell to the floor and began to energetically vomit. Within a month, she was promoted at work, became the lead singer in her singing group, found a new house, and was given a car. "Her energy had been stuck," Stiene explained, "but she opened up to her true self."

The willingness to open up may explain why some people heal spontaneously. Love and joy certainly work wonders, as journalist and UCLA professor Norman Cousins illustrated. He cured his heart disease by taking megadoses of vitamin C and belly-laughing his way through Marx Brothers' films.

Spontaneous healings often occur in meditation, as shown in hundreds of studies. Mindfulness meditation is particularly useful for pain control, according to Jon Kabat–Zinn, PhD, who has successfully introduced this form of meditation—centered on attentional focus and self-reflective awareness—to hospitals, addiction and trauma centers, physician's offices, schools, and businesses throughout the United States.

Oschman points out in his book, *Energy Medicine*, that both the cause and the effect of the illness must be removed for healing to work. If the cause is not addressed, the effect will return. The cause is always in the mind, as Edgar Cayce said in the oft-quoted phrase, " . . . for the spirit is life; the mind is the builder; the physical is the result . . . " (349-4) Cayce made this and other similar statements decades before the mind–body connection was widely recognized.

Soul guidance is the way to clear mental–emotional issues that obstruct physical healing. Inside the deeper, core self, we dialogue with the mind, heart, and body to find out what each part wants and needs. Providing what's needed clears away tangled energies and unites the inner being into a *single spirit*.

When the eye is single, the whole body can be filled with light, as Jesus phrased it in Matthew 6:22. This verse refers to clear intention, focus, and emptying the cup of fear and worry so the spirit can heal itself and be healed. At that point, a healer can clear residual patterns of vibrational discord in the body to reinstate health and wholeness.

How does a healer heal? Deepening into the resonant alpha–theta frequencies in the brain, the healer attunes to the brainwaves of the earth and to the Field, all of which by harmonic resonance can supply the body with any missing frequencies. In mystical terms, the soul turns its hidden eye to nature and God, so the angelic, higher self can write its pattern of perfection on the body of the soul.

And how do we handle discordant fields around us? Centered in the heart, we simply open up to our wholeness and allow that coherent energy field to flow with love. Negative vibrations can then travel through the empty spaces in our atoms and beyond us without attachment, while we remain open and loving. This loving, compassionate non–attachment enables us to live in the light of the soul, whose primary entanglement is with other enlightened spirits.

Global Fields of Healing

Along with the Institute of HeartMath, the most convincing studies on global healing have been conducted by physicist John Hagelin, PhD, a devotee of the late Maharishi Mahesh Yogi, the founder of Transcendental Meditation in America. Consequently, Hagelin's studies are referred to as the Maharishi Effect.

In more than six hundred experiments, Dr. Hagelin has proved that the energies of group meditation produce resonant fields that ripple out and reduce violent crime in the vicinity by an average of twenty percent. One group curbed crime by twenty-five percent in Washington, DC! A detailed meta-study on the Maharishi Effect is available on the Web site permanentpeace.org. You will also find on this Web site Dr. Hagelin's plan to use meditation to bring about global peace.

By now you know that meditation and energy healing arouse a highly intuitive field of energy: the calm, peaceful heart couples with resonant fields that amplify in strength, and this high-amplitude field projects into infinity, losing its strength only over distance. Coherent fields benefit our planet, too, according to studies on the relationship of human consciousness to geomagnetic events and solar flares carried out by the Institute of HeartMath's Global Coherence Initiative.

The Global Coherence Initiative (GCI) states that the ionosphere, part of the earth's atmosphere, is of vital interest to everyone, since increased solar activity and solar flares can compress the earth's magnetosphere and thereby change the Schumann resonance. Researchers working in many nations have found that solar and geomagnetic disturbances change heart and brain patterns. When the earth's frequencies undergo change in the geomagnetic pulsation range of 1 to 40 hertz, these changes profoundly affect every form of life on earth.

Changes in the Schumann resonance have corresponded with increased hospital admissions for heart attacks, strokes, suicide, homicide, increased accidents, violence, and mental disorders, as well as changes in memory, attention, migraine headaches, and hormone levels. Studies show, however, that these changes are weaker in people with strong adaptability skills, such as meditators. In clear agreement with remote-viewing research, GCI studies show that solar and geomagnetic changes also influence intuition, which is received by the body's most finely tuned oscillators—first the heart and then the brain.

These extraordinary studies on the interrelationship of solar activity, the earth's Schumann resonance, and life on this planet prompted the Institute of HeartMath to implement the Global Coherence Initiative. The eye-opening statistics collected by GCI prompted this organization to connect almost forty thousand people in fifty-six countries, who gather in an online Global Care Room to send out a worldwide wave of heart coherence to people and nations experiencing distress. Everyone is invited to join this intentional community in its global effort to curb catastrophic weather, wars, and epidemics.

The Global Coherence Monitoring System, which is part of GCI, is placing magnetometer sensors at various points on the planet in order to map the relationship of planetary and solar phenomena to personal well-being as well as the converse relationship of human emotion to global health.

Still more far-reaching, the Institute of HeartMath is collaborating with the Institute of Noetic Sciences (IONS) and Princeton University's Global Consciousness Project to place random-number generators at each sensor site to further measure the earth's energetics. Someday, their body of research will convince even the most skeptical people of our interconnectedness with the cosmos and the pressing need for planetary harmony.

Could millions, even billions, of people focused on a single healing intention cause a dramatic shift in physical reality? In this quantum sea of light, could we prevent catastrophic weather in the same way we center our attention in the heart to raise healing light in self and others?

Wisdom traditions—and Edgar Cayce's readings—have always believed so. John Hagelin's peace project states that the square root of one percent of the world's population is enough to make a change—and that's only a few thousand people.

Despite the evidence, years and perhaps generations will pass before mainstream scientists unanimously agree on the nature of reality, if they ever do. Meanwhile, research pioneers like IONS, the Institute of HeartMath, GCI, and others will continue to blaze trails that will eventually become numinous enough for scientists and world leaders to follow.

Regardless of what scientists report, we can use our intelligence, intuition, and instinct to evolve our own consciousness. Reaching out with compassion to help and heal others will generate resonant fields that will heal our planet and all who live on it.

Science will attain its proof about the nature of reality. And we psychic souls will be doing our work on earth by rising into the loving intelligence of the universal Creative Forces.

11

Living the Intuitive Life

" . . . it is not what the mind knows but what the mind applies or does about that it knows, *that makes for soul, mental or material advancements."—Edgar Cayce reading 444-1*

Not much needs to be said in this chapter, since the key to living the intuitive life is to live intuitively!

You learned about biophotons in the last chapter and why it's so important to charge up your energy field with light. Everything is composed of light, so staying healthy and psychically open is a matter of taking in fresh air, water, sunlight, and vibrant living foods. If you want to power up your intuition, eat primarily fruits and vegetables so your diet tends toward alkalinity and your endocrine and nervous systems are healthy and strong. Consider the occasional fast, and meditate for twenty minutes to an hour each day to stay clear, lucid, peaceful, and in touch with your spirit. Send healing light to others at the end of meditation and be sure to receive it yourself.

When you walk in nature, use all of your senses to experience her rich and varied beauty. If you can't walk outdoors or stretch and exercise for health, you can use your sensory intuitive imagination to increase the flow of electricity in your body in order to power up your superconscious brain and mind. Connect with each force and form in nature–the "holy angels" of the earth, as the ancient, mystical Essenes referred to the energetic patterns that give rise to the manifest world.

Standing in a natural landscape with your feet spread comfortably apart, breathe deeply and draw into your bioenergetic field the currents of energy in water, earth, trees, fire, and minerals. Immerse yourself in these energies, one at a time, and pull them into your body. For example, imagine yourself swimming in a sparkling river, standing under a waterfall, or drinking clear, pure water. Sit next to a tree, absorb the fire of the sun, and pull the energy of crystals up out of the earth into your hands and feet. This Essene/Five Elements Chi Kung meditation will strengthen your connection with Mother Earth, sensitize you to subtle energies, and harmonize your body, mind, and spirit.

The good life is the balanced life, so create what excites you, laugh and play with people you love, and open-heartedly serve each soul in your life. Peak moments of illumination brought about by your constant connection with Source will attract to you even more joy and abundance. Live in this flow of happiness and consciously radiate it to others.

The currents of peace, love, and light flowing so naturally in heaven and earth will draw you to the life of your dreams–and our collective dream of a new earth.

A New Human, a New Earth

Somewhere near the beginning of time, the immortal souls descended into the earth and, deciding to play, were trapped in dense animal forms, according to the Edgar Cayce readings. The readings say that we are still trying to free ourselves from this heavy energy in order to return as light-filled souls to the Creative Forces. Every single event in life serves to purify and refine the soul, so that it may someday ascend into the light whence it came.

In this era of rank materialism and greed, corporate corruption, climate change, political wars, and global strife–a time like any other–we are faced with enormous challenges and opportunities. Yet everything we need is right here at hand, in the quiet mind and its omniscient spirit, which waits and wants to show us the way back home.

Where is home? It is in the psychic soul, where the sixth sense resonates with the light and wisdom in the superconscious and channels this higher vibration into a new human and a new reality.

This new reality is already being born, as scientific studies on the brain, meditation and consciousness ripple into the media airwaves and awaken people to their untapped possibilities and potential. Signs of this awakening are cropping up in every nation. In the United States, commercial publishers attending Book Expo America 2001 in New York City declared that they were moving out of the Age of Intellect into the Age of Soul. This shift in focus followed the discovery of a new marketing demographic, the Cultural Creatives, whose members read an average of twenty-five books per year on personal development, spirituality, green economies, and sustainable living, compared to the mainstream's average of three books on random topics. Commercial publishers also identified this time as the new Age of Soul because massive numbers of people had begun to self-publish books on spirituality.

According to Lifestyles of Health and Sustainability, the organization that is tracking these trends, Cultural Creatives composed one-fifth of the adult population in America in 2001. The latest statistics say that in 2005, their numbers jumped to one-fourth of the US adult population, amounting to more than 62 million people. Because Cultural Creatives buy products that support their values and beliefs, from yoga mats and nutritional supplements to organic clothing, electric cars, and solar-powered homes, their choices are defining market trends and thus are changing every aspect of this nation. These same changes are occurring worldwide.

We are also seeing signs of a new reality in the emergence of incredibly psychic children, calmer and more rational adults, and a civilization that is widely contemplating the quality of its regard for others and the earth. Guided by the soul's direct intuitive experiences, a new, superconscious human is manifesting faster than the speed of light, and so is the inevitability of a paradigm shift from competition and conflict to compassion and cooperation. Rational and spiritual in character, our new reality is flowing out of the soul's conscious communion with the mind *and* heart of God.

In these tumultuous times, wherein the new reality is struggling to be born as the old ways fight to maintain control, many people find it hard to believe that this is a period of constructive change. And yet, on a higher level we see the truth: the challenges we face inspire us to search the psychic soul for solutions, and in the light-filled higher self, we find the wisdom and insight we need to surmount any difficulty. Embracing the soul's sixth sense is the *impetus* of our evolution.

The Quantum Leap in Consciousness

Today, with the conscious mind's intelligence relying on its deeper intuition and instinct, a quantum evolutionary leap into a new humanity and a happier, more equitable world is inevitable.

Even the timing of this global shift in consciousness is in perfect order, as the stars and planets in the celestial clock wheel us into the Aquarian Age whose keynote is humanitarian love. By destiny, desire, and intention we are birthing the fifth root race predicted by Edgar Cayce: a new human in a new earth.

Perhaps you can feel on a deep unconscious level the evolutionary shift that is underway. Some say that we came here for this shift. If that feels true to you, I hope you will take up a daily meditation practice and host a spiritual study group or Psychic Circle. Only your commitment and cooperation with like-minded people can bring about the spiritual awakening that is so near.

Soon the day will come–and indeed is now at hand–when the whole world learns to quiet itself and listen to the still, small voice of the soul, which has beckoned us to this unprecedented point in time to guide us to the pure Spirit that is who we are in our essence. In the light of this love, we are home.

Resources:

A Special Dinner, *a celebratory guided meditation with big band music and the chance to dance and sing as never before.*

(For the above meditation, *see* Selected Bibliography for track information regarding: Pennington, Judith. *The Meditation Experience: Listening to
Your Psychic Soul.* CDs)

**Visit Judith online and enjoy articles
on meditation, dreams, and inspired writing
at www.YourPsychicSoul.com**

Appendix A

Sensory Exercises

Visual Imagery

1. Walk in nature and experience every aspect with your eyes. Notice colors, textures and forms, patterns of light and shadow, and visual contrast and definition. Etch these details in your mind.

2. Close your eyes and envision a place of great beauty, one that you know and care about. Walk around in this place, and notice the colors, textures, patterns, forms, and the play of light and shadow. Add visual and other sensory details wherever possible.

3. Find a full-color picture that captures your imagination. Place the image in front of you and describe every detail in it. Close your eyes and repeat your description. If you do not see anything with your eyes closed, repeat out loud your earlier verbal description, and begin to sense visual impressions as if you can see what you are describing. You may sense subtle stirrings in the area of your forehead. If so, this is an

awakening of your mind's eye, or third chakra.

4.   After you have worked with re-creating images in your mind's eye, envision those images three-dimensionally, and imagine yourself moving through this 3-D world. Imagine looking at objects from different angles and different sides. After several of these sessions, you will begin to "see" internal visual images, perhaps as a brief flicker to begin with. Soon, you will be able to sustain the image, just as in waking life.

Inner Feeling

1.   While visiting a place that is special to you, whether it is in nature or in the landscape of your mind, notice any sensations of warmth or cold, and experience these in every way possible. What else do you feel here? Attune completely to your feelings.

2.   Feel the energy of another person. Is this person relaxed or agitated? Calm or turbulent? Happy or sad? Make mental notes of your own impressions, and then delicately ask the person to describe his or her state of mind; afterward, make a comparison to check your accuracy. Do this with friends and family, knowing that you are building your psychic empathy and don't have to keep the feelings you experience. Your *intention* releases external energies.

3.   While walking in nature, touch a leaf, walk barefoot on the earth, dip your toes in the water, and feel everything you can.

4.   In your mind's eye, imagine flying in the air or outer space. Add details to your vision.

Inner Hearing

1.   Sit quietly and listen to the sounds around you. Is there a refrigerator or air conditioner humming? A chirping bird? Can you hear the sound of your own breathing or the swish of your clothing as your lungs empty and fill? In this "bare attention" meditation, allow yourself to follow and hear whatever the mind is attracted to. Once you have

deeply relaxed, evoke these sounds in your mind's ear.

2.   Using your own voice, record and play back in contemplative si-lence a litany of images that you have created. Look around in nature for these images and sensations, or reimagine what evokes your senses of taste, touch, smell, sight, and hearing. Arrange your impressions in a list, and enjoy flexing your sensory muscles.

Multi-Sensory Awareness

1.   When out in nature, luxuriate in what you see, hear, feel, taste, and smell. Listen for your inner voice. Is it full of mind-chatter, or is there a quiet, steady stream of impressions? Learn to "listen" all of the time in order to discern the difference in your inner voices. At opposite ex-tremes, one inner voice nags and criticizes; the other voice speaks lov-ingly of universal laws containing insightful guidance. Which one do you want to hear? The voice you choose will be the one that speaks up to communicate with you.

2.   Place a glass of water on a table in front of you, and relax your body and mind. Open your eyes, jiggle the glass slightly, and watch the light ripple on the water as it moves, listening to any sounds the water makes. Feel the texture of the glass in your hand and its warmth or coolness. Raise the glass to your mouth and taste the water, tracing its path down your throat and into your stomach. Next, close your eyes and reimagine the experience of looking at, listening to, and tasting the water in the glass. Repeat this exercise with your outer and inner senses, each time sharpening your experience of drinking the water.

3.   Count sheep when you go to bed at night. Watch the sheep leap over the fence, and then call one or two of them to your side. Run your fingers through their fleece, stroke their heads, listen to them baa, and enjoy these fuzzy creatures with all of your senses. Do this exercise with any animal. You will surely slip into an alpha state that's not far away from sleep. Alpha waves will put you to sleep very quickly, and you will have expanded your sensory intuition along the way!

Appendix B
Guide to Meditation

Preparation.
Shower or wash your hands and drink water to purify yourself.
Light candles or use incense to purify the space.

Relax your body.
Loosen up with gentle stretching. Standing up, stretch like a cat or do head-and-neck rolls to relax your muscles.

Find a position.
Sit with your back straight and your feet flat on the floor. Loosen any binding clothing. Position your hands comfortably, and rest the tip of your tongue in the roof of your mouth or against the back of your teeth.

Connect with your spirit.
Recite the Lord's Prayer, chant Om, and/or read an inspiring message.

Withdraw into yourself.
Do some alternate-nostril breathing to further relax. Set aside your earthly self: grasp it and set it firmly outside your body.

Connect with light.
Sense the presence of light above your head, and draw it down to surround any remaining thoughts in your mind.
Now usher these thoughts down into your heart. Linger in light and memories of joy.

Connect with Universal Awareness.
Breathe light up through your chakra system and pause to let the light at your crown stream into your head.
Exhale slowly and bathe the light into your chakras—back down your spine.

Repeat seven times, saying "Arise my soul and enter the Oneness" to attune to divine light.

Expand outward.
Holding your attention on your third eye chakra, expand your focus outward into Universal Awareness. Feel yourself moving out into the universe toward your Source. Embrace the infinite with your heart, saying "Not my will, but thine be done, O Lord." Rest in pure awareness.

Meditate in the silence.
If thoughts arise, repeat your ideal as a mantra.
Stay connected and receive the light.

Send your light outward to heal all sentient beings, including the Earth.

Close your meditation.
Find a "landmark" representing how you feel.
Give thanks in creative prayer or recite the Twenty-Third Psalm. Chant Om.
Distribute the energy and ground with a sharp, full exhalation and a full-body stretch.

Bibliography

Agee, Doris. *Edgar Cayce on ESP.* Edited by Hugh Lynn Cayce. New York: Warner Books Inc., 1988.

Begley, Sharon. *Train Your Mind, Change Your Brain: How a New Science Reveals Our Extraordinary Potential to Transform Ourselves.* New York: Ballantine Books, 2007.

Bentov, Itzhak. *Stalking the Wild Pendulum: On the Mechanics of Consciousness.*

Rochester, VT: Destiny Books (Inner Traditions International), 1988.

Brennan, Barbara. *Hands of Light: A Guide to Healing Through the Human Energy Field.* New York: Bantam Books, 1988.

———. *Light Emerging: The Journey of Personal Healing.* New York: Bantam Books, 1993.

Bruyere, Rosalyn L. *Wheels of Light: Chakras, Auras, and the Healing Energy of the Body.* New York: Fireside Book: Simon & Schuster, 1994.

Bucke, Richard Maurice, MD. *Cosmic Consciousness.* New York: Penguin Putnam, 1901.

Burr, Dr. Harold Saxton. *The Fields of Life: Our Links with the Universe.* New York: Ballantine Books, 1973.

Cade, C. Maxwell and Nona Coxhead. *The Awakened Mind: Biofeedback and the Development of Higher States of Awareness.* Shaftesbury, Dorset, England: Element Books, 1989.

Cayce, Edgar. *A Search for God, Books I and II, 50th Anniversary Edition.* Virginia Beach, VA: Edgar Cayce Foundation (A.R.E. Press), 1992.

Cayce, Edgar. *Auras.* Virginia Beach, VA: Edgar Cayce Foundation (A.R.E. Press), 1978.

———. *The Edgar Cayce Collection: Four Volumes in One.* Edited by Hugh Lynn Cayce. New York: Bonanza Books, 1986. (Edgar Cayce on Dreams,

Edgar Cayce on Healing, Edgar Cayce on Diet and Health, Edgar Cayce on ESP)

———— . *The Psychic Sense: How to Awaken Your Sixth Sense to Solve Life's Problems and Seize Opportunities.* Virginia Beach, VA: A.R.E. Press, 2006.

Cousens, Gabriel, MD. *Spiritual Nutrition: Six Foundations for Spiritual Life and the Awakening of Kundalini.* Berkeley, CA: North Atlantic Books, 2005.

Dispenza, Joe, DC. *Evolve Your Brain: The Science of Changing Your Mind.* Deerfield Beach, FL: Health Communications, Inc., 2007.

Doidge, Norman, MD. *The Brain That Changes Itself: Stories of Personal Triumph from the Frontiers of Brain Science.* New York: Viking Penguin, 2007.

Dossey, Larry, MD. *Healing Beyond the Body: Medicine and the Infinite Reach of the Mind.* Boston: Shambhala Publications, 2001.

———— . *Space, Time & Medicine.* Boulder, CO: Shambhala Publications, 1982.

Goleman, Daniel, PhD. *The Meditative Mind: The Varieties of Meditative Experience.* New York: Jeremy Tarcher/Putnam, 1988.

Green, Elmer and Alyce Green. *Beyond Biofeedback.* San Francisco: Delacorte Press, 1977.

Hagerty, Barbara Bradley. *Fingerprints of God: The Search for the Science of Spirituality.* New York: Riverhead Books, 2009.

Kirkpatrick, Sidney. *Edgar Cayce: An American Prophet.* New York City: Riverhead Trade, 2001.

McTaggart, Lynne. *The Field: The Quest for the Secret Force of the Universe.* Great Britain: HarperCollins Publishers, 2001.

Mind & Life Institute. *Destruction Emotions* and *The Science and Clinical Applications of Meditation, Investigating the Mind 2005.*

Newberg, Andrew, MD, Eugene D'Aquili, and Vince Rause. *Why God Won't*

Go Away: Brain Science & The Biology of Belief. New York: A Ballantine Book: Random House Publishing, 2001.

O'Neill, Kim. *The Calling: My Journey with the Angels.* Virginia Beach, VA: 4th Dimension Press, 2012.

Pennington, Judith. *The Meditation Experience: Listening to Your Psychic Soul.* Virginia Beach, VA: A.R.E. Press, 2011, CDs.

Volume 1:
The Lake of Inner Peace
The Inner Temple
The Healing Garden

Volume 2:
Creative Light
Gifts of Insight
Journey of Transformation

Volume 3:
Breathing Light
Woods and Water
The Illuminated Door

Volume 4:
The Heart of Meditation
Autumn Woods
What Instrument Am I?
Orange Trees by the Ocean
A Special Dinner

———. *The Voice of the Soul: A Journey into Wisdom and the Physics of God.* Bloomington, IN: 1st Books Library, 2001.

Puryear, Herbert B., PhD, and Mark A. Thurston, PhD. *Meditation and the Mind of Man.* Virginia Beach, VA: A.R.E. Press, 1975.

Radin, Dean, PhD. *Entangled Minds: Extrasensory Experiences in a Quantum Reality.* New York: Simon & Schuster, 2006.

Rama, Swami, Dr. Rudolph Ballentine, and Dr. Alan Hymes. *Science of Breath:*

A Practical Guide. Honesdale, PA: The Himalayan Institute Press, 2005.

Robbins, Jim. *A Symphony in the Brain: The Evolution of the New Brain Wave Biofeedback.* New York: Grove Press, 2000.

Sanders, Pete A., Jr. *You Are Psychic!* New York: Fawcett/Random House Books, 1989.

Sannella, Lee, MD. *The Kundalini Experience: Psychosis or Transcendence.* Lower Lake, CA: Integral Publishing, 1976.

Sechrist, Elsie. *Meditation: Gateway to Light.* Virginia Beach, VA: A.R.E. Press, 1972.

Sugrue, Thomas. *The Story of Edgar Cayce: There Is a River.* Virginia Beach, VA: A.R.E. Press, 1997.

Thurston, Mark, PhD. *Understand and Develop Your ESP.* Virginia Beach, VA: A.R.E. Press, 1988.

Todeschi, Kevin J. *Dream Images and Symbols: A Dictionary.* Virginia Beach, VA: A.R.E. Press, 2003.

——— . *Edgar Cayce on the Akashic Records: The Book of Life.* Virginia Beach, VA: A.R.E. Press, 1998.

Todeschi, Kevin J. and Carol Ann Liaros. *Edgar Cayce on Auras & Colors.* Virginia Beach, VA: A.R.E. Press, 2012.

Van Auken, John and Edgar Cayce. *Toward A Deeper Meditation: Rejuvenating the Body, Illuminating the Mind, Experiencing the Spirit.* Virginia Beach, VA: A.R.E. Press, 2007.

Wilhelm, Richard, Translator, with commentary by C.G. Jung. *The Secret of the Golden Flower: A Chinese Book of Life.* Orlando, FL: A Harvest Book (Harcourt Brace & Company), 1963.

Wise, Anna. *The High-Performance Mind: Mastering Brainwaves for Insight, Healing and Creativity.* New York: Penguin Putnam Inc., 1995.

—— . *Awakening the Mind: A Guide to Mastering the Power of Your Brain Waves*. New York: Penguin Putnam Inc., 2002.

Yogananda, Paramahansa. *Autobiography of a Yogi*. Los Angeles: Self-Realization Fellowship, 1974.

A.R.E. PRESS

Edgar Cayce (1877–1945) founded the non-profit Association for Research and Enlightenment (A.R.E.) in 1931, to explore spirituality, holistic health, intuition, dream interpretation, psychic development, reincarnation, and ancient mysteries—all subjects that frequently came up in the more than 14,000 documented psychic readings given by Cayce.

Edgar Cayce's A.R.E. provides individuals from all walks of life and a variety of religious backgrounds with tools for personal transformation and healing at all levels—body, mind, and spirit.

A.R.E. Press has been publishing since 1931 as well, with the mission of furthering the work of A.R.E. by publishing books, DVDs, and CDs to support the organization's goal of helping people to change their lives for the better physically, mentally, and spiritually.

In 2009, A.R.E. Press launched its second imprint, 4th Dimension Press. While A.R.E. Press features topics directly related to the work of Edgar Cayce and often includes excerpts from the Cayce readings, 4th Dimension Press allows us to take our publishing efforts further with like-minded and expansive explorations into the mysteries and spirituality of our existence without direct reference to Cayce-specific content.

A.R.E. Press/4th Dimension Press
215 67th Street
Virginia Beach, VA 23451

Learn more at EdgarCayce.org. Visit ARECatalog.com to browse and purchase additional titles.

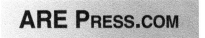

Who Was Edgar Cayce?
Twentieth Century Psychic and Medical Clairvoyant

Edgar Cayce (pronounced Kay-Cee, 1877-1945) has been called the "sleeping prophet," the "father of holistic medicine," and the most-documented psychic of the 20th century. For more than 40 years of his adult life, Cayce gave psychic "readings" to thousands of seekers while in an unconscious state, diagnosing illnesses and revealing lives lived in the past and prophecies yet to come. But who, exactly, was Edgar Cayce?

Cayce was born on a farm in Hopkinsville, Kentucky, in 1877, and his psychic abilities began to appear as early as his childhood. He was able to see and talk to his late grandfather's spirit, and often played with "imaginary friends" whom he said were spirits on the other side. He also displayed an uncanny ability to memorize the pages of a book simply by sleeping on it. These gifts labeled the young Cayce as strange, but all Cayce really wanted was to help others, especially children.

Later in life, Cayce would find that he had the ability to put himself into a sleep-like state by lying down on a couch, closing his eyes, and folding his hands over his stomach. In this state of relaxation and meditation, he was able to place his mind in contact with all time and space—the universal consciousness, also known as the super-conscious mind. From there, he could respond to questions as broad as, "What are the secrets of the universe?" and "What is my purpose in life?" to as specific as, "What can I do to help my arthritis?" and "How were the pyramids of Egypt built?" His responses to these questions came to be called "readings," and their insights offer practical help and advice to individuals even today.

The majority of Edgar Cayce's readings deal with holistic health and the treatment of illness. Yet, although best known for this material, the sleeping Cayce did not seem to be limited to concerns about the physical body. In fact, in their entirety, the readings discuss an astonishing 10,000 different topics. This vast array of subject matter can be narrowed down into a smaller group of topics that, when compiled together, deal with the following five categories: (1) Health-Related Information; (2) Philosophy and Reincarnation; (3) Dreams and Dream Interpretation; (4) ESP and Psychic Phenomena; and (5) Spiritual Growth, Meditation, and Prayer.

Learn more at EdgarCayce.org.

What Is A.R.E.?

Edgar Cayce founded the non-profit Association for Research and Enlightenment, Inc. (A.R.E.®) in 1931, to explore spirituality, holistic health, intuition, dream interpretation, psychic development, reincarnation, and ancient mysteries—all subjects that frequently came up in the more than 14,000 documented psychic readings given by Cayce.

The Mission of the A.R.E. is to help people transform their lives for the better, through research, education, and application of core concepts found in the Edgar Cayce readings and kindred materials that seek to manifest the love of God and all people and promote the purposefulness of life, the oneness of God, the spiritual nature of humankind, and the connection of body, mind, and spirit.

With an international headquarters in Virginia Beach, Va., regional representatives throughout the U.S., Edgar Cayce Centers in more than thirty countries, and individual members in more than seventy countries, the A.R.E. community is a global network of individuals.

A.R.E. conferences, international tours, camps for children and adults, regional activities, and study groups allow like-minded people to gather for educational and fellowship opportunities worldwide.

A.R.E. offers membership benefits and services that include a quarterly body-mind-spirit member magazine, *Venture Inward,* a member newsletter covering the major topics of the readings, and access to the entire set of readings in an exclusive online database.

Learn more at EdgarCayce.org.